THE POLITICS OF INSURGENCY
The Farm Worker Movement
in the 1960s

THE POLITICS OF INSURGENCY

The Farm Worker Movement in the 1960s

J. Craig Jenkins

COLUMBIA UNIVERSITY PRESS
NEW YORK   1985

Columbia University Press
New York   Guildford, Surrey
Copyright © 1985 Columbia University Press
All rights reserved

Printed in the United States of America

Library of Congress Cataloging in Publication Data

Jenkins, J. Craig, 1948–
    The politics of insurgency.

    Bibliography: p.
    Includes index.
    1. United Farm Workers—History.   2. Trade-unions—
Agricultural laborers—California—History—20th century.
3. Agricultural laborers—California—Political activity—
History—20th century.   4. Social movements—United States
—History—20th century.   I. Title.
HD6515.A292C34   1985   331.88'13'09794   84-27509
ISBN 0-231-05692-3
ISBN 0-231-05693-1 (pbk.)

Book design by Ken Venezio

Contents

Acknowledgments

This book owes its origins to the confluence of several fortunate events. In the spring of 1966, John Logue did me the inestimable favor of dragging me off to the United Farm Worker march on the Texas state capitol, giving me my first introduction to the spirit of la causa. The determined marchers with their colorful banners, peasant garb, and Spanish songs spiked my curiosity. Why were they marching on the capitol? Why were these supposedly contented, simple workers rising up against their supposedly protective benefactors? Why, despite his reputation as a Texas moderate, did then-Governor John Connally defy the marchers, meeting them briefly along the road rather than at the capitol? What did the prominence of clerics, labor leaders, and student activists among the marchers signify? Answers to these questions did not begin to gel until almost a decade later while I was working with Charles Perrow on a research project on the social movements of the 1960s. As I delved deeper into the history of farm worker insurgency and the United Farm Worker story in particular, I began to realize that the answers required a complete rethinking of theories of social movements and political power. It was at this point that my liaison with Chick Perrow really began to pay off. Over the next six years, Chick served as an ideal mentor, playing the role of constructive critic, supportive colleague, and general guide through the thicket of research and academe. By the time I emerged with firm answers, I found it increasingly difficult to separate my own ideas from his.

This book also owes its genesis to the unflagging spirit of the farm workers. Without their heroic efforts as foot soldiers of rebellion, there would be no story to tell. By dedicating this book to the sons and daughters of la causa, I offer but a token return. The future now lies in their hands as the second generation of la causa comes of age. Several individuals in la causa deserve special mention. Dolores Huerta, Chris Hartmire, Richard Chavez, Jim Drake, Phil Vera Cruz, Vic Salandini, Mark

Day, and Don Watson were extraordinarily patient with demands on their scarce time and my naive questions. This book owes much to their spirit of camaraderie as well as to the cooperation of numerous others in la causa whose names I have since lost or never known. H. L. Mitchell (or "Mitch" as his friends know him) and Hank Hasiwar filled me in on their misadventures with the National Farm Labor Union. Chris Paige was invaluable at a critical point, providing access to his farm labor collection and helping me clarify the farm worker powerlessness thesis. Ed Walsh had the patience to drive me all about central California, introducing me to the "grass roots" while conducting his own study of the Teamsters Union and then had the audacity to quarrel with me about the importance of external support.

My thesis readers at Stony Brook—Lewis Coser, Gerry Suttles, Woody Dill (now deceased), and Gene Lebovics—provided critical stimulus throughout the initial work. Michael Schwartz quarreled with me about the powerlessness of the underclass and the new directions of social movement theory, and Jim Rule passed on several working pieces that crystallized the direction of my research. The transformation of the dissertation into a book was pushed forward by the patient criticism of Tony Orum, who responded to an early version of the introduction, and the detailed comments on the entire manuscript by Tony Oberschall, Chuck Tilly, Bill Friedland, and an anonymous reviewer. Jim McCartney, John Hall, Mayer Zald, Jo Freeman, Linda Majka, and Theo Majka eyed particular chapters. Sid Tarrow stimulated the crystallization of the "turmoil" argument. Doug McAdams' *Political Process and the Development of Black Insurgency* (1982) forced me to sharpen several of my arguments. Although my critics did not win all their points, the virtues of the final product owe much to their efforts. The research itself was facilitated by financial support from the National Institute of Mental Health (5 RO1 MH20006-04 SSR), the National Science Foundation (Dissertation Improvement Grant #1SOC 75-08476), the Research Foundation of the State University of New York, and the Graduate School, University of Missouri-Columbia. My colleagues at the University of Missouri-Columbia provided a supportive environment and waited patiently for the completion of another overdue book. Susie Lindsay, Sharon Ely, and Mona Childers worked under tight time schedules to turn indecipherable draft into polished manuscript. Not least, my wife Mary Ellen cheerfully bore the burdens of being a book widow while my sons, Sean and Todd, found ways to divert me from the work underfoot.

Agenda and Objectives

Neoconservative critics celebrate its demise. Former sympathizers pause momentarily to note its passing and then furtively move on to other subjects. Old activists look back on their past as a moment of youthful idealism and, having crossed that magic age barrier of thirty, silently pass into the political mainstream. From virtually all sides of the political spectrum, it is as if the social movements of the 1960s had occurred on the other side of historical memory. Pointing to the political headlines of the late 1970s, commentators of various stripes forecast the rest of the twentieth century as an age of political conservatism and quiescence. An inflation-squeezed middle-class supports a tax revolt and broad cuts in governmental spending. Disillusioned voters withdraw from the electoral process, leaving reform oriented politicians stranded before the conservative onslaught. The growth of the sunbelt strengthens the "new right" revolt as cultural conservatives rally to defeat the ERA, restrict access to abortions, reintroduce prayer in the schools, halt "moral decay," and strengthen the arm of the "national security state." If the 1960s represented a period of political turmoil and reform, the 1970s a period of disillusionment and accommodation, then the 1980s would seem cast as a period of retrenchment and quiescence.

Yet signs abound that deny that judgment. In November 1981, almost a million marchers descended on the nation's capitol in a display of solidarity against the newly inaugurated Reagan administration, an event that would have been unimaginable without the mass marches and organizational alliances forged during the civil rights and antiwar movements of the 1960s. Six months later, another million strong amassed at the foot of the United Nations building in New York to demand a freeze on the "new cold war" and the nuclear arms race, this time linked by direct organizational heritage to the antiwar movement of the 1960s. At the same time, hundreds of thousands of community activists have been at work in a "backyard revolution" pressing for local tax reforms, control

ix

over nuclear power, the development of alternative energy resources, restrictions on industrial polluters, and the decentralization of economic and political decisions to a human scale. Meanwhile the raging issues of the time—busing, affirmative action, abortion, the ERA, military adventurism abroad—remain those initially raised by the social movements of the 1960s. If these are taken as reliable signposts to the future, the "spirit of the sixties" would seem to be very much alive.

This book offers an interpretation of the politics of this stormy decade. What were the social and political forces that gave rise to the social movements of the 1960s? What processes created the generalized political turmoil of this tumultuous period? What impact did these social movements have on American politics, culture, and social institutions? Why did some of these movements succeed while others seemingly failed?

This is a broad agenda. In making this agenda manageable, I have concentrated on the experience of one of the more prominent and successful of the social movements of the 1960s: the farm worker movement centered in the United Farm Workers Union (or, more simply, the UFW) under the indefatigable leadership of Cesar Chavez. The UFW began in humble origins. In the spring of 1961 a young community organizer named Cesar Estrada Chavez set out to build an organization of Mexican-American farm workers. Adopting the unassuming name of the Farm Workers Association, Chavez patiently built up a permanent membership association based on a consumer co-op, burial insurance, and a credit union. By a combination of diligence, shrewd organizing, and sustained sponsorship from churches and unions, the Association was gradually transformed into the United Farm Workers Union, the organizational center of an aggressive union movement with a mass following and the capacity to mobilize major strikes, large-scale boycotts, and effective political protests. By the late 1970s, the United Farm Workers had become the first successful farm worker union in U.S. history, permanently altering the structure of political and economic power in rural California.

The United Farm Worker story is significant for three reasons. In general terms, the UFW exemplified the basic goals and strategies of the social movements of the stormy sixties. The major social movements of the period were insurgencies, that is, organized attempts to bring the interests of previously unorganized and excluded groups into centers of economic and political power.[1] By organizing farm workers, the UFW took up the interests of one of the more disorganized and marginal seg-

x

ments of American society. By pressing for unionization and alliances with the Democratic party, the UFW sought routine access to centers of economic and political decision making. In terms of tactics, the social movements of the 1960s drew on the venerable American tradition of militant reformism. By using militant tactics to pursue moderate goals, the UFW maximized pressure on its antagonists while strengthening its political alliances. The UFW also made extraordinarily effective use of that distinctive *ruse de guerre* of the sixties movements—protest actions designed to mobilize external support and push forward the development of generalized political turmoil.[2]

The second reason for telling the UFW story is its promise as a model for organizing the powerless. Of the various struggles of the poor and excluded during the 1960s, the UFW was one of the most successful in overriding the barriers of poverty, social disorganization and a heritage of cultural subordination and political exclusion. Moreover, it did so by building a permanent membership association that used the power of organized numbers as a basis for economic and political change. Although farm workers are a relatively advantaged segment of the American underclass, the UFW experience offers instructive lessons for organizing other sections of the powerless.

The third reason for tracing the UFW experience is its contribution to rethinking our theories of social movements and political power. The upsurge of social movements during the 1960s caught the scholarly community seriously off guard. The traditional theories of social movements—what I will call the classical model—had been molded by the academic attack of such center-liberal luminaries as Talcott Parsons, Edward Shils, Daniel Bell, William Kornhauser, and Neil Smelser against the international rise of fascism and bolshevism in the 1920s and 1930s and the domestic "radical right" of the 1950s. As the defenders of threatened liberal values, these analysts had offered a series of formulations— mass society theory, collective behavior theory, relative deprivation and status inconsistency theories—that contested the viability of social movements as vehicles for social change and treated the American political system as an approximation to the pluralist ideal of an open polity. In the face of the onslaught of the new insurgencies of the 1960s, the mettle of these theories began to weaken as they failed to provide an accurate guide to the developing struggle for political power. A new group of scholars inspired by these new social movements advanced a new perspective—a resource mobilization theory of social movements—that emphasized the critical role of social movements in bringing about social change and the restrictiveness of the American polity.

It is worth spending a moment with this debate because it underlies so much of the argument to follow. In this classical model of social movements,[3] support for movements was seen as due to sharp increases in short-term individual discontents (e.g. anomie, relative deprivation, cognitive inconsistency) that were generated by the structural strains of rapid social change (cf. Gusfield 1968). In other words, the underlying discontents were individual and transitory rather than collective and structural. Their origins lay in overly rapid social change rather than structural antagonisms. Second, social movement participants were seen as a-rational, if not outright irrational, responding to the quasi-mystical "generalized beliefs" (Smelser 1963) and the *Ersatzgemeinschaft* or "substitute community" (Selznick 1970) offered by the social movement. Participation, then, was primarily therapeutic rather than political, and participants acted with less than their normal cognitive faculties. Third, a sharp distinction was seen to exist between social movement actions and conventional political actions giving rise to a bifurcation between social movement politics and routine politics. The study of social movements fell into the field of "collective behavior" with its emphasis on transient events and unstructured social action as opposed to political sociology with its focus on long-term social changes and structures of power and authority. Fourth, and flowing by implication from this bifurcation, institutionalized political power in the United States was seen as highly pluralistic. Multiple elites competed for power, guaranteeing the existence of extensive opportunities for all groups with genuine and long-standing grievances to secure access to centers of power. Cohesive and powerful elites, then, were not a significant obstacle to bringing about social changes. Fifth, social movements were seen as peripheral to the processes of structural social change. At most, they were symptomatic, prefiguring effective political action by identifying for elites the sources and location of strains and tensions. Ameliorative reforms were ultimately in the hands of public spirited elites rather than social movements.

The new insurgencies of the 1960s challenged these assertions, creating a wide-ranging debate over the nature and importance of social movements and the structure of political power in American society. The most important product of this debate has been the development of a new theoretical perspective—the resource mobilization theory of social movements—that has emphasized the centrality of social movements in the processes of social change and the restrictiveness of the American political system.[4] In general terms, the analysts drawing on this perspective adopted a sympathetic stance towards the problems and goals of social movements. Grievances were seen as collective and derived from structural antagonisms built into social institutions. Grievances were real and significant, but the central factors explaining the emergence of social movements were increases in organizational capacities and political opportunities, not the intensity of individual discontents. Similarly, social movement participants were seen as rational actors, pursuing collective interests rather than "acting out" their inner psychic dispositions.[5] Given this line of argument, it was only logical that the sharp boundary between social movement politics and routine politics, and therefore between the study of social movements and political sociology, should dissolve. Centralized political institutions controlled by cohesive and powerful elites loomed as the major barrier to social change. Social movements were seen as the major agencies of social change, their disruptiveness as essential means for bringing about social reforms and the democratization of social power. William Gamson caught the switch in mood quite well when he argued: "In place of the old duality of extremist politics and pluralist politics, there is simply politics. . . . Rebellion, in this view, is simply politics by other means. . . . The relations between political challengers and members of the polity is more a fight with few holds barred than it is a contest under well-defined rules" (1975:138–42).

These five premises—the structural bases of grievances, the rationality of movement participation, the basic identity of routine and social movement politics, the obstructive role of political elites, and social movements as the central agencies of social reform—frame the analysis that follows. Drawing on this resource mobilization theory of social movements, this book compares the emergence, development and outcome of the three major farm worker insurgencies of the post-World War II period: that associated with the National Farm Labor Union (or NFLU) that was active in the fields of California from 1947 through 1952; that of the Agricultural Workers Organizing Committee (or AWOC) that ran an off-and-on organizing campaign from 1958 through 1966; and the United Farm Workers. Few studies of insurgency have actually compared challenges, yet comparison is essential if one wants to isolate the processes that create sustained, successful insurgency. Each farm worker movement had the same basic goals, namely, bringing farm workers into centers of economic and political power. All three challenges confronted similar obstacles, chiefly the exclusion and powerlessness of the farm workers and the entrenched political power of the growers. The UFW succeeded while the others failed. The major reasons, I will argue, were the UFW's strategy of mobilization and the changed political environment that the challenge confronted, especially the ascendance of a center-left governing coalition and the development of generalized political turmoil.

This book, then, has four major objectives. Chapter 1 reviews recent developments in social movement theory, outlining the theory of resource mobilization and briefly contrasting it with classical arguments. Resource mobilization theory is, of course, a broad label that has covered a wide variety of arguments, ranging from the essentially organizational theory advanced by John McCarthy and Mayer Zald (1973, 1977) to the political process theory forged by Anthony Obershall (1973), William Gamson (1968a, 1975), Michael Schwartz (1976), and Charles Tilly (1978). Because my overview highlights the contrast between resource mobilization theory and the classical model, differences among resource mobilization analysts are given short shrift. Those interested in a more detailed review are invited to look further on their own (Perrow 1979; Jenkins 1981, 1983b; McAdam 1982; Garner and Zald 1983).

Second, the book contributes to the ongoing debate over the structure of political power in the United States. Traditionally this debate has been cast in terms of the clash between pluralist, elitist, and Marxist perspectives. As will become obvious, none of these perspectives has provided a satisfactory interpretation of the politics of insurgency. Marxist theorists have correctly emphasized the role of the state as the central barrier to social change but have not provided a satisfactory interpretation of the processes by which the state can be neutralized and social changes institutionalized. Elite theorists have correctly recognized the role of institutionalized political actors in mediating social reforms but have neglected the impetus from political outsiders. Pluralists have correctly stressed the opportunities for social change provided by liberal democracies but erroneously argued that these regimes are structurally permeable. The institutional theory of the state outlined in chapter 1 and elaborated throughout the book moves beyond these theories by distinguishing the political processes that restrict or expand opportunities for insurgency.

Third, the book offers an interpretation of the success and failure of what Piven and Cloward (1977) have called "poor people's movements" by comparing the major post-World War II farm worker insurgencies. My major argument is that by building a permanent membership association around the collective incentives of solidarity and consciousness and mounting the challenge during a period of political realignment and generalized political turmoil, the UFW mounted a sustained challenge and eventually brought about major social reforms. The first step of the story, however, starts on the other foot by explaining the failure of farm worker insurgencies. Chapters 2 and 3 provide a partial explanation of failure by showing how the structure of California agriculture and the political power of the growers have excluded farm workers and left them structurally powerless. Excluded segments of the working class are an unpromising basis for sustained insurgency. Yet the United Farm Workers eventually succeeded in precisely such a context. Obviously these barriers are not completely insurmountable. The second step entails defining the strategic factors and political processes that set off the UFW challenge from its predecessors. Chapters 4 and 5 trace the travails of the National Farm Labor Union and the Agricultural Workers Organizing Committee, showing that misguided strategies and restrictive political environments blocked both of these challenges. The UFW overrode these two problems by a different mobilization strategy and mounting the challenge during the generalized turmoil of the late 1960s and early 1970s (chapters 6 and 7).

A fourth objective is interpreting the generalized political turmoil that ran from the early 1960s through the mid-1970s. A full interpretation will have to await another book, but if I am correct about the importance of generalized turmoil in the UFW success, then the issue deserves attention. Any number of social structural interpretations of this turbulent decade are now available. One can have demographic overload theories focusing on the "invasion of the barbarians" and the failure of socialization institutions leading to a loosening of the "organizational harness" on youth (Bell 1976). Or one can emphasize the rise of new groups and the spread of new values, the "greening of America" (Reich 1970; Roszak 1969) and the rise of the "new class" (Inglehart 1977; Kirkpatrick 1977; Kristol

1979). Useful as these perspectives are in capturing facilitative structural trends, they fail to analyze the political dynamics involved in the expansion and contraction of political turmoil. Chapter 8 sketches a political interpretation of the stormy sixties and seventies and highlights the importance of turmoil in creating opportunities for successful insurgency.

Of course, a book such as this has political objectives as well. These are easy to identify. By analyzing the obstacles to successful insurgency and the conditions that lead to social movement success, this study can, I hope, play a small role in sustaining the spirit of the sixties and re-creating a period of generalized turmoil where the democratization of social power once again becomes the paramount question of the day.

THE POLITICS OF INSURGENCY
The Farm Worker Movement
in the 1960s

"When that damn eagle flies, the problems of the farm workers will be solved!"

> Manuel Chavez
> NFWA founding Convention (1962)

1

Theories of Insurgency

Every theory of insurgency is ultimately rooted in an underlying theory of society—in a vision of the social world that defines the major issues for analysis and the factors that enter into useful explanations. The two approaches that have dominated recent studies of insurgency—resource mobilization theory and the various classical formulations—have drawn on different visions of society. Resource mobilization theory has drawn its primary inspiration from the conflict theory tradition of Karl Marx and Max Weber. The major issue in this vision of society has been the explanation of social change, especially the transformation of structures of economic and political power. The major explanations of insurgency, then, are cast in terms of social power: structures of dominance that contain antagonistic interests, changes in political power that create opportunities for collective action, the mobilization of resources for sustained challenges, and power struggles that bring about changes in institutional structures. At the heart of this theory is the assumption that insurgency is a ubiquitous form of political action and that it constitutes a set of rational collective actions by excluded groups to advance their interests in the context of a restrictive polity. Insurgencies emerge, develop, and succeed or fail primarily because of changes in structures of social power.

The various formulations of the classical model have drawn on quite different theoretical premises, primarily those of the structural-functionalist tradition rooted in the work of Emile Durkheim and Vilfredo Pareto and the interactionist tradition of early Chicago sociology. The major issue in these theoretical traditions has been the explanation of social order, typically in terms of functional interdependence and the emergence of shared meanings and collective identities. The major explanations of insurgency, then, are cast in terms of the disruption and recreation of a shared normative order and set of collective identities, and processes that lead to the eventual collapse and absorption of these actions. At the heart of this classical model is the assumption that insurgency is of marginal social and political importance and that it constitutes a set of expressive actions generated by short-term disruptions in the moral fabric of society. Insurgencies are important chiefly because of the problem of social control that they pose to the established sociopolitical order.

Although the clash between these perspectives has created a wide-ranging debate, the key points have centered on two issues: the processes leading to the generation of sustained insurgency, and the factors shaping the outcome of challenges, especially their success and failure.[1]

The Generation of Insurgency

The sine qua non of the study of social movements has traditionally been the question of the emergence or generation of sustained insurgency. The classical theories have centered on explanations of discontent, arguing that insurgency emerges because of sudden and widespread increases in short-term individual grievances. In most versions, discontents are generated by the pressures or "strains" of rapid social change. These theories have borrowed the rather simple and highly misleading metaphor of a "pressure cooker." The assumption is that discontents mount up like the pressures inside the confined spaces of a pressure cooker, becoming more and more intense until they create an explosion. Although the classical analysts have emphasized different causes of discontent, the general argument has been the same. Rapid social changes impinge on existing social relations, creating "strains" or inconsistencies in the social order. The more rapid and profound these changes, the more severe the "strains" and therefore the greater the intensity and scope of the discontents. As these discontents build up, they overload the normal tension-reduction mechanisms and create explosions of individual aggression.

Insurgency, then, is simply an organized extension of more elementary forms of disorderly action. In mass society theory, for example, the discontents of anomie emerge because of the social dislocations generated by rapid industrialization, wars, and large-scale economic depres-

2

sions which "uproot" individuals from the intermediary social relations that normally integrate them into larger social structures, thereby making them available for "extremist" politics (Kornhauser 1959). Collective behavior theories have provided a more eclectic formulation, identifying a wide variety of social changes—economic crises, wars, mass migrations, the diffusion of new ideas and techniques—that create "normative ambiguities" (Smelser 1963) or "problematic situations" (Turner and Killian 1957, 1972) in which old norms are suddenly found to be inappropriate, leading to collective searches for new norms and social identities (cf. Aiken et al. 1968; Cohn 1961). Similarly, relative deprivation and status inconsistency theories have argued that rapid economic developments, urbanization, extensive social mobility, and sudden exposure to the standards of new reference groups create inconsistencies between expectations and satisfactions or cognitive dissonance, both of which create intense and widespread discontents leading to support for social movements (Davies 1969, 1971; Feierabend, Feierabend and Nesvold 1969; Gurr 1970; Geschwender 1971; Kriesberg 1973: 70–76; Miller et al. 1977). Gusfield captured the general thesis quite well in his classic review for the *Encyclopedia of the Social Sciences* when he argued:

A major hypothesis in the field is that social movements are the products of social change. Circumstances arise in which long established relationships are no longer appropriate; the result of this strain between old and new is discontent. One of the sociologist's tasks in analyzing a movement is to identify the social changes that have generated discontent and to specify their relation to the movement. (1968:446)

This is not the point to argue the merits of particular versions of this classical model. An extensive critical literature already exists pointing out specific empirical and conceptual weaknesses.[2] My concern here is the general assumptions that underlie these classical theories. Each has built on the pressure cooker metaphor, arguing that the intensity and scale of discontent is the central factor in the generation of insurgency. Discontents have been seen as short-term, individual grievances that derive from exogenous social changes such as economic depressions, wars, and natural calamities. Insurgency itself has therefore been seen as a sharp break from the existing social order, as a sudden spontaneous explosion of the outraged masses.

In contrast, the resource mobilization theory of social movements is based on an analysis of social power. Insurgencies emerge and become

3

sustained, not because of sudden and widespread discontents, but because of favorable changes in the structure of social power. The basic image is that of excluded groups organizing and pooling resources in response to increased resources and opportunities. Discontents are seen as indigenous features of social institutions that are ultimately rooted in underlying structural antagonisms rather than transient grievances produced by social dislocations. Insurgencies, then, are direct extensions of ongoing institutional processes rather than explosions produced by fractures in the social order. Although insurgency may initially emerge from spontaneous processes, sustained challenges require concerted organizing and strategic planning, in other words, leaders and social movement organizations. Rather than being a sudden explosion, a sustained insurgency rests on a gradual cumulative process of resource mobilization that typically requires long time periods. As the Tillys have argued, pointing to the long-run effects of industrialization and urbanization on the generation of insurgency during the rebellious century between 1830 and 1930: "instead of short-term generation of strain, followed by protest, we find long-run transformation of power and collective action" (1975:254). Long-standing social antagonisms defined the major actors and issues under contention. Sustained insurgency developed because of favorable changes in power relations, especially increases in the mobilization potential and strategic position of excluded groups, the adoption of effective mobilization strategies and the development of favorable political alignments that altered the collectively perceived costs and rewards of collective action.

What then is the role of discontents? Several analysts have recently argued that discontents are irrelevant because they are structural constants produced by objective social inequalities or the organizing efforts of political entrepreneurs. McCarthy and Zald, for example, have argued that "there is always enough discontent in any society to supply the grass-roots support for a movement" (1977:1215) and that entrepreneurs simply manufacture the discontents: "the definition of grievances will expand to meet the funds and support personnel available" (1973:13). Similarly, John Wilson has argued that discontents are a necessary but not sufficient condition "because certain tensions seem to be endemic to society" (1973:55). Speaking specifically of excluded groups, my own previous work has argued that "grievances are relatively constant and pervasive. . . . What changes, giving rise to insurgency, is the amount of social resources available to unorganized but aggrieved groups" (Jenkins and Perrow 1977:266, 250).

Although discontents are secondary, neither formulation can ultimately stand as a general explanation of insurgency. Discontents are, after all, a question of subjective definitions rather than simple objective deprivations. Excluded groups are always objectively deprived but this does not mean that they will uniformly perceive these conditions as socially unjust and alterable. As Barrington Moore (1978) has argued, the development of insurgency requires that subordinants collectively redefine existing conditions as socially unjust and mutable. Elites have to be perceived as responsible, as having violated their social responsibilities. Objectionable conditions have to be seen as alterable. Normally, however, such definitions of social injustice are blocked or cannot be converted into collective images. Past experiences of failed insurgency, elite control of information and socialization processes, disorganization and lack of "free spaces" for creating alternative definitions of reality, and simple psychological adaptation to the state of powerlessness create quiescent attitudes among the excluded towards their objective deprivations. "Given the onus of choice, the powerless internalize their impossible situation and internalize their guilt. . . . The slave often identified with his master and accepted society's estimate of himself as being without worth. . . . The less complete but nonetheless pervasive powerlessness of blacks in America's northern ghettoes has similar effects" (Katznelson 1973:198). The most powerless of the Appalachian mineworkers studied by Gaventa (1980) were the most docile and the least likely to label their objective deprivations as injustices. Although theories of social antagonism can show how objective social inequalities lead to structural conflicts of interest and hence the objective potential for insurgency, these conflicts are structural constants and hence cannot explain variations in discontents (cf. Oberschall 1978b:291–294; Jenkins 1981:113–114). Objective social inequalities have to be collectively redefined as the source of social injustices that can be remedied by collective action. In short, the excluded group has to experience a "cognitive liberation" (Ash-Garner 1977) that transforms its collective consciousness.

How does this come about? In the entrepreneurial theory, the transformation of consciousness is simply manufactured by organizers. The greater the resources invested in the organizing campaign, the greater the intensity and scale of the discontents. Like Lenin's classic formulation of class as opposed to trade union consciousness, the transformation is mechanically imported from the outside. But this leaves the link of insurgent consciousness to structural antagonisms problematic, denies spontaneous processes, and treats grievances as simple, linear products of entrepreneurial definition rather than as products of the actual process of social conflict.

A more fruitful theory of discontent begins with the premise that the consciousness of excluded groups is dual or, to use Gramsci's (1957:67) term, "contradictory." An insurgent consciousness based on a sense of social injustice coexists alongside a contradictory deferential consciousness that highlights the "fairness" and immutability of the prevailing order. These contradictory belief systems coexist and, because of the dominance of elites and the powerlessness of the excluded, the former becomes private while the latter is public knowledge. The result is the political passivity of the excluded. However, changes in power relations will bring the consciousness of injustice to the fore, making it the dominant and collective definition of reality. In other words, increases in the intensity and scale of discontents are produced by changes in the structure of social power.

A second premise in such a revised theory of discontents is that social conflict is a routine part of social relations. As Ralf Dahrendorf once put it: "social conflict is ubiquitous" (1959:162). Social conflict, however, is not the same as insurgency. Most conflicts are small-scale, isolated acts of insubordination, such as work slow-downs and minor violations of institutional rules, that test the armor of the power structure but, like prepolitical peasant rebellions (Hobsbawm 1959), do not articulate a clear sense of injustice, much less a coherent set of remedies. Rule and Tilly (1975) have appropriately labeled these "testing actions." Since they are randomly distributed, these testing actions continuously explore the protective armor of the power structure. Once chinks are discovered, disruptive actions tend to escalate to fill the open space. Outside cadres are attracted, grass-roots organizers are trained, and excluded groups develop an enhanced sense of their political efficacy, thereby supporting expanded disruptions. In the course of escalating disruptions, the collectively perceived costs and rewards of these actions are gradually transformed. Conditions that were previously perceived as immutable and fair are collectively redefined as mutable and unjust. In short, a consciousness of social injustice moves to the fore. The key question, then, is identifying the changes in the structure of power that set off the escalation of disruptions and the transformation of the consciousness of the excluded.

Four major aspects of the structure of power shape the generation of insurgency: the mobilization potential of the excluded group; its strategic position in routine institutional processes; the strategies of mobilization adopted by organizers; and opportunities created by the structure of political alignments. The first is essentially a question of the indigenous organizational capacity or readiness of the group as shaped by its resources, its indigenous organization, and the institutional controls of its main antagonists. The second determines the disruptive potential of the group; groups that are functionally important to their antagonists, whose antagonists control resources, and who are lodged in central social institutions have greater strategic leverage. These potentials are put into motion by organizers who, in interaction with spontaneous processes, define strategies of mobilization for the assembly and management of resources. The structure of political alignments is essentially a question of how the relations among politically powerful groups create opportunities for the excluded to organize and act collectively on their interests. Unless there are significant opportunities, a deferential consciousness will remain the dominant definition of social reality. Before specifying the ways in which these factors interact, we need to first look at each separately.

Mobilization Potential. To speak of the potentials of a group is to point to the social structural conditions that shape their capacities prior to actual insurgency, what Coleman (1969) has referred to as their "conversion potential." The most important considerations are the indigenous resources of the group, its internal or indigenous organization, and the institutional controls of its main antagonists. In general, the more economically secure the group, the more the indigenous resources and organization and the less the institutional controls, the greater the likelihood of mobilization. As Tilly (1978:145–51) has argued, resourceful groups are more readily mobilized and more likely to support preparatory mobilization prior to open contests while deprived groups respond more gradually and in a defensive manner. More directly linked to mobilization campaigns are organizing resources, especially experienced organizers, recognized leaders, and means of communication such as newspapers and meeting facilities. Organizers and leaders are generally grass-

7

roots volunteers drawn from the indigenous community or the fallout of proximate social movements. Motivated by a "missionary impulse" (Freeman 1983), their major role is to coordinate actions and knit together existing groups by creating a sense of solidarity and commitment to an alternative vision of social justice. Generally, organizers are indigenous "opinion leaders" (Lazarsfeld et al. 1955), often leaders of social clubs and economic benefit associations. As Lipset (1950:195–205) found in his study of Saskatchewan socialism, these are typically the earliest and most central recruits. A group endowed with natural leaders or receiving an infusion of outside organizers is more likely to mobilize. In addition, these leaders need means of communications to reach the masses and protected locations for carrying out organizing efforts. To the extent to which the group enjoys "free spaces" (Boyte 1980), the group is more likely to mobilize.

Indigenous organization is probably the most important single factor, providing a communications network for coordinating actions and diffusing an insurgent consciousness, strengthening collective perceptions of efficacy by creating awareness of the number of potential supporters (Berk 1974; Granovetter 1978), facilitating collecting redefinitions of conditions as mutable and unjust, and furnishing the context for collective incentives that mitigate the problem of free-riders. As Oberschall (1973:119) has argued, an organizational base is necessary if isolated ephemeral testing actions such as riots and crowd outbursts are to be transformed into sustained insurgency.

Indigenous organization can be defined simply as the extent to which a category of people sharing some characteristic or interest in common are aware of this interest and linked together by interpersonal bonds or social networks (Tilly 1978:62–63). These networks can have two distinct bases, solidary networks defined by natural groups such as kinship and friendship ties, and membership in formal community organizations such as churches, benefit associations, and social clubs. A social movement organization (or SMO) is, in contrast, a formal association that attempts to interject the interests of excluded groups into centers of power (Zald and Ash 1966; McCarthy and Zald 1977:1218). Its major task is extending and deepening indigenous organization while harnessing it to the goals of insurgency. Even in advanced phases of insurgency, however, the social movement organization is never coterminous with the movement itself, much less the organization of the group.

8

The greater the density of indigenous organization, the greater the potential for mobilization. Indigenous organization has two dimensions: inclusiveness or the extent to which social networks link the group together and absorb the time, energies, and social interaction of members, and exclusiveness or the extent to which these networks are isolated from other categories of actors, especially antagonists. Jackson et al. (1960) found that the absence of such an indigenous network among property taxpayers in Los Angeles in the late 1950s prevented a tax revolt from emerging despite strong but disorganized interest in tax reforms. Conversely, working class insurgency is critically facilitated by the solidarities forged by community ties and work affiliations. Among nineteenth-century English workers, for example, Foster (1974) found that the more extensive and exclusive the local community ties to pubs, fraternal clubs, and extended families, the more likely the development of an insurgent consciousness and collective action. Similarly, the ecological concentration of the working class in separate neighborhoods of large cities has facilitated strikes and union organization (Lodhi and Tilly 1973; Britt and Galle 1972, 1974; Lincoln 1978; Shorter and Tilly 1974:287–295). These networks are often the creation of previous movements or political mobilization efforts. Freeman (1975:44–70) found that the development of inclusive networks among participants in the President's Commission on the Status of Women in the mid-1960s created the basis for launching the National Organization for Women. Likewise, the informal networks among radical women involved in the student movement in the late 1960s created the organizational basis of the radical wing of the women's movement (Freeman 1973; Evans 1979).

Indigenous organization is also decisive in overriding the free-rider problem. As Mancur Olson (1965) has argued, individuals rationally pursuing their self-interest will often refrain from collective actions because they stand to gain whether or not they participate. All workers might gain by a union contract, but only those who strike actually pay for this collective benefit. According to Olson, the rational course of action is to free-ride on the contributions of others. Of course, if all individuals acted this rationally, there would be no collective benefits. Thus, according to Olson, organizers of collective action have to provide "selective incentives" such as strike funds and promises of jobs to those, and only those, who pay the costs of collective action.[3] Selective incentives, however, are a weak basis for mobilizing insurgency. Excluded groups lack re-

9

sources, and although external contributions can help, such sponsors are, as the civil rights movement found, frequently unreliable in the long run (Lipsky 1968; Garrow 1978). Moreover, as Gamson (1975:66–71) has pointed out, Olson's narrow self-interest scheme does not explain the contributions of sponsors. Nor does Olson's theory account for the efforts of organizers, unless one adopts the rather implausible explanation that they are pursuing the ephemeral gains of public recognition and career advancement (cf. Frohlich et al. 1971). In most cases, there are more promising avenues for personal advancement.

A more persuasive theory of collective action that links indigenous organization to mobilization has been offered by James Q. Wilson (1973:33–51) in his discussion of solidary and purposive incentives. Solidary incentives rest on emotional commitments, their receipt on the maintenance of valued social relations. They can be experienced only through the actual process of participating in collective actions, either as the major aim of the action or its direct by-product. These incentives may be selective, such as the special honors and recognition handed out to movement leaders, or collective, such as the exhilaration that comes from participating in demonstrations and marches or collective actions that assert the social respectability of the group as a whole. Purposive incentives differ in deriving from actions that conform to an internalized moral code. In this sense, they are inherently collective, resting on the moral commitments that link the individual to the group. In effect, internalizing a moral code redefines self-interest in terms of collective interest. Significantly, both sets of incentives are ultimately based on indigenous organization. Solidarities and internalized values are largely structured by the social networks of everyday life. In other words, the more cohesive the group in terms of common networks and sentiments, the stronger the indigenous social infrastructure for the operation of these incentives (Fireman and Gamson 1979; Moe 1980; Jenkins 1983a).

These social networks also have to be cooptable to the goals of the movement. Here the critical factor is their exclusiveness and the particular values attached to the networks. Von Eschen, Kirk and Pinard (1971), for example, found that networks defined by membership in conservative political associations such as the Urban League and major political parties discouraged support for civil rights protests while those linked to more liberal associations such as the NAACP and the Americans for Democratic Action facilitated participation. Similarly, Freeman (1983:24-

25) has argued that support for the contemporary women's movement has been structured by women's networks that are linked to a conception of independent female status while the more traditional networks of sororities and women's professional clubs have inhibited support. The more exclusive the networks, the more likely they are to serve as consciousness transforming and mobilizing channels. Foster (1974) found that working class communities with extensive cross-class ties experienced little insurgency while exclusive communities were centers of insurgency.

Vertical networks between elites and subordinates are frequently the basis for institutional controls while free spaces provide the basis for mobilization. The most controlled environment is a "total institution" (Goffman 1961) in which the entire lives of subordinants and their networks are enveloped by structures controlled by their antagonists. Free spaces for developing solidarities and alternative definitions of social justice are eliminated. Antagonists develop highly personalized, paternalistic controls over their subordinates and promote intensive competition among them. These ties inculcate a view of the naturalness and justice of the existing order as well as provide informal controls for coopting initial testing actions. Competition blocks in-group solidarity and the transformation of collective consciousness. In contrast, free spaces constructed around sites of autonomous group interaction provide a potent basis for developing alternative definitions of social justice and developing the solidary and cultural bases for mobilization. Poor peasants and tenants are often controlled by intense rivalries and patron-client ties (Migdal 1974:33–42; Paige 1975:24–25). Conversely, middle peasants who own their own land and live in independent villages possess the open space and solidarities for mounting challenges (Wolf 1969:284–293; Skocpol 1979:128–132). Similarly, the paternalistic authority and totalistic controls of slaveowners in the antebellum American South provided virtually complete dominance over their houseservants while fieldhands, especially skilled slaves who worked independently, were less controllable (Genovese 1973). In the same vein, meritocratic hierarchies promote competition by providing privileges on the purported basis of individual merit while egalitarian rewards create solidarity. White collar workers have generally resisted unionization because of their sense of greater worth and the perks of respectability, clean work and job security, while flat hierarchies among teachers and nurses have encouraged unionization (Lockwood 1956). Similarly, employers have used ethnicity to create rivalries yet ethnic

11

bonds have frequently furnished the basis for unionization (Brody 1960; Aronowitz 1973).

These institutional controls are, of course, reinforced by direct coercive sanctions. Striking workers are fired, dissident peasants evicted, and slave rebellions crushed with beatings and armed violence. Coercion is generally not used until insurgency has already emerged but, where the memory of repression is direct and fresh, the mere threat often serves as a powerful deterrent. As long as the state monopoly on the means of legitimate violence remains intact, clear and visible signals of support by political elites for the antagonist are often sufficient. The southern cotton plantations during slavery and the tenancy era often resembled armed concentration camps in which plantation owners had virtually unrestricted control over the means of violence and, if challenged, could count on quick, solid backing from local police and courts (Raper 1969; W. J. Wilson 1973:65–73). In contrast, weakening this state monopoly or even signals of elite indifference often leads to the rapid development of multiple insurgencies (cf. Skocpol 1979).

Strategic Position. All groups, even the most abject and powerless, have some minimum of strategic leverage. At the least they can refuse to cooperate with ongoing institutional processes, supporting "mass defiance" that "violates the traditions and laws to which they ordinarily acquiesce, and flaunt the authorities to whom they ordinarily defer" (Piven and Cloward 1977:4). The strike and the riot are the classic forms, workers withdrawing their labor from production and citizens throwing off their normal civility. Waskow (1967) referred to the "creative disorder" of civil rights protests as creating leverage against political authorities and Wilson (1961) saw it as the core feature of civil rights protest strategies.

The leverage afforded by mass defiance, however, varies widely. The compliance of some groups with ongoing institutional routines is simply more important than that of others. Moreover, some antagonists control more resources and can therefore more readily make concessions. And some social institutions are more central in the functioning of the larger society, magnifying the significance of disruptions. In general, these conditions reinforce one another. Central institutions control more resources and are more dependent on the cooperation of subordinates. Excluded groups, however, are not generally favored by these considerations. Strikes by skilled workers deprive employers of a critical resource, but those by unskilled menial workers who perform marginal functions have few repercussions. Similarly, protests by the unemployed and welfare recipients have little significance other than temporarily disturbing the tranquility of a few marginal governmental agencies. In the same vein, the antagonists of "poor people's" movements often do not control sufficient resources to make major concessions and are implacably opposed to concessions. Slumlords frequently lack the finances to repair their buildings, and the owners of marginal enterprises cannot pay high wages without bankrupting their firms. As we will see, California growers have determinedly resisted farm worker unions, resorting to extreme measures in their battles against insurgency. Finally, excluded groups are typically embedded in marginal social institutions. Strikes against the large corporations in the core sector of the American economy shake the entire society, but the reverberations of protests against welfare officials, school administrators, and slumlords are largely confined to particular institutions. Of course, these conditions change as institutions decline or become more socially prominent. The industrial enterprise was insignificant in the early nineteenth-century American economy but had become the core of the national economy by the 1930s. Early industrial strikes had little leverage, but the wave of industrial strikes in the 1930s shook the entire sociopolitical order.

Strategies of Mobilization. Although spontaneous processes are often sufficient to initiate insurgency, concerted organizing and deliberate mobilization strategies are necessary to sustain challenges. In fact, in settings where resources are scarce and indigenous networks are weakly developed or only partially cooptable, organizers are often necessary to even initiate challenges because the group is simply too disorganized and dominated by its antagonists. All three of the farm worker movements we will examine were initiated by professional organizers, as were most of the urban social movements of the late 1960s and early 1970s (Ballis 1974; Jackson and Johnson 1974; Lancourt 1977). The major contribution of organizers, however, is sustaining mobilization. As Fainstein and Fainstein (1974:202-206) found, a formal movement organization with a professional staff, membership lists, and meeting facilities is often necessary to sustain interest during lulls in spontaneous activity. And, as Gamson (1975:89-99) and Tilly (1978:154-155) have argued, a formal movement organization increases the combat readiness of a challenge and provides a more flexible tactical repertoire, both of which promise more effective actions and thereby sustained mobilization.

13

The highly charged debate over the role of social movement organizations has been due in part to the failure to distinguish organizers from formal leaders.[4] Organizers are generally highly committed "grass-roots" supporters receiving little or no pay. Their efforts are focused on knitting together isolated groups, instilling consciousness of social injustices, offering tactical advice, and pushing forward disruptive actions. Formal leaders, in contrast, hold formal positions in social movement organizations and are more concerned with the articulation of formal goals and negotiating relations with institutional elites. Organizers help expand institutional disruptions while leaders articulate goals and negotiate formal institutional access.

In general, social movements with professional or full-time paid organizers are advantaged. Organizing efforts are more sustained and, as Oliver (1982) has argued, commitment levels are higher. The rapid growth of the Southern Farmers Alliance in the 1880s, for example, was based on full-time salaried organizers (Schwartz 1976:128-136) as was the proliferation of industrial strikes in the mid-1930s (Derber and Young 1957:20). Similarly, professional community organizers in the 1960s transformed sporadic testing actions into more sustained challenges against corporations and big city political machines (Silberman 1972:279; Bailey 1974; Peterson and Greenstone 1977). As Freeman has concluded: "Even in something as seemingly spontaneous as a social movement, the professional is more valuable than the amateur" (1983:27).

The mobilization strategies adopted by these organizers vary widely in their effectiveness. Organizers can tap two constituencies: direct beneficiaries or the group itself, and external or third parties. Although a sustained challenge ultimately depends on indigenous support, external support can be a critical facilitator, especially among deprived groups who lack specialized resources such as organizing facilities, legal advice, and political contacts. In general, a dual strategy that mobilizes both constituencies is more effective.

Studies of group mobilization have repeatedly found that organizers using "bloc" recruitment methods are more successful because they build on the group's indigenous solidarities and culture (Oberschall 1973:117-8, 125-129; Snow, Zurcher and Eckland-Olson 1980; Jenkins 1983a). As in conventional community organizing, the existing solidary groups of everyday life and their natural leaders are recruited intact and converted into the active cells or structural units of the movement. Conversely,

14

organizers who shun the more solidary groupings, reject prevailing cultural understandings, and insist on their own radical programs will find deaf ears (Brill 1971; Boyte 1980). Similarly, organizers who make use of collective incentives by holding solidary events and inaugurating ideological training programs can override the free-rider problem, while those emphasizing selective material benefits will often receive only transitory support. As we will see, the United Farm Workers generated sustained farm worker support by focusing on existing solidary groups and emphasizing solidarity and consciousness. In contrast, the National Welfare Rights Organization, organizing a roughly similar population, experienced debilitating turn-over rates because it relied on the selective incentive of access to special welfare benefits (Ballis 1974).

Organizers are also critical to pyramiding resources and actions. By limiting actions to less ambitious but successful projects that fit the capacities of the challenge, insurgencies can use small successes to gradually mobilize support and eventually escalate to more demanding actions (Alinsky 1971). In the mid-1970s, for example, the citizens' organization Massachusetts Fair Share launched an overly ambitious tax referendum campaign that almost exhausted the nascent challenge while ACORN, organizing in a less favorable environment, has successfully pyramided its projects into larger scale contests (Kopkind 1978).

Insurgencies also build off external resources, a point completely neglected in the classic literature (McCarthy and Zald 1973). The emergence of the student and antiwar movements of the 1960s depended heavily on the cooptation of the mass media to spread their message and recruit supporters (Oberschall 1978a; Gitlin 1980). Similarly, the civil rights and urban movements staged dramatic protests that captured the attention of more powerful groups, "socializing" the conflicts (Schattschneider 1960) and generating significant external support for the challenges (Lipsky 1969, 1971; Garrow 1978). At the height of the political turmoil of the late 1960s, liberal social service organizations such as the National Council of Churches, the Ford Foundation, and the YMCA became general sponsors of insurgency, supporting the development of a wide array of new challengers (Jenkins 1977; Kotz and Kotz 1977; West 1981).

External support, however, entails significant limits. Bids for support have to be framed in terms of principles accepted by supporters, such as legal due process and equality of opportunity, that can restrict movement goals and actions. The liberal supporters of the civil rights movement, for example, were repelled by the urban riots and the demands for black power and withdrew their support (Garrow 1978:158-160; McAdam 1982: 208-213). Similarly, the National Council of Churches refused to support the Movement for Economic Justice because of its radical demands for economic redistribution (cf. West 1982). As Lipsky (1971) found in urban rent strikes, external supporters are also often satisfied with quick symbolic victories that provide little basis for a sustained challenge. The receptiveness of potential sponsors also varies widely. Periods of economic prosperity provide slack resources and facilitate rapid growth in the social welfare bureaucracies that house the "organizational intellectuals" (Zald and McCarthy 1975) who are likely sponsors of new challenges. As we will see, the prosperity of the early 1960s was a critical structural facilitator in creating the external support for insurgencies. Probably the most decisive factor, though, is a favorable shift in the structure of political alignments that give potential sponsors more political power and increases their short-term interests in supporting a challenge.

Structure of Political Alignments. The fundamental distinction around which political systems are organized is that between polity insiders or members who possess routine, low-cost access to centers of state power, and polity outsiders or exluded groups who do not (Tilly 1978:55). Members have a stake in blocking challenges and maintaining the existing system of polity rules which guarantee their access; excluded groups, in seizing opportunities to mobilize and seeking the transformation of these rules or at least their application to themselves. Polity members will, of course, use their access to block direct challenges, but even members not directly affected by a challenge will generally perceive insurgency as threatening simply because it raises the possibility of a restructuring of access rules and, by acting outside existing channels, violates these rules. This, coupled with the inherent conservatism of the state as an institution fundamentally committed to the maintenance of social order, imparts an intrinsic restrictiveness to political systems. As McAdam has put it, "*all* social movements pose a threat to existing institutional arrangements in society [because they] raise the spectre of a restructuring of polity membership" (1982:26). The state, then, is institutionally biased against insurgency. Short of a general collapse of state power, political elites will normally move to prevent the development of sustained challenges.

The structure of liberal democratic regimes, however, tempers this bias of the state by allowing routine political realignments that periodically create opportunities for the emergence of challenges. Contrary to most theories of liberal democracy, however, the major basis is not the formal protections on speech and assembly and voting rights enshrined in liberal democratic constitutions. These protections are routinely extended only to polity members. The major factor is realignments inside of the polity, structured largely through the electoral system, that encourage coalitions between polity members and excluded groups and thereby create opportunities for the mobilization of insurgency. In effect, liberal democratic rules rationalize the struggle for political power by converting it into a series of routinized electoral contests between contending factions supported by voting coalitions of polity members. Routine competitive elections insure that political elites have to periodically attend to the views of the groups inside the system. If these groups find that bringing an outsider into the system will bring electoral or other advantages, their sponsorship can create opportunities for mounting a sustained challenge. Political elites may temporarily lift the institutional controls conventionally used to keep the excluded in check and may even sponsor insurgent organizations. Insurgents can then use demonstrations and marches to signal their base of support and promise as an electoral ally. As McAdam (1982:83-86, 146-149, 156-163) has shown, the rise of the civil rights movement was facilitated by several decades of increasing federal protections of black civil rights, especially restrictions on lynchings and denial of voting rights, and increasing infusions of white liberal support for black colleges and churches. Similarly, the development of the movements of the unemployed and industrial workers during the 1930s depended heavily on the support of the Democratic party and middle class liberal reformers (Piven and Cloward 1977: chs. 2 and 3). In both cases, political realignments triggered the expansion of new political opportunities.

The scope of these realignments determines the scale and duration of the opportunities. The most dramatic opportunities develop out of generalized realignments and periods of intense struggle among polity members. In closely divided polities in which roughly equal political coalitions compete for governmental power, the solidarity among polity members is reduced and the potential value of outsiders as political allies is increased (Tilly 1978:200–204). The more intense this internal power struggle, the greater the likelihood of generalized sponsorship. Sponsorship can also grow out of more limited realignments. An antagonist loses its political footing and becomes more vulnerable to attack or a single polity member decides to support a challenge. Sponsorship also typically emerges at particular points in the process of realignments. If sponsors are part of a political coalition acquiring increased governmental power, their ability to provide support and their interest in the entry of new groups is greater. The close electoral battles of the early 1930s made the votes of previously marginal white ethnics and blue collar workers a valuable resource, leading Democratic politicians to support the movements of the unemployed and industrial workers. At the same time, increasing dominance by the Democratic party and the declining importance of business confidence as a structural constraint gave political elites more room to support insurgencies (Andersen 1979; Skocpol 1980). Similarly, as I will argue below, the closely fought electoral battles and the Democratic victories of the early 1960s and the restructuring of peripheral sector capitalist firms created a conducive context for the development of new challenges among blacks and other excluded groups.

The emergence of successful challenges also stimulates new insurgencies. Organizers branch out to new causes. New models of collective action are developed and new resource bases identified. Dramatic successes boost the excluded's sense of political efficacy, and as long as movements do not challenge their allies, reform-oriented political parties and governing coalitions are strengthened. Movement organizers vie for recognition, and as the political pulse escalates, the scope of insurgent demands expands. Polity members become less secure, longstanding coalitions break up, and the entire field of political action becomes more fluid. In such a context, virtually all groups possessing even a modicum of resources and organization will rise up, making their own bids for entry. The successes of the civil rights and student movements in the mid-1960s stimulated challenges from virtually all sides, creating a period of generalized political turmoil. Insurgencies were launched among groups such as homosexuals and school children who had never previously organized and those, such as the urban underclass, who possessed few resources and little organizational base or strategic position. Of course, such periods of turmoil are rare, precipitated by polity-wide realignments that dramatically restructure the boundaries and rules of the system. Generally, the dynamic of expanding insurgency is halted in the early stages, limiting the changes to the entry of single groups and lesser reforms.

How do these four factors—the mobilization potential, strategic position and mobilization strategies of insurgents, and shifting alignments in the polity—interact in the development of sustained challenges? In broad terms, each dimension is shaped by long-term structural social changes. Capitalist development brought about urbanization and industrialization which, in turn, increased the organizational strength of the industrial working class and their strategic position in the economy as a whole (Korpi 1978). In this context, working class organizers gradually perfected strategies of mobilization, developing more effective devices for mobilizing collective action. Simultaneously, the gradual entry of new groups, especially the industrial working class (Therborn 1978), has democratized liberal democratic states, extending the franchise, legitimating new forms of action and creating broader, more diverse mass based political parties and governing coalitions that have been more willing to support challenges. In other words, long-term structural changes have gradually increased the mobilization potential and strategic position of excluded groups, and these groups have gradually evolved new mobilization strategies and enjoyed increased political opportunities. In the short run, however, the specific changes setting off a challenge can come along any of these four dimensions. Gamson, Fireman, and Rytina (1982) have provided a convenient way of thinking about the interaction of these factors by offering a "threshold" model of movement emergence. Each factor has to be at minimum threshold point before a sustained challenge will emerge. Within limits, surpluses in some dimensions, such as organizing resources, can compensate for deficiencies in others, such as indigenous organization. Considered independently, the threshold level for each factor is a necessary but not sufficient condition. If all factors reach their threshold, then the necessary and sufficient conditions exist for the development of a sustained challenge.

The Outcome of Insurgency

The major goal of insurgency is the interjection of the interests of previously excluded groups into centers of economic and political power. The major criteria for success, then, center on changes in the structure of social power. Social power is, of course, a complex, multi-

19

dimensional phenomenon. No simple scale or single dimension can capture the full range of changes potentially entailed by insurgent success. Because challenges are defined primarily in terms of specific institutional antagonisms, the primary successes lie in changing the structure of the master or, as Schwartz (1976:172–176) has called it, "parent" institution that directly molds the lives of the excluded. As Piven and Cloward have argued, "people experience deprivation and oppression within a concrete setting, not as the end product of large and abstract processes. . . . Workers experience the factory, the speeding rhythm of the assembly line, the foreman, the spies and the guards, the owner and the paycheck. They do not experience monopoly capitalism" (1977:20). In order to cement these gains, however, insurgency also has to expand to a broader arena, securing routine access to the polity. Because the state is the primary institution for guaranteeing social claims, the excluded have to secure routine access to the political arena. Otherwise, their antagonists will eventually turn back their newly won rights and gains. A firm independent handle on the ballot box and routine access to legislative chambers and administrative elites are the basic measures.

The structure of social power also has multiple levels or dimensions, setting off different types of insurgent successes. Drawing on the theory of social power outlined by Lukes (1974) and Domhoff (1979:121–150), we can distinguish three different dimensions of insurgent success.[5] Insurgents can secure policy successes by altering the content of official decisions, such as new Congressional legislation or changes in the investment and hiring policies of corporations. The signal of success lies in tangible gains won in direct and open contests of wills. Insurgents can also score regime successes by altering the processes that routinely define the agenda for decision-making. The principal objective here is transforming the institutional processes that routinely bias decision-making, excluding controversial issues and dissident perspectives from the agenda. Alterations in the channels of elite socialization and recruitment, the articulation of new issues and prespectives, and the introduction of new rules defining legitimate actors and forms of collective action fall into this dimension. A transformation of the issues and perspectives brought to bear in policy-making mark the victories here. Finally, insurgencies can generate distributional successes, redistributing socially valued goods to the advantage of previously excluded groups. Transformations in the distribution of economic resources, alterations in the structure of social prestige, and the decentralization of political power fall into this dimension. The signal mark here is a change in the structural conditions that allow groups to mobilize and realize their interests.

Changes in these three dimensions are, of course, interdependent. Full success comes from altering all three dimensions, while lesser measures begin with policy changes and build toward regime and distributional gains. Although there is no necessary time sequence for these changes, victories generally begin with policy successes and culminate in distributional gains. Successful insurgencies generally have to be contented with partial measures. In general, the more favorable the circumstances and the more powerful the movement, the greater the degree of success.

In the classical literature, the issue of insurgent success has virtually been ignored. Given the tendency to view social movements as apolitical expressive actions, this should be no surprise. Insofar as there has been an argument, it has been about the inevitability of the collapse and eventual failure of social movements. Insofar as success is gauged, it is in terms of the self-defined goals or utopias advanced by charismatic leaders. Gauged by the ideals of utopian beliefs, social movements inevitably fall short. In most classical analyses, social movements are seen as inevitably undergoing an endogenously determined natural development or life cycle leading from unstructured spontaneity to ossification and collapse or institutional accommodation (Hopper 1959; Lang and Lang 1961). Political processes are seen as basically irrelevant because, at least in the American polity, power is decentralized, elites are receptive, and the regime is structurally open or, in Gamson's (1975) terms, "permeable" (cf. Dahl 1967; Rose 1967). Because insurgencies are essentially expressive actions, their contribution to actual social change is marginal. Elites, parties, and interest organizations operating within the existing rules of the game are the principal architects of social reforms.

The development and outcome of challenges is far more complex and politically channelled than this classical model has allowed. Insurgencies inevitably decline, but this is often due to successes as well as failures. The classical theories have correctly stressed internal developments such as organizational restructuring and strategic shifts, but as Turner (1964) has argued, interactions with authorities, antagonists, supporters, and bystanders are frequently decisive. Political power is centralized and generally the polity is closed, elites supporting antagonists while potential supporters watch quietly on the sidelines. Because of the antagonistic nature of their demands, insurgents have to step outside the rules of the game to create significant leverage. Theodore Lowi captured the situation quite well when he argued: "The proper image of our society has never been a melting pot. In bad times, it is a boiling pot; in good times, it is a tossed salad. For those who are *in*, this is all very well. But the price has always been paid by those who are *out*, and when they do get in, they do not always get in through a process of mutual accommodation under a broad umbrella of consensus" (1971:53).

In general, a straightforward continuation of the favorable conditions that lead to the emergence of a sustained challenge creates the most favorable circumstances for its further development and success. Since we have discussed these in detail, they require little further elaboration. What does merit further attention are strategic decisions and the development of further political realignments, especially those creating generalized political turmoil. Action strategies have to maximize the leverage against antagonists while minimizing the challenge's vulnerability to social controls. Because there are always multiple targets, insurgents frequently confront conflicting priorities and dilemmas. As for political opportunities, limited realignments created the initial opportunities for mounting the challenge. Dramatic successes typically require further reshuffling inside the polity and the development of generalized political turmoil.

Strategies of Action. In the course of a challenge, the direction becomes increasingly independent of the generating forces, becoming an object for internal debate and explicit deliberations. The social movement organization emerges as the primary arena for these collective decisions, placing organizers and movement leaders in the center of major strategic decisions. The pivotal choices are over alternative organizational structures, the scope of insurgent demands and the tactical repertoire. Challenges have to develop durable organizational structures that increase mobilization levels while minimizing their vulnerability to repression. Insurgents also confront what Ash-Garner (1977:12–13) has called the "optimizing problem" of choosing whether to pursue marginal incremental gains that are more readily obtained or broader structural changes that will provoke intense opposition and open repression. The basic tactical choice lies between making innovative use of existing institutional procedures and intensified institutional disruptions.

In the course of insurgency, social movements almost invariably move in the direction of greater formalization and centralized control. As Gamson's (1975:89-110) study has shown, clear rules and centralized resource management are major pluses in routinizing the flow of resources, reducing the likelihood of debilitating factional disputes and maximizing general combat readiness. The problem, however, is that these same processes can also strip the challenge of its spontaneity, eating away at the missionary impulse that drives organizers and ties them to the mass base, weakening mass solidarity and commitments to the challenge consciousness, and strengthening tendencies towards oligarchization and cooptation. This is especially true for insurgencies among deprived and severely disorganized groups, because they are less likely to sustain support and leaders often find themselves dependent on external support. The National Welfare Rights Organization and its successor, the Movement for Economic Justice, both experienced these strains (Kotz and Kotz 1977; West 1981). Centralized control and formalization also make the challenge more vulnerable, creating a single target for repression, and by reducing internal diversity and competition among organizers, temper the missionary impulse (Gerlach and Hine 1970). Insurgencies, then, are seemingly caught on the horns of an organizational dilemma, pushed towards increased centralization and formalization and towards decentralized informal structures.

This is not, however, an insoluble dilemma. Lawson (1983) has argued that insurgencies with multiple structural levels can enjoy the advantages of both centralized and decentralized structures. A centralized social movement organization operating on a national or polity-wide level can coordinate actions and articulate broad demands yet, by preserving loose links to independent grass-roots locals with their own resources, can retain its spontaneity and diversity. In Lawson's case, the tenant movement in New York has thrown up umbrella-type coordinating organizations that have coordinated political demands and provided technical support while retaining a highly decentralized structure of grass-roots locals in specific tenement buildings that conduct mobilization campaigns and organize strikes. Similarly, the loosely structured Leadership Conference on Civil Rights has coordinated national civil rights lobbying while leaving each segment of the movement to pursue its own distinctive programs on a local level (McAdam 1982:151-156). As we will see, a similar rough balance between centripetal and centrifugal forces was also at work in the more successful stages of the United Farm Worker insurgency.

The optimizing problem is less resolvable. As Gamson (1975:38-55) has argued, insurgencies that restrict their goals to single issues and leave the existing structure of authority uncontested are more likely to secure tangible gains. Those with broader, diffuse goals, especially those that demand the displacement of their antagonists, will provoke intense opposition and repressive controls. Probably the most persuasive tract for cleaving to the conservative side of the optimizing problem is Gelb and Palley's (1982) analysis of the women's movement. By focusing on incremental, single issue reforms that built on institutionalized conceptions of social justice, the moderate wing of the movement has successfully brought about policy successes in the form of legislation and administrative reforms. Meanwhile, the demands of the radical wing for alternative institutions and new standards of equity have provoked a powerful backlash and elite hostility. This argument for thinking small is limited, however, by what it ignores. Insurgent demands are not fixed, emerging full blown in the initial stages of a challenge. Goals develop out of the process of insurgency. Moreover, demands tend to expand in response to successes and increasing opportunities. In the middle 1960s, the successful attack by the civil rights movement on the Jim Crow system led to broader demands for solutions to powerlessness and poverty. Instead of Southern white racists, the target became the corporations, the urban political machines, and the secure white middle class. Although radicalization alienated sympathetic polity members and provoked repression, it also temporarily heightened the pressure on the moderates to produce tangible results and softened up elites to accept significant reforms. In the long run, however, radicalization did have debilitating repercussions, destroying the informal consensus and loose coordination that had held the movement together and generating a white backlash that eventually pushed national political alignments in a conservative direction (McAdam 1982:181-229, 1983).

Insurgencies also choose between unruly disruptive actions and reliance on existing institutional channels. Unruliness works through negative sanctions that create direct leverage but have the long-term negative effect of alienating targets and provoking repression. The urban riots of the 1960s created short-term policy gains (Button 1978; Jennings 1981;

24

Isaac and Kelly 1981) but alienated white sympathizers who then withdrew support from the civil rights movement and licensed wholesale official repression in many riot-torn cities (Schumaker 1978; Burstein 1979, 1981; McAdam 1982:208-229). Existing channels, in contrast, work through persuasion and positive inducements, thereby creating more durable relations (Etzioni 1961). The problem for insurgents, however, is that their demands and resources generally rule out successes based solely on using existing channels. Persuasion depends on shared values and exchange on the control of valuable resources (cf. Turner 1973). Insurgent demands are at odds with the interests of their antagonists, shattering normative agreements. Although positive inducements such as smoother labor relations and voter support are useful, these presuppose that the antagonist has already accepted the challenger as a legitimate bargaining partner. In other words, insurgents have to first secure a degree of access before serious negotiations will be possible. Moreover, insurgents generally have to first use negative measures merely to make their offers of cooperation desirable. Success requires unruliness at some point.

These are not, however, exclusive options. In fact, social movements rarely rely on a single tactical repertoire. The most effective approach has been tactical escalation, beginning with moderate tactics and then escalating towards disruptiveness. As Geschwender (1983) found in the Hawaiian land use dispute, the movement's exhaustion of remedies through existing channels created external support for disruptive measures. Challenges that begin with major disruptions are likely to confront devastating repression.

Structure of Political Alignments. The history of U.S. politics is studded with challenges that made a significant beginning only to be destroyed by political repression (Goldstein 1978). The success of insurgencies is even more dependent on favorable political alignments than the generation of challenges. At a minimum, success entails changes in public policies. More durable changes require the development of routine political access. The key questions are the strength of the coalitions forged between insurgents and polity members and the access of this reform coalition to centers of political power.

The stronger the coalition, the more directly polity members become involved in the outcome of actual conflicts. Sponsors often limit their contributions to organizing resources, helping to generate a challenge but leaving its prospects uncertain. Others become more directly involved,

25

providing political protection and openly attacking antagonists. As we will see, farm worker movements have traditionally received meager organizing support and even less political protection. The UFW was distinctive because it received extensive political protection as well as organizing support and, by organizing widely supported boycotts, brought sponsors directly into the fray. Similarly, the civil rights movement received significant organizing support from liberal foundations, church agencies, and labor unions, but only with federal restrictions on the activities of the Ku Klux Klan and the White Citizens Councils and the sustained legal attack by the American Bar Association and the American Civil Liberties Union on southern state governments was it able to organize successful voter registration drives (Thayer 1968; Navasky 1974; Lawson 1976).

The strength of these member-challenger coalitions depends on the bases for support and the reform coalition's position in the broader struggle for political power. Polity members have to perceive a clear and direct advantage to extend sustained support. In liberal democratic polities, the key consideration is the electoral calculus of bringing new groups into the polity in the context of shifting or unstable electoral alignments and closely contested elections. Reform coalitions coming to power also have more political influence and a larger stake in bringing new groups into the polity. The Democratic party has historically been the major supporter of new groups. In the 1930s, critical Democratic support for the industrial worker movement stemmed from the importance of blue collar votes in the shifting electoral alignments of the early 1930s (Andersen 1979; Piven and Cloward 1977). Likewise, their electoral victories strengthened their ability to institutionalize the political access of unions. Similarly, black ballots were strategically important in the closely contested elections of the late 1950s and early 1960s, leading to Democratic support for the civil rights movement. As the Democratic party expanded its electoral margin, its ability to institute incorporative social reforms such as the Civil Rights Acts of 1964 and 1965 increased. The UFW victories stemmed, as we will see, from the same realignments and political coalitions.

The most dramatic insurgent successes flow from generalized realignments that are intertwined with the development of generalized political turmoil. Favorable realignments and insurgent successes spur the development of new challenges. The proliferation of social movements and the spread of institutional disruptions maximize the pressure for further reforms. Electoral coalitions become unpredictable, intensifying party competition for mass loyalties and weakening the hold of entrenched opponents. Sponsors become more optimistic about the prospects for further reforms and step up their sponsorship. Political elites sponsor the entry of the more powerful insurgencies and institutionalize social reforms that, in part, address their demands. Just as the political realignments and turmoil of the 1930s gave rise to a series of labor and social welfare reforms and the entry of new groups into the polity, we will argue that the successes of the UFW depended on the political realignments and generalized turmoil of the late 1960s and early 1970s.

Summary

The resource mobilization theory of social movements offers a distinctive analysis of the generation and outcome of insurgencies. In contrast with the classical theories, it emphasizes the indigenous resources, organization, and strategic position of excluded groups and the creation of political opportunities by political realignments. The images of mass explosions stemming from intense, widespread discontents and inevitable movement collapse have been replaced by those of excluded groups pursuing their collective interests in a restrictive polity. Insurgencies are seen as the major agencies of social change and their success as stemming from effective strategies of mobilization and action and from the political opportunities created by political realignments. The central issues in the study of social movements, then, are questions of power and politics, not the social psychology of grievances and the exotic character of insurgent beliefs.

2

California Agriculture and Grower Power

". . . a history of greed, of perjury, of corruption, of spoilation, and high-handed robbery for which it will be difficult to find a parallel."

Henry George (1871)

"Ill fares the land, to hastening ills a prey,
Where wealth accumulates, and men decay."

Oliver Goldsmith (1770)

In the spring of 1880, Karl Marx wrote his American friend Friedrich Sorge, bidding information on the transformation of California agriculture. "California is important because nowhere else has the upheaval shamelessly caused by capitalist centralization taken place with such speed" (1979:330). A half century later, Carey McWilliams, a muckraking journalist and political activist, returned to the theme, tracing the historical processes that gave rise to the "great exception" of the *Factories in the Field* (1939). Although the concentration of American agriculture has since reduced the distinctiveness of rural California (Vogeler 1981), Marx and McWilliams were correct about the exceptional character of early California agriculture. Capitalist development came early to California and occurred with such a swift vengeance that the egalitarian cultural and political traditions laid down elsewhere in the United States by family farming never caught hold. California agriculture was, as it were, born in old age. Concentrated ownership, large-scale factory production, and a massive proletariat of impoverished migratory workers have been features since the mid-nineteenth century. Marx and Mc-Williams were also right about another feature. Capitalist centralization brought in its wake social upheaval: extreme concentration of economic wealth and power, racist ideologies legitimizing farm worker subordination, and a closed political system dominated by the growers.

Of the two analysts, Carey McWilliams has proven the more durable. Like many contemporary analysts, Marx assumed that capitalist centralization flowed directly from the evolutionary development of the means of production. In this view, the course of economic development was regulated by market competition, insuring the eventual dominance of the most efficient enterprises. In his two classics, *Factories in the Fields* (1939) and *Ill Fares the Land* (1942), McWilliams thoroughly punctured these myths, demonstrating the centrality of grower power in the development of the "great exception." A handful of land barons seized the arable lands, mobilized an army of farm workers to operate the vast estates, secured governmental programs to tame the arid environment and chaotic markets, and freely used repression to block challenges. This centrality of grower power also undermined another of Marx's predictions. Marx assumed that capitalist centralization would create an organized, class-conscious working class capable of mounting successful challenges. But grower power created a disorganized, impoverished body of workers that, at least until recently, has been unable to mount a sustained challenge.

The following two chapters analyze the structure of California agriculture as a system of power. This chapter deals with the dominant side of the system, analyzing the bases of grower power and the sources of their intransigent resistance to insurgency. Chapter 3 turns to the farm worker side, examining the bases of farm worker powerlessness and recent changes in their strategic position and potential for mobilization.

The Structure of California Agriculture

The structure of any economic system is fixed by two major axes: the property system that defines the claims on the economic goods produced and the political supports required to maintain these claims—what Marx called the "relations of production"—and the technology that shapes the actual production activities that take place inside particular enterprises—the "forces of production." In rural California, the dominant agricultural enterprise has been what Paige (1975) has called the "migratory labor estate." Capitalist relations and the technology of so-called specialty crop production, chiefly fruits and vegetables, have created a distinctive system of power and class conflict.

The core feature of a capitalist enterprise is the wage-labor/capital relationship. The grower owns the means of production and hires wage workers to carry out actual production tasks, extracting and economic surplus for personal consumption and future investments out of the difference between expenses and receipts from the sales of farm commodities. This sets up a series of antagonisms between grower and worker over the control of the production process and the distribution of the net product. Growers favor a rapid and predictable production pace that maximizes their flexibility and minimizes capital investments and labor costs. Workers, in contrast, favor secure employment, a less intense production pace, and maximum wages.

The technology of specialty crop production has sharpened the basic antagonisms, creating an underlying profit squeeze, insecure employment, and harsh working conditions. The major specialty crops are fruits, nuts, and vegetables. The production cycle of these crops is highly discontinuous, creating sharp seasonal fluctuations in jobs. Employment is highly unstable, work coming in brief fits and starts. Particular tasks such as girdling grape vines or hoeing onions often last only a week or two at a time, and, to insure their production schedule, growers prefer hiring excess workers, thereby aggravating employment insecurity.[1] The great estates, then, have depended on a vast army of seasonal farm workers who either migrate from area to area with the crop cycle or fill out the season with work in other industries and enforced idleness. As I will argue in chapter 3, erratic employment and migrancy have deprived farm workers of a secure livelihood and solidarity, thereby contributing to farm worker powerlessness and exclusion. Yet, paradoxically, this has also weakened the growers' institutional controls over their workers. Strong controls depend on a long-term employment relationship. Under tenancy, for example, the landowners can use paternalistic controls, extending personal favors such as cheap housing, emergency loans and a show of personal concern in exchange for personal loyalty. Similarly, on large ranches and plantations, the owners use bureaucratic structures and longer job tenure to create a more loyal and cooperative labor force (cf. Stinchcombe 1961; Paige 1975). The discontinuous character of specialty production undermines these controls, leaving the growers relatively vulnerable to challenges.

The discontinuous production cycle has also depressed the rate of profit. As Mann and Dickinson (1978, 1980) have argued, discontinuous production means that fixed capital investments in buildings, machines, and land improvement frequently stand idle, raising the total capital costs of the enterprise and thereby lowering the average rate of profit. Although this is relevant for production agriculture as a whole, this profit squeeze is even greater for specialty crops because the discontinuities are more and fixed investments are higher than in other agricultural sectors. The specialty crop growers, then, have to strengthen their control over the most malleable production factor, namely, direct labor-power. As Paige (1975:66–70) has argued, the grower/worker antagonism on the migratory estates resembles a zero-sum game in which both parties can advance their interests only at the expense of the other. Conflicts are intense, and the issues range across the board from the pace and organization of production to wages and employment security.

A second feature of specialty crop production is its labor-intensiveness and the general lack of technical progress. This has been due to two factors: the inherent obstacles to rationalizing production and the availability of so-called cheap docile labor. Crops of highly variable size, maturation cycle, and perishability make it difficult to improve productivity by greater division of tasks or introduction of machinery. In fact, new technology generally requires the development of new crop varieties. In addition, the depressed level of farm wages and the general surplus of docile workers have greatly reduced the incentive for improved labor productivity. The introduction of vacuum packing of head lettuce and machine harvest of tomatoes illustrate the basic pattern. In the late 1950s, Bud Antle, the largest head lettuce grower in the Salinas Valley, introduced a new method for packing lettuce, vacuum packing in the fields in place of traditional ice packing in sheds. The impetus came from a series of packingshed strikes and the availability of cheap docile braceros (Spanish for "arms") imported from Mexico to handle field tasks. The gain came from the lower wages paid to braceros, not increased labor productivity or cheaper machines (Glass 1966). Similarly, the introduction of machine-harvested tomatoes in the 1970s stemmed from labor insurgency. In this case, a lone inventor had developed a new tomato variety and harvest machinery as early as 1963, but few growers adopted the

31

new method because of lower crop quality and available cheap labor. Mass insurgency in the tomato harvest in the early 1970s prompted wholesale mechanization and, in this case, significant improvements in labor productivity (Hightower 1973; Friedland, Barton, and Thomas 1981). Overall, however, labor productivity in specialty crops has been stagnant over the past half century, especially compared to the technology revolution that has taken place in the rest of production agriculture (see figure 2.1). Direct labor costs still constitute the largest single farm expense, frequently one third to half of total expenses, and the ratio of labor inputs to total production has changed little (Goldsmidt 1947:34-40; California Senate 1961; Kasimatis 1967:36; USDA, State Farm Income Statistics, 1976). In effect, the profit margin in specialty production still depends on "sweating out" the workers and holding the lid on wages rather than reorganizing production tasks or substituting machines for direct laborpower. This, of course, has reinforced the squeeze on profits and aggravated the zero-sum character of the grower/worker antagonism.

The perishability of most specialty crops also makes the estates highly vulnerable to disruption. Although the scheduling of the harvest on some crops such as oranges and grapefruit is quite flexible, most fruits and vegetables ripen during a short and often unpredictable time period. The harvest then constitutes a bottleneck in the production cycle, giving the harvest workers considerable leverage. This leverage is magnified by the fact that the entire investment in the standing crop rides on a successful harvest. In response, many growers have tried to instill loyalty among their seasonal workers by wage premiums and cheap housing. Yet because of high labor turnover, the growers have had to fall back on more direct coercive controls.

The profit squeeze also stems from the marketing characteristics of specialty crops. Consumer demand for most fruit and vegetables is price inelastic. In other words, price cuts do not bring out increased purchases that would stabilize price declines. The commodity markets are easily flooded at the harvest peak, producing intense price competition and extremely narrow profit margins. The growers who market their crops early make fabulous profits, but the rest reap narrow margins. The notorious fluctuations in the prices of head lettuce, for example, have earned it the nickname "green gold" and enveloped it in the mythology of Las Vegas gambling casinos with their high risks, tides of fortune, and famine (Friedland, Barton and Thomas 1981). Moreover, like the rest of

Figure 2.1
Trends in Labor Efficiency

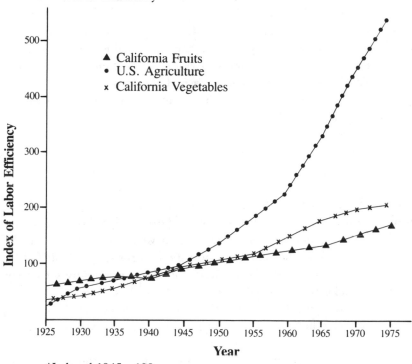

▲ California Fruits
• U.S. Agriculture
× California Vegetables

*Indexed 1945 = 100

SOURCE: USDA Agricultural Statistics, 1925–1978.

production agriculture, the great fruit and vegetable estates are in the periphery of the national economy (Averitt 1968). Their market position vis-à-vis the suppliers of credit and machinery and the large grocery chains and food processors is weak. The growers have therefore faced a long-term "cost-price" squeeze that has narrowed their profit margins and increased their risks (California Senate 1961; Wilcox et al. 1973:236–248). Although market rationalization through marketing order quotas and cooperative selling has reduced the severity of price fluctuations and strengthened the growers' hand in the marketplace, the average returns from most specialty crops have remained extremely narrow.

These structural features of the migratory labor estates have created a profit squeeze while leaving the estates highly vulnerable to worker disruptions. In response, the growers have strengthened their controls

by recruiting a large pool of docile, cheap labor that is amenable to erratic seasonal employment. Docility is important because the growers have
lacked institutional controls and have been vulnerable to harvest strikes.
Cheap labor purchased at rates below labor-power of comparable productivity is important because of the stagnant production methods and
the long-term "cost-price" squeeze. Erratic seasonal employment is due
to the discontinuous production cycle and the large size of the typical
enterprise. Chapter 3 will look in detail at the traditional measures for
securing access to this labor base.

The interplay of these factors has created intransigent resistance among
the growers to any improvements in worker conditions (figure 2.2). In
fact, the growers have treated virtually any signs of worker independence, much less open organizing or mass defiance, as a fundamental
threat to their property rights. As John Steinbeck's legendary grower Hines
replied to worker queries about his wage rates: " 'A *red* is any son-of-a-
bitch that wants thirty cents an hour when we're payin' twenty-five!' "
(1939:329). Because the controls inside the enterprise are weak and the
growers share most of the labor force, they have frequently set up collective agencies to recruit labor and combat strikes. Because of the se-
riousness of the perceived threat, the growers have viewed virtually any
measures—including armed violence and vigilante attacks—as legitimate
controls.

A major support of this production system has been the grower's monopoly over the politics of the rural communities. The growers are local
residents but the majority of the workers are not, and the immigrants
lack basic citizenship rights. The imbalance in organization and structural access is even greater. The growers are highly mobilized, and because of their importance to the rural communities, local officials automatically take their interests into account in making decisions. The
workers, by contrast, are disorganized and viewed by local officials with
contempt and derision. As one police chief in the 1930s commented: "The
workers are like pigs! We herd them!" (Dunne 1967:117).

Community politics is especially important to the growers because the
major agencies that control the labor markets—the county labor bureaus, labor associations, and labor placement offices—are arms of local
government or regional quasi-public agencies such as irrigation districts
and crop marketing boards. The local courts and police have also provided the first line of defense in labor conflicts, harassing organizers,

Figure 2.2

The Logic of Grower Intransigence

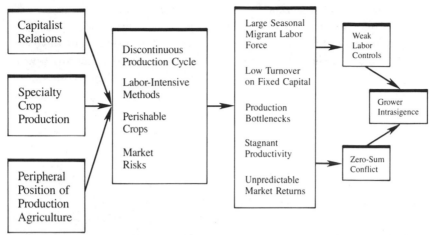

outlawing peaceful demonstrations and strikes, and deterring organizing drives by guaranteeing the growers' right to restrict access to their private labor camps. In general, this grower political monopoly has been sufficiently impregnable that most insurgencies have not been sustained beyond a few isolated strikes.

The Rise of the Factory Farm

The story of the rise of the factory farm as the dominant institution in rural California is a tale that is part heroic epic and part tragedy. Heroic epic because, against major odds, an arid marginal frontier was transformed almost overnight into a bountiful, seemingly endless Garden of Eden. Tragedy because, despite this cornucopia, the majority of the rural populace have been excluded from its fruits.

In 1850 California was admitted to the Union as a sparsely settled, economically marginal frontier state. A few large rancheros owned by Mexican landholders or *Californios* and staffed by a handful of Indian and mestizo ranch hands raised cattle and sheep, alongside the gold and silver prospectors and a growing contingent of small farmers. By the end of the nineteenth century, the economic base of the state had been radically transformed. California had become a major wheat exporter, the leading wheat producer in the United States, and the second largest agricultural state. The quiet rancheros that had dotted the fertile valleys had long disappeared, replaced by two rival institutions—the large migratory labor estates worked by a swelling army of migratory farm workers, and the family farms of the newly arrived settlers. Those two types of agricultural enterprise contained the seed of two divergent developmental paths. If the large capitalist estates prevailed, economic power would become centralized and the division between owner and worker would give rise to intense class conflicts. If the family farm prevailed, economic power would become decentralized and a relatively egalitarian rural society might emerge. The rivalry was short-lived. By the 1930s the large estates had won out, leaving the small farmers to make do with the margins and creating a vast and troublesome agricultural proletariat.

There have been two major schools of interpretations of this "great transformation" of California agriculture. The historical school, best represented by Jamieson (1945), Cleland (1944, 1947, 1951, 1963) and Gregor (1962, 1969, 1970a, 1970b), has emphasized the central importance of the heritage created by the colonial land system. Four centuries of Spanish and Mexican colonial rule created a centralized land tenure system. Economic development was therefore channeled towards a centralized economy dominated by large capitalist enterprises. The more conventional economic school has emphasized the superior productive efficiency of the large estates, especially in an arid terrain. The large estates could absorb the risks of unpredictable harvests (Rasmussen 1975; Wik 1975), tackle large-scale and expensive land improvements such as irrigation projects and erosion control (Nash 1959; Dumke 1944; Maass and Anderson 1978), and make maximum use of advanced technology (Higbee 1963; Rusmussen 1975; Rodman 1975).

Neither of these interpretations is fully adequate. The historical interpretation has been more fruitful, emphasizing the importance of early land concentration and the exclusion of the small farmers. This overstates, however, the weight of historical tradition and understates the diverse bases of grower power. The economic interpretation, despite its greater popularity, is far weaker. It has ignored the central role of grower power and has erroneously assumed that the large estates are more efficient.

The major factor behind the rise of the great estates has been the power of the growers. There were two stages in the "great transformation." The first, from statehood through roughly 1900, was shaped primarily by the

Figure 2.3

Average Size of California and U.S. Farms

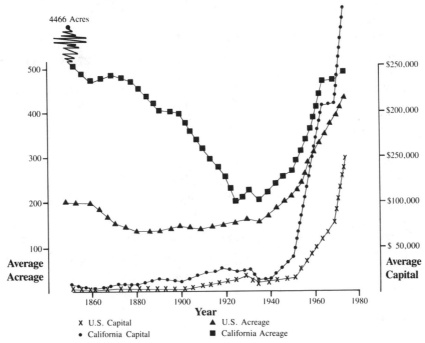

SOURCE: U.S. Agricultural Census, 1960–1974.

colonial land heritage and extensive corruption in the sales of public lands. By 1900, a small group of large investors controlled the most valuable farm lands, having seized the colonial estates and kept public lands out of the hands of small settlers. The second stage came with the conversion to specialty crops. Between 1900 and the 1930s, the great landowners successfully externalized a major share of their production costs through governmental programs that provided irrigation subsidies and rationalized chaotic commodity markets. Most critical of all, mass unemployment created access to plentiful supplies of cheap docile labor.

The basic contours of this "great transformation" can be gauged from the trend in the size of California farms. Figure 2.3 and table 2.1 chart changes in average landholding, capital investments, and land concentration over the past century. In 1850 California entered the Union with an average farm size of over 4,000 acres—over twenty times that of the average U.S. farm. Average farm value was $8,400—three times the na-

Table 2.1

Land Concentration in California and U.S. Agriculture

California Farms Acreage	1860	1880	1900	1930	1950	1974
10	5.9%	3.4%	9.4%	21.3%	27.3%	19.9%
10–49	24.5	11.7	29.5	25.3	37.8	35.7
50–99	17.3	11.0	11.1	12.1	11.1	12.3
100–499	46.6	56.3	36.1	17.3	15.9	19.4
a. 100–174	—	—	(18.2)	(8.5)	(7.8)	(8.8)
b. 175–259	—	—	(6.4)	(3.7)	(3.3)	(4.3)
c. 260–499	—	—	(11.5)	(5.1)	(4.8)	(6.3)
500–999	3.8	8.6	7.3	3.6	3.5	5.2
1000	1.9	7.0	6.5	3.7	4.4	8.5
	100.0	100.0	100.0	100.0	100.0	100.0

U.S. Farms Acreage	1860	1880	1900	1930	1950	1974
10	2.8%	3.5%	4.7%	5.7%	8.9%	5.5%
10–49	39.8	25.8	29.0	31.8	27.5	16.4
59–99	31.1	25.8	23.8	21.9	19.4	16.6
100–499	24.9	42.3	39.9	36.8	38.5	45.7
a. 100–174	—	—	(24.8)	(21.4)	(20.5)	(19.1)
b. 175–259	—	—	(8.5)	(8.3)	(9.1)	(10.9)
c. 260–499	—	—	(6.6)	(7.2)	(8.9)	(15.7)
500–999	1.0	1.9	1.8	2.5	3.4	9.0
1000	0.4	0.7	0.8	1.3	2.3	6.7
	100.0	100.0	100.0	100.0	100.0	100.0

Source: *U.S. Census* (1860–1930); *Census of Agriculture* (1950, 1974).

tional average. Capitalist centralization was not, however, a continuous linear development. Between statehood and the turn of the century, California agriculture actually became slightly decentralized. Average farm size dropped to less than 400 acres, two and a half times the national average, while average value rose to $10,000, still about one-third the national norm. In effect, the door had been opened by ever so narrow a crack to small settlers, who purchased smaller, less valuable farms and substituted their own sweat for hired labor and expensive machinery. Small farms of less than 100 acres increased to almost half of all farms by 1860 and peaked at two-thirds around 1900. Still the large estates (over 1,000 acres) did not actually decline, rising from 262 or less than two percent of all farms to 2,531 or almost seven percent. By 1900, a third of all arable acreage lay within these mammoth estates. The competition between these two conflicting trends continued through the 1930s when the capitalist estates firmly told hold. The Great Depression expanded access to cheap docile labor, new public irrigation projects provided vast water subsidies, and New Deal policies created market controls that reduced price fluctuations, thereby allowing the great estates to shift to specialty crop production.

The Colonial Land Heritage.   The Spanish began colonizing southern California in the late sixteenth century, establishing a series of haciendas or church missions containing a military garrison and 20,000 to 30,000 acres (Cleland 1944; Shrode 1956). The haciendas rested on manorial labor, using imported Spanish peasants and native Indians who had been coerced into the service of the priests. In return for political protection and access to subsistence plots, the peons provided corvee labor on the mission lands. The chief products were grain and goats, largely for direct consumption. Private holdings were rare. The Spanish made only twenty-five private land grants during three centuries of colonial rule. Because of the arid terrain, the haciendas were clustered in the river valleys and along the coast line. Irrigation was poorly developed, although one large hacienda in the Imperial Valley built a primitive system, diverting the Colorado River water onto the rich bottom lands.

In 1821 Mexico declared its independence from Spain and reorganized the land system to promote further settlement. The haciendas provided little tax revenue, and encroachments by Russian and U.S. settlers threatened Mexican hold on the territory. The Mexican governors began distributing large private land grants with the sole proviso that the land actually be settled and turned to productive use. Most of the grants were used for ranching, providing grazing lands for large herds of cattle and sheep (Cleland 1951; Hutchinson 1969). Like the haciendas, the rancheros were based on peonage and production was subsistence oriented with the chief commercial product being cattle hides.

In 1828 the Mexican governors launched an attack on the haciendas, stepping up their tax collection efforts and, in 1833, abolished the missions outright under the Secularization Act, opening them to private denouncement. The peon labor system was preserved but all lands were converted to private ownership. Land grants were limited to between 4,500 and 50,000 acres, the range considered ideal for cattle ranching.

Between 1833 and 1846, over eight hundred new land grants were made transferring over eight million acres of land largely in the southern section of the California territory. Spanish and Mexican colonial rule created a highly concentrated system of land tenure, but because most of the prime lands in the northern valleys remained unclaimed, the direction of land development remained open.

Statehood to the Great Land Wars. U.S. encroachment intensified in the 1840s and, in 1846, U.S. troops under Colonel Stephen Kearny finally subdued the last Mexican military resistance, annexing California to the United States. In terms of agricultural development, there were two major options: capitalist development based on increasing the number of large estates and importing vast numbers of landless workers; and small farmer development based on dismantling the estates and opening unclaimed lands exclusively to small settlers. Although several estate owners flirted with the option of slavery, the majority preferred peonage or free labor as a more efficient labor base. The major question, then, was the land tenure system. Over the next five decades, this issue gave rise to a plethora of court battles, electoral campaigns, and vigilante land seizures. At the center of these battles were two prizes—the large estates of the Mexican californios in the south and the vast unclaimed public lands in the north and central valleys. At its core, the struggle was essentially a three-way battle between the colonial estate holders attempting to hold onto their claims, the swelling flood of small settlers seeking to dislodge them and claim the open lands, and an emerging class of Anglo land barons bent on seizing the colonial estates and controlling the allocation of public lands.

The Treaty of Guadalupe Hidalgo (1848) set the basic direction, guaranteeing the claims of holders of Mexican land grants. Peonage was protected but slavery prohibited. In 1850, California entered the Union as a free state with an agricultural economy dominated by the large landowners. The average farm contained over 4,400 acres with less than two percent of the population holding more than half the arable lands. At the center of this land monopoly stood the colonial estate holders or californios, an economic elite numbering less than 200 families and owning over 14 million acres in parcels of 20,000 to 30,000 acres (McWilliams 1949:20–23; Pitt 1966:87).

The battle then shifted to the courts and legislature. Many of the Mexican claims lacked solid legal footing, having been hastily filed in the closing months of Mexican rule in anticipation of the U.S. annexation. Others predated accurate surveys, lacking clear definitions of boundaries and water rights. Many had never even been registered. Overlapping claims were common. On top of this, several large estate owners had set about expanding their domain, floating the boundaries of their claims through court maneuvers and forgeries so as to seize gold claims, land improvements, and water rights. The situation was so confused that in 1851 the U.S. Congress established the California Land Commission to adjudicate conflicting claims. Any claims not confirmed by the Commission within five years were declared invalid and opened to settlement as public lands (Allen 1935; Gates 1959, 1967: Ch. 1).

The colonial land grants were concentrated in the southern part of the state but most of the disputes were in the north. The gold rush had enticed settlers to the north, and the terrain was generally better suited to small homesteading. The northern californios were also more vulnerable, a fact which the Anglo settlers quickly recognized. Ignoring the Land Commission, the small settlers flooded the local courts with legal complaints contesting the colonial claims and the efforts to extend them. Many turned to open squatting, seizing choice sections and hoping with numbers and organization to make their claims stick. In one dramatic case, over 1,000 settlers, armed to the teeth, ambushed without distinction land surveyors, estate owners, and a sheriff's posse dispatched to clear the squatters from one of the large estates (Pitt 1966:228–230).

Despite occasional settler victories, the Commission left most of the large estates intact. When it finished its work in 1856, it had reviewed 813 claims covering over 14 million acres and, in 588 cases, ruled in favor of the original claimant, confirming over 8.9 million acres or nine percent of the state's total acreage (Taylor 1975:159). Yet most of the estates changed hands during this tumultuous period. The northern californios were one by one overwhelmed by the settlers. In many cases they lost their estates to the Anglo lawyers and bankers simply because of the legal costs of defending their claims. Others lost in front of prejudiced judges or following vigilante attacks (Pitt 1966). By 1860, the northern californios had been vanquished. In the south, the californios held on through the early 1870s when prolonged droughts, expensive legal battles, and high usury rates forced massive land sales. Anglo bankers and large investors were the major buyers, often picking up the estates for pennies an acre (Cleland 1963: Ch. 7). The demise of the californios, however, did not mean that the large estates were broken up. Instead it meant the rise of a new class of Anglo land barons, who reorganized the estates as capitalist enterprises and shifted to production for the market and use of hired labor.

The possibility of small farm settlement was not, however, foreclosed. The State of California still controlled vast tracts of public lands, sufficient to create over 50,000 farms of 160 to 200 acres. While these were not the choice lands, most of the public land was in the north and suitable for homesteading. The question was how it would be allocated. Operating under laws that trumpeted the moral and economic superiority of the small farmer, the public land offices channeled most of the public land into the hands of the new land barons. The devices ranged from the use of dummy entrymen hired by large investors to purchase small plots, to lax statutes and administration in the state land office, to outright corruption. Between 1865 and 1875, over eight million acres of public land were distributed by the California land office, creating 7008 large farms of 100,000 or more acres (Gates 1975).

An indication of the general pattern of public land development is given by the Swamplands Act of 1850. By special Congressional legislation passed in 1855, the state of California acquired control of all "swamp and overflow" sections of public lands. These lands were to be sold off to small settlers in plots of 320 acres at $1.15 to $1.25 per acre with the proceeds to be set aside for the construction of levees and drains to make them arable. The statutes, however, contained no criteria defining swamplands, leaving the issue to the imagination of the state land officers. Because land sales were administered by part-time officers paid on a bounty basis for the quantity of land sold, the officers preferred a loose definition of swamplands. As an additional boon to land speculators, a claim required initial payment of only twenty percent of the purchase price with the balance defrayed for five years. Since this payment schedule was rarely enforced, land speculators removed vast tracts for the token fee of twenty cents an acre, fulfilling payment only after land prices had risen. To bypass the acreage restriction, large investors hired dummy entrymen who, once the claim was secure, resold the claim to the investor. Additional opportunities were created by the absence of clear land surveys. Disputes over the colonial estates meant that most California public lands remained unsurveyed until the 1860s. Claimants handled their own surveys, subject to certification by the state land agents who rarely went out in the field. As a result many swamplands entries contained previously claimed land.

Irregularities in the sales of swamplands and other public lands were so severe that in 1871 the California legislature finally investigated the sales of state lands. The hearings revealed widespread violations of the federal statutes and the amassing of vast tracts of public lands by large land speculators. A group of thirty "swamplands thieves," as the editor of the *Alta Californian* called them, had entered claims for over 430,000 acres, an average of over 16,000 acres apiece. The most flagrant violations were carried out by a cabal of San Francisco financiers headed by Henry Miller and Charles Lux. Working closely with officials in the state land office who had been well rewarded for their cooperation, the land corporation organized by Miller and Lux secured patents for a total of 80,350 acres of swamplands. Another pair, James Ben Ali Haggin and Lloyd Tevis, laid hands on over 34,000 acres, the initial basis for the mammoth Kern County Land Company. To evade the acreage restrictions, Haggin had scouted the San Francisco barrooms, hiring drifters and unemployed cowhands at a dollar a head to serve as dummy entrymen. Nor were most of the lands actually swamplands. As the muckracking journalist Horace Greeley claimed, the so-called swamplands often contained "not muck enough on the surface to accommodate a single fair-sized frog" (cited in McWilliams 1949:96). In one notorious case, Henry Miller vouched for his "swamplands" by hitching a team of horses up to a boat and having himself towed about his vast tracts. According to the state land agent who verified Miller's claim, any land over which a boat could pass constituted "swampland" (McWilliams 1939: ch. 4, 1949:95–97; Gates 1959:326–328, 1975:161–163).

The same pattern of land concentration and corruption held on the other public land programs—the public school lands, the Morrill Act lands, those of the various acts to finance the contruction of public buildings (including the state capitol), the Desert Land Act of 1877, and the Stone and Timber Acts (Gates 1960, 1975). Additional public lands were also handed over to finance railway construction, most of which remained in the hands of the railway magnates (McWilliams 1949:94–96). By the turn of the century, the land tenure system was essentially fixed. A new class of Anglo land barons had amassed large estates by seizing the colonial land grants and manipulating the sales of public lands. Typical of the new land barons were Henry Miller and Charles Lux, a pair of land pirates who had successfully acquired joint control of 223,000 acres of Mexican land grants, 181,132 acres of federal lands, and over 120,000 of state school and improvement lands. By 1891, the Miller and Lux partnership held over 750,000 acres. There was also the Kern County Land Company organized by Haggin and Tevis, an empire that contained over 400,000 acres in the San Joaquin Valley alone—183,000 acres of desert lands, 33,868 acres purchased from the Southern Pacific, 59,252 acres from state school and improvement sales, 17,151 from various federal scripts, plus an additional 54,000 acres purchased from private owners. There were the holdings of William Chapman and Issac Friedlander, acclaimed by the press respectively as the "king of the desert lands thieves" and "the wheat king," who had amassed some 632,000 acres of federal lands and 22,000 of school lands, most of the latter during the period that Chapman was on the Board of Regents of the University of California (Gates 1975:167–178). Henry George, writing in 1871 before the scale of the public land frauds had become fully evident, claimed:

California is not a country of farms but a country of plantations and estates. Agriculture is speculation. There is no state in the Union in which settlers in good faith have been so persecuted, so robbed, as in California. Men have grown rich, and men still make a regular business of blackmailing settlers upon the public land, of appropriating their homes, and this by power of the law and in the name of justice. (cited in McWilliams 1949:99)

In 1900, the agricultural census revealed 4,753 large estates of over 1,000 acres that contained almost two-thirds of all farmland, accounted for one-third of fixed farm capital, produced one-third of all commercial crops, and provided over one-third of farm employment. Lord Bryce's epigram had become even more relevant: "Latifundia perdunt California!"

Land concentration did not go uncontested, but the small farmers proved too few and politically weak. The influx of small settlers increased in the 1870s as the railways and land speculators launched promotional efforts. But most of the settlers were forced onto marginal lands in the northern foothills and the arid southern San Joaquin. Land prices averaged ten times those in the midwest (Shanon 1968:162–165). The first serious settler challenge came in the 1870s when the Grange, extolling cooperation and scientific husbandry, grew to over 15,000 members. In 1873, the People's Independent Party was organized, making demands for public regulation of the railways, land taxes to break up the estates, and a restructuring of water rights. In 1876 the small farmers managed to force a constitutional convention, only to lose control of the convention when they refused to ally with representatives of the urban workers.

The few successful reforms proved blunt instruments. The State Board of Equalization, for example, was created to implement Henry George's "single tax" measure, raising the taxes on the great baronies so as to force them into the marketplace. Although a few developers had to set up "colony" settlements (cf. Dumke 1944), most of the land barons either shifted to more profitable intensive cultivation or evaded the new tax assessors. Haggin and Tevis, for example, installed irrigation and planted acres of orchards and grape vines. Other land barons bribed the new tax collectors. Some reforms were simply corrupted. The Railroad Commission was designed to force down rail rates, but William Herrin, the major owner of the Southern Pacific Railway, found that the newly appointed populist commissioners were easily purchased with bribes (Delmatier et al. 1970: ch. 3). Nor did the populist surge of the 1890s alter the scene, putting the Democratic party into disarray with its fusion tactics (Gates 1962, 1967; Cleland 1944: ch. 19).

The Specialty Crop Revolution.   About the same time, the great land owners began experimenting with new crops and production methods. By 1860 most of the large estates had been reorganized as capitalist enterprises, but cattle ranching remained the primary activity, requiring only few workers and little division of labor. The first genuine factory farms were San Joaquin Valley wheat farms established in the 1870s that used large gangs of seasonal workers, mostly Chinese immigrants recently released from railway construction, and heavy machinery to cultivate vast fields of grain. Between 1852 and 1874 wheat exports from the San Joaquin grew from 112,000 to over 7.5 million bushels. The estates were vast, one being worked by plow teams that traveled seventeen miles in each direction, using a whole day to traverse the fields. The wheat barons secured strong fencing laws, making stock owners liable for crop damages by wandering livestock.

When the wheat boom peaked in the mid-1880s, the estate owners began shifting to what would prove the mainstray of the factory farms— the production of specialty crops and sugar beets. By 1894 wheat exports had dropped to 7.3 million bushels while fruit orchards and vegetable fields, previously mere adjuncts to the wheat farms, spread throughout

Table 2.2
The Growth of Specialty Crops in California

		Value of California Specialty Crops	California as % of U.S. Specialty Crops	% of Total California Agricultural Production
1850	Vegetables,	$ 75,275	1.0%	.5%
	fruits, and nuts	17,700	.3	1
1879	Vegetables,	796,663	4	1
	fruits, and nuts	2,017,314	4	3
1900	Vegetables,	93,641,334	39	3
	fruits, and nuts	28,280,104	22	21
1929	Vegetables,	100,234,599	16	14
	fruits, and nuts	218,048,463	26	35
1949	Vegetables,	180,862,162	30	17
	fruits, and nuts	350,327,312	44	33
1969	Vegetables,	457,519,217	36	12
	fruits, and nuts	785,829,154	46	20

Source: *U.S. Census* (1860–1930); *Census of Agriculture* (1950–1969).

the Valley. In 1879 specialty crops accounted for less than four percent of commercial agricultural products but, by 1900, comprised one-quarter, making California the nation's leading producer of specialty crops (table 2.2). Sugar beets were the other major crop, based on Japanese labor and protected by strong tariffs. When the agricultural slump of the 1930s came, the labor surplus created by mass unemployment facilitated the shift to labor-intensive specialty crops (Reed 1956; Shear 1956; Knott 1956; Shanon 1968). Soon specialty crops defined the major crop regions and made up over a third of the state's commercial agriculture.

The specialty crop revolution was rooted in the power of the great land barons. Specialty crops required vast amounts of water on a controllable schedule. Large-scale irrigation was the ideal arrangement. The land barons organized private works and pressed for publicly subsidized projects. Specialty crops were also highly perishable, and because of the inelasticity of consumer demand, maximum profits depended on matching supply with existing demand. So the land barons established marketing cooperatives and pressed for governmental controls to rationalize the markets. Most important of all, the specialty crops were labor-intensive. Although the mass unemployment of the 1930s provided sufficient labor,

Map 1

Crop Regions in California

SACRAMENTO
VALLEY

Scale of Miles

0   50   100

Peaches
Yuba City ● ● Wheatland
Grain

● Sacramento
Cherries
Asparagus ● Stockton
San Francisco ● ● Tracy
Tomatoes
SANTA CLARA ● San Jose
VALLEY *Apricots*
Prunes *Cotton* ● Madera
Plums
Artichokes **SAN JOAQUIN VALLEY**
SALINAS VALLEY *Strawberries* *Olives* *Oranges*
● Strathmore

Lettuce ● Delano
Cotton *Grapes*
Potatoes ● Arvin

Lemons
● Oxnard
● Los Angeles *Grapes*
COACHELLA VALLEY
Vegetables
IMPERIAL VALLEY
El Centro ● *Cantaloupes*

the growers had to develop a substitute labor base once economic prosperity returned in the 1940s.

The Great Water Wars. Irrigation was hardly new to California. As early as the sixteenth century, the Spanish padres had used narrow ditches to cart water from the rivers. What was novel was the extent of irrigation that laid the base of the specialty crop revolution. State intervention was essential. Before 1890 irrigation had been entirely private, generally done by larger farmers with direct water access and sufficient capital to construct ditches and pumps. James Ben Ali Haggin, for example, organized a water company transport and sell water to small farmers. In addition, several irrigated colonies of small farms were established from the 1850s through the 1870s, such as Anaheim, Riverside, Palisades, and Fresno (Dumke 1944: ch. 19; Schrode 1956; Hutchinson 1965: ch. 9; Maass and Anderson 1978:157–172). Most of the colonies failed, however, because of insufficient capital and engineering knowledge. At this point politics became central. The State of California began promoting irrigation, first by a series of court rulings affirming "prior appropriation" water rights and later by actually constructing irrigation projects. In the United States, water rights have generally rested on the "riparian rights" doctrine that rights accrue solely to holders of land contiguous to the natural watercourse. Rights are relative to those of other contiguous landowners, meaning that any increase or decline in waterflow is shared equally and that no contiguous owner can impair the equal access of other contiguous landowners. Prior appropriation instead assigns rights to the party making first use. In other words, the first party to use water of a certain quantity holds exclusive rights to that amount regardless of subsequent users. Moreover, water rights can be fixed and sold independent of fluctuations in stream flow. Later riparian owners could be excluded if the water flow dropped. Although prior appropriation benefited small settlers in areas where land speculators had sat on their lands (Stephenson 1937; Gaffney 1969; Maass and Anderson 1978), generally the advantage accrued to the largest owners who had the capital and earlier access to construct the first irrigation works.

The major impetus came after the Wright Act of 1887 and the Newlands Act of 1902. The Wright Act strengthened irrigation by authorizing the creation of semi-public irrigation districts. Irrigation districts could, therefore, market tax-exempt bonds, levy land taxes, enter into binding contracts with water buyers and suppliers, and compel hold-out landowners to join (Maass and Anderson 1978:173–175). Within a decade, a majority of the private projects, including a number of mutual companies and private water corporations, had been reorganized as irrigation districts (Goodall et al. 1978).

In 1902 the U.S. Congress passed the Newlands Act, setting aside the proceeds from public land sales in the west to finance the construction of irrigation projects. Modeled on the Desert Land Act of 1877, it had small farmers again as the intended beneficiary. Farms were supposed to be limited to a maximum of 160 acres, and the owner-operator had to reside within fifty miles of the project. If owners held excess lands above the 160 acres, these were to be sold off by the end of the ten-year repayment period at a price fixed to eliminate any windfall profit. The Bureau of Reclamation was created to construct the projects which were to be repaid in full over a ten-year period. Current operating costs on the projects were to be recouped by water use fees based on the volume of water usage (Taylor 1949; Gates 1968:685–686). The construction of mammoth projects such as the Central Valley Project built in the 1930s rapidly accelerated irrigation expansion. According to the Agricultural Census, between 1900 and 1940 irrigated acreage grew from around ten percent to two-thirds of all croplands.

It should be no surprise that the major beneficiaries proved to be the large estate owners. In effect, the irrigation projects were converted into huge public subsidies for the land barons. Under the original Newlands Act Statutes, the only subsidy lay in the interest-free ten-year financing for the projects. The first measure extended the interest-free repayment period. In 1908 the repayment period was extended to twenty years, in 1926 to forty, and, in 1939, to fifty with a complete exemption for any repayments during the first ten years. Then the Bureau of Reclamation moved into the electricity business, using project water to generate hydroelectric power. The major customers were urban users, who were charged at prevailing commercial rates double and triple those paid by the farmers. In effect, the general taxpayer who footed the interest-free construction and the urban consumers of project electricity paid most of the project costs, creating subsidies that have been estimated as varying between $3.50 to $14 per acre foot of water or, converted to farmed acreage, between $35 to $135 per irrigated acre annually (Gates 1968:685–90; Berkman and Viscusi 1971:136; Taylor 1971:254–255; Howe and Easter 1971:136; Bain et al. 1966:206). Considering that covered farms ranged from 1000 to 10,000 acres, the average subsidy per farm during the past three decades has been around $100,000 per year. Unfortunately, precise figures on the size of subsidies are unavailable, in large part because the Bureau of Reclamation policy has been to avoid the controversial issue of acreage limits. As Senator Claire Engle, the major Congressional spokesman for repeal of the 160-acre limitation during the 1950s, observed:

You start looking into the 160-acre limitation and it is like inspecting the rear end of a mule: you want to do it from a safe distance because you might get kicked through the side of a barn. But it can be done with circumspection, and I hope we can exercise circumspection.(1955:495)

Despite considerable "circumspection," the available evidence shows unmistakably that the principal beneficiaries have been largest landowners. Small landowners have, of course, also benefited. In one of its few moments of disclosure, the Bureau of Reclamation reported a 1969 survey of landholding in the Central Valley Project, identifying 11,434 farms out of a total of 12,941 that were within the 160-acre limit and an additional 971 farms of 160 to 320 acres. In other words, significant violators of the limit were less than one-half of one percent of all landholders. Yet, more significantly, these 636 "excess" landholders owned 53 percent of all the lands, and 18 of these farms contained more than 5,000 acres each (Taylor 1971:252; Maass and Anderson 1978:270–272). Moreover, despite statues requiring sales of excess land, enforcement has been lax. Large corporations such as the Southern Pacific Railway, the Kern County Land Company of Haggin and Tevis fame, the Tenneco Corporation, and the Chandler family of the *Los Angeles Times* have benefited from the projects (McWilliams 1949:330–332; Taylor, 1971:252).

There are several additional avenues for circumventing the 160-acre limit. The tried method of dummy ownership is common, with leases used to centralize actual farming operations. The Bureau has also redefined the acreage limit to mean 160 acres per family member. In 1911, the Newlands Act was amended to allow sales of surplus project waters at cost to outside landowners who were exempted from the acreage limit. Neighboring estate owners have thereby secured access to the water subsidy without actually joining the projects, as have continguous landowners whose ground water level is indirectly raised by the irrigation works (Bates 1967:689–696; Taylor 1958, 1971, 1975; Berkman and Viscusi 1971:164–178). More secure, though, have been legal exemptions from the acreage rules. The Imperial Valley Irrigation District, for example, was established in 1911 to repair the private canals destroyed by the 1905–06 flooding of the Colorado River. Because the project had originally been privately owned by the Southern Pacific Railway, the Bureau authorized a complete exemption (Hosmer 1966; Hudley 1975: ch. 2). Likewise, exemptions have been extended to the neighboring Coachella Irrigation District, which was linked to the Imperial Valley canalworks in 1946. Further exemptions in the Central Valley Project

50

have stemmed from the conglomeration of Bureau projects with private canals and Army Corps of Engineers flood control projects (Taylor 1949:249; McWilliams 1949:332). More recently, the California State Water Plan has funded irrigation works freed from any acreage restrictions, thereby covering the very largest estates with some of the largest subsidies, the most prominent being the Westlands District where the subsidy rate runs double that of federal projects (Bain et al. 1966:206; Ballis 1960; Taylor 1971; Goodall et al. 1978).

The political power of the growers has been key to these subsidies and exemptions. An "iron triangle of power" (Maass 1951) composed of grower associations, specialized Congressional committees recruited from implicated districts, and semi-autonomous governmental bureaus has controlled the major irrigation and land development policies. Because all three parties have an interest in expanding the size of public subsidies and excluding broader constituencies, an insulated policy subsystem based on log-rolling compromises and mutual accomodation has developed (cf. Lowi 1964; Ripley and Franklin 1978). The interests of insiders are advanced while those of broader constituencies such as the urban taxpayer, the farm worker, or the consumer in the grocery market are systematically excluded.

An essential feature of this triangular alliance has been the virtually uncontested dominance of the largest landowners inside the irrigation associations. Although strict enforcement of the acreage and residency requirements would benefit the small landowners, the large growers have repeatedly used their leverage, prestige, and the rhetoric of local control to mobilize the small farmers against any effort to enforce the acreage rules (Goodall et al. 1978; Maass 1978:272). In addition, the irrigation district associations have operated on a "one acre-one vote" rule as opposed to a more democratic "one farmer-one vote" basis, thereby reinforcing the dominance of the land barons (Goodall et al. 1978).

Rationalizing the Marketplace. One of the major ironies of American politics is that precisely at the moment that capitalists were turning state power to the task of rationalizing markets and taming their political opponents, the rhetoric of laissez faire free enterprise and market competition reached peak intensity (Kolko 1963; Wolfe 1977). Although California growers were hardly innovators, they likewise turned to rationalizing measures while holding to laissez faire rhetoric. The initial targets for rationalization were product and supply markets. Product markets were initially more important because the initial expansion of specialty crop production depended on generating controlled access to national markets and, at least until the 1950s, purchases of supplies were less central to overall profits. The growers rationalized product markets through several measures. At the minimum, they needed a predictable delivery system and assurances that perishable crops would be accepted by wholesalers and ultimately consumers. A method for rationalizing the timing of shipments was also desirable. In addition to the danger of spoilage, the chronic problem of market gluts and depressed prices during peak harvests followed by windfall profits during the off-season worked to the advantage of the middlemen. Less important was the rationalization of supplies, chiefly the use of collective buying to secure volume discounts and substitutes for expensive manufactured products.

The least significant measures proved the easiest. The initial push came as early as the 1870s with the organization of the first cooperatives, but it was not until the 1930s when the New Deal agricultural policies created the market-order system that product market controls were actually installed. The major obstacle was the "collective goods" problem (Olson 1965). The first successful co-ops were centered among growers of particular fruits or vegetables, most likely a crop that was confined to a small growing area such as dates or olives. By bargaining collectively with suppliers, wholesalers, and shippers, the growers attempted to strengthen their overall market position. Their initial successes, however, were limited to creating predictable acceptance of their shipments. By creating voluntary grading systems to insure produce quality, the co-ops opened up distant markets and created the basis for mass advertising and trade brands. The wholesalers repeatedly beat back co-op attempts to control commodity prices, but collective purchasing and labor recruitment by co-ops such as the California Fruit Growers Exchange (popularly known as Sunkist) were fabulously successful (Cumberland 1917; Erdmann 1958; Blackford 1978:15–21). Amidst the market gluts of the early 1930s, the California legislature attempted to create market controls through compulsory restrictions on fruit production, but interstate competition proved too great. In 1938, amendments to the Agricultural Adjustment Act finally created federal-level governmental controls in the form of a market-order system that depended on ratification by two-thirds of the growers of a particular crop. Growers in particular crop areas were organized into marketing associations and empowered to regulate shipments based on market condition reports compiled by the Federal Marketing Service. In this way, the growers preserved their independence while securing market controls (Blackford 1978:19–25). Since most specialty crops were concentrated in a limited area, the two-thirds approval was relatively easy to secure. By the 1950s, half of California specialty crops were protected. In general, market rationalization worked to the advantage of the largest growers. Although all growers benefited from the price stabilization, the larger used their size advantage to rationalize internal operations. In some crops, most notably cotton, acreage limits rather than price controls were installed, giving a clear edge to the larger landowners who could set aside their more marginal lands. In addition, the marketing associations strengthened the organization of the growers and created new political alliances with the food wholesalers, processors, and distributors.

The Labor Base. The most central factor in the rise of the migratory labor estates was the availability of a massive army of farm workers amenable to erratic, seasonal employment at cheap wages who would not rebel. This labor base allowed great land barons to keep their estates intact and gradually shift to labor-intensive specialty crops. In fact, cheap docile labor has been so central to California agriculture that, since the late nineteenth century, land prices have largely reflected access to this labor pool (Fuller 1940).

This labor base was created by large-scale immigration, mass unemployment, and concerted recruitment efforts. The earliest workers were Chinese immigrants, originally imported as indentured servants by the railway companies. With the completion of the transcontinental rail links in the late 1870s, the railway companies abandoned the Chinese in the rural hinterland. Destitute, excluded from the more desirable jobs, and dependent on bilingual labor contractors who exploited their vulnerability, the Chinese accepted the low wages, erratic employment, and harsh working conditions. By 1890 the 100,000 Chinese made up around half of the agricultural labor force. In the 1890s, economic depression and mass unemployment lead to nativist labor agitation, and the domestic workers marched into the countryside, demanding their jobs. The growers hired the domestic workers at half the Chinese wage, and the Chinese fled to the urban slums where they eked out a livelihood as domestic servants and launderers.

When prosperity returned and the domestic workers moved back to the cities, the growers recruited a new base of immigrant workers from Japan. By 1910, the Japanese made up over a third of the labor force. Mass unemployment lead again to nativist labor agitation and exclusion of the Japanese. This time the growers recruited immigrants who could not be so readily excluded: Filipinos from a U.S. protectorate; dustbowl immigrants from the drought-stricken midwest; and, most important of all, Mexican workers who could return to their homeland during the off-season. The model farm worker was an immigrant, lacking citizenship rights, culturally set off from domestic workers, the target of racial attacks and discrimination, and sufficiently destitute to accept the cheap wages, erratic employment and harsh working conditions. In his *The Grapes of Wrath,* John Steinbeck aptly dubbed them "imported slaves."

The growers have confronted two major problems in holding onto their labor base. The immigrants have gradually become acculturated, moving on to new opportunities and losing their inhibitions about strikes and unions. The Japanese were highly successful small farmers and, like the Filipinos and Mexicans, organized powerful strikes. The immigrant workers have also been vulnerable to exclusion. During periods of mass unemployment, domestic workers have demanded immigrant exclusion but, once prosperity returned, drifted off to better jobs. The growers have organized labor associations to recruit workers and pressed for public policies to promote immigration and exempt farm workers from protective labor and welfare legislation. In 1920, the growers in the San Joaquin Valley created a labor bureau to recruit workers for the grape and vegetable harvest. By the 1930s, labor associations existed throughout the state were using labor drummers and mass advertising to entice workers from Mexico and the midwestern dustbowl. In the early 1940s, the associations became the backbone of the most novel recruitment system—the bracero program—a governmental program for importing temporary seasonal workers from Mexico. When the bracero program came to an end in 1965, the growers returned to traditional measures, keeping the Border Patrol ineffective and supporting a lax system of immigration controls (Galarza 1964; Craig 1971; Corwin, 1978). The growers also secured special exemptions from major pieces of protective labor and welfare legislation. The Wagner Act of 1934, the Social Security Act of 1935, and the Fair Labor Standards Act of 1938 each exempted production agriculture from new standards (Tangri 1967; Dunbar and Kravitz 1976). If agencies attempted to protect farm workers, they immediately became the target of attack. When the Farm Security Administration attempted to resettle migrants and small farmers onto new farms, in the late 1930s, the growers stripped the agency of its funding and authority (McConnell 1953). Only with the successful insurgencies of the late 1960s and 1970s has protective social legislation been extended to farm workers.

The Agribusiness Oligarchy

Capitalist centralization created an agricultural production system controlled by an agribusiness oligarchy with three semi-distinct segments: a grower elite of the largest estate owners; an industrial elite controlling the corporations and banks supplying inputs to the farm sector; and a mercantile elite in the processing and marketing of agricultural commodities. Centralization has been greater among the last two segments, gradually shifting control outside the farm sector and reinforcing the centralization of production agriculture.

Centralization within the grower elite can be gauged in two ways: the concentration of landholding and its links to the ownership of fixed capital, commercial production, and hiring; and the concentration of commercial production in the hands of large-scale producers. Each taps an important but distinct aspect. Land concentration reflects on the control of long-term land development. Market concentration captures short-term production capacity. Figures 2.4 through 2.7 and tables 2.3 and 2.4 chart the centralization of California and U.S. agriculture. Large estates of 1000 or more acres have represented only a small percentage of California farms yet have held two-thirds of farmland and roughly a third of fixed farm capital, and produced two-fifths of commerical commodities and farm employment. Significantly, large acreage alone does not set off capitalist enterprises from family farms. As table 2.3 shows, small acreage farms have also been major employers, typically by using more intensive production methods. The historic trend has been towards increased inequality, placing farmland and capital in the hands of fewer and fewer owners (figures 2.4 and 2.5) and making California agriculture one of the most concentrated sectors of U.S. agriculture (figures 2.6 and 2.7). The pattern is also visible from measures of commercial output (table 2.4). In 1974 the top fifteen percent of all farms in terms of sales had an average capital value of around $2.5 million and produced 60 percent of all commercial output. These commercial giants were also the primary employ-

Table 2.3
Small and Large Acreage in California, 1900–1969

	% Farms	% Farmland	% Farm Capital	% Farm Production	% Hired Labor
Small farms (>50 acres) constituted:					
1900	38.0	1.8	17.0	18.7	12.8
1930	63.3	4.8	33.6	N.A.	N.A.
1950	65.1	3.8	29.8	25.5	17.1
1969	57.3	2.1	12.0	16.8	23.6
Large farms (1000 + acres) constituted:					
1900	6.5	61.8	34.1	30.8	34.2
1930	3.7	63.5	19.8	N.A.	N.A.
1950	4.4	70.7	25.2	28.3	31.8
1969	7.1	79.6	46.9	34.2	38.4

Source: *U.S. Census* (1900–1930) and *U.S. Census of Agriculture* (1950–1969).

ers of farm workers and controlled almost one-third of total fixed farm investments.

In fact, several other studies of economic centralization indicate that these figures underestimate the actual extent of capitalist centralization.[2] The most thorough study is by the Nader Task Force on California Land Use (Fellmeth 1973). Drawing on the data from county tax records, news items, financial directories, county atlases, and miscellaneous governmental surveys, the Task Force concluded that 325 owners or less than half of one percent of California farmers held over 10.6 million acres, slightly over thirty percent of the state's agricultural lands. Heading up the list were giant corporate farmers such as the Newhall Land and Farming Corporation with 1.6 million acres; the Tenneco Corporation, in 1970 the 34th largest corporation in the United States with assets of over $4.3 billion and activities in oil production, manufacturing of farm equipment, and shipbuilding as well as its 400,000 acres of farming; the Tejon Ranch Corporation, owned by the Chandler family of the Los Angeles Times-Mirror Company, containing 348,000 acres; the Southern Pacific Company with over 2.4 million acres of which 810,000 were agricultural; Standard Oil of California with over 306,000 acres; the Irvine Company, holder of the 97,000 acre Irvine Ranch; J. G. Boswell Company, holder of 108,000 acres including the 37,000 acre Boston Ranch in Kern County; the infamous Miller & Lux, Inc. with 93,058 acres; the

Figure 2.4

Land Concentration in California Agriculture

Gini Index for 1900 = .79
Gini Index for 1930 = .81
Gini Index for 1969 = .85

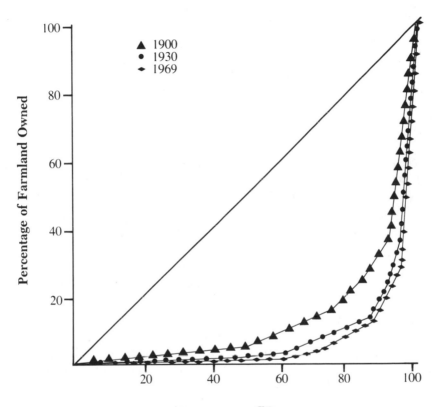

▲ 1900
● 1930
◆ 1969

Percentage of Owners

SOURCE: U.S. Census, 1900, 1930 4:125; U.S. Agricultural Census, 1969.

DiGiorgio Corporation, the largest producer and shipper of fresh fruit and vegetables in the United States, with 27,000 acres; and the Del Monte Corporation, the world's largest canner, with 21,200 acres (Fellmeth 1973:10–12, 515–530; see also Moore and Snyder 1970; Goffman 1971; Kotz 1971a, 1971b; Barnes 1971; Krebs 1971, 1972, 1973; Ballis 1972; Baker and Taylor 1972; Galarza 1977:22).

The pinnacle of this grower elite, then, consists of a handful of mam-

Table 2.4
Large Commercial Farms in California, 1974

Size of Farms	% Farms	Average Value of Farm Capital	% Total Farm Capital	% Total Production	% Total Labor Expenses
$2500– 4999	5.5	$145,494	5.6	.3	1.0
$5000– 9999	8.0	146,034	5.3	.7	.7
$10,000– 19,999	9.0	184,605	7.1	1.5	1.6
$20,000– 39,999	16.5	213,079	8.0	3.0	3.0
$40,000– 99,999	15.2	334,507	13.8	7.3	7.8
$100,000– 199,999	15.5	511,287	11.5	8.7	8.6
$200,000– 499,999	14.7	793,470	15.9	17.3	15.9
>$500,000	15.6	2,402,814	32.8	61.2	61.4

Source: *U.S. Agricultural Census: California Summaries* (1974).

moth corporate farms that link the growers to the other sectors of the agribusiness oligarchy. Large corporations such as the DiGiorgio Fruit Corporation and the Boswell Corporation have forward integrated their farming with canning, fruit exchanges, and farm machinery sales. At the same time, large corporations involved in other sectors of the food and fiber industry, such as the Heublein Corporation, have backward integrated by purchasing vineyards and vegetable fields. Although the incentive has partially been to "tax farm" the tax laws (National Planning Association 1972; Vogeler 1981:147–162), the major advantages lie in the rationalization of supply and increased control over product markets. In a parallel way the bureaucratization of the marketing cooperatives has centralized production, subordinating farming to marketing and distribution and leaving the former grower as an uninvolved paper owner (Goldberg 1972:111–112; Kravitz 1972).

In general, capitalist centralization has been more dramatic outside production agriculture. By recent estimates, over ninety percent of national retail food sales are handled by a handful of large grocery chains and allied independents, making the grocery business the most concen-

Figure 2.5

Capital Concentration in California Agriculture

Gini Index for 1900 = .46
Gini Index for 1930 = .47
Gini Index for 1969 = .51

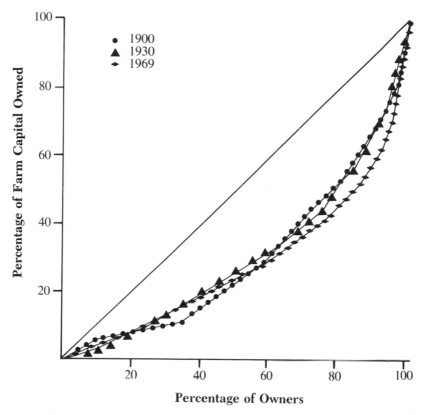

SOURCE: U.S. Census, 1900, 1930 4:127–129; U.S. Agricultural Census, 1969.

trated sector of the entire food and fibre industry (Mueller 1969; USDA, Economic Research Service, 1971, 1972; Vogeler 1981:105–136). The chains establish the delivery schedule, set quality standards, and, through multimillion dollar advertising campaigns, promote trade labels that stablize market demand. The most extreme form of market concentration is "forward contracting," an arrangement under which the grower essentially abrogates entrepreneurial independence by contracting as much as a year in advance to deliver a specified quantity and quality of product

Figure 2.6
Land Concentration in California and U.S. Agriculture, 1969

Gini Index for California = .85
Gini Index for the U.S. = .76

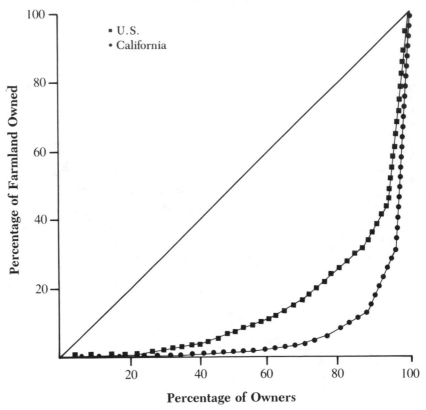

SOURCE: U.S. Agricultural Census, 1969.

at a fixed wholesale price. The most affected crops have been specialties. In 1970, over half of all fresh vegetables were marketed under forward contracts: 95 percent of processed vegetables; 70 percent of potatoes; and 40 percent of citrus fruits (Kyle, Sundquist, and Guither 1972:5–8; Mitchell and Hoofnagle 1972). Likewise, the markets for farm supplies—machinery, fertilizer, credit—have become highly concentrated, placing production agriculture in the periphery of the national economy.

The Myth of Efficiency

The seemingly relentless drive towards capitalist centralization has led several analysts to assume that the dominance of the large estates is due to greater technical efficiency. In fact, this has been a central contention in the most interpretations of the development of California agriculture. Recent studies, however, have thoroughly punctured this myth of efficiency. The classic study is Madden's (1967) review of input-output efficiencies in agricultural production. Consistently, farms

Figure 2.7
Capital Concentration in California and U.S. Agriculture, 1969

Gini Index for California = .51
Gini Index for for U.S. = .23

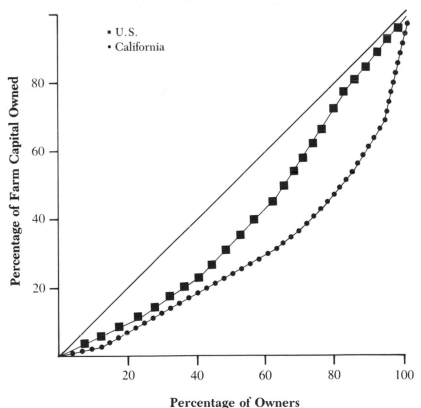

SOURCE: U.S. Agricultural Census, 1969.

of more than 600 acres were less efficient than medium-sized 500–600 acre farms. In fact, on California specialty crop farms, maximum efficiency is generally reached with far less—60 acres in cling peaches, for example; 600 acres in tomatoes; 640 in Imperial Valley lettuce farms (Madden and Patenheimer 1972). In general, there are negative economies of scale beyond 600 acres.

The efficiency of the large estates is, to trade on Thorstein Veblen's (1917) language, their pecuniary efficiency, not their resource efficiency (cf. Perelman 1978; Vogeler 1981:89–104). To be sure, the large-scale capitalist farmers generate higher profit margins. This, however, is not because of economies of scale in the use of resources, but because of institutional advantages. Large operators secure higher volume discounts on credit and supplies (Perelman and Shea 1972), greater public subsidies from federal commodity support programs (Bonnen 1968) and irrigation projects (Taylor 1972), and greater protection from market rationalization. They use new technology developed at public expense (Hightower 1973, 1975), pay lower rates on property and corporate income taxes (Ballis 1972), and, perhaps most important of all, reap the benefits of plentiful cheap docile labor that allows them to underbid smaller, especially family-sized farms (Fuller 1969; Fuller and Van Vuuren 1972).

The Structure of Agripolitics

The political power of the great land barons was decisive in the development of California agriculture. The rise of the great estates depended on extensive political corruption, cheap labor, public subsidies, and favorable institutional practices like volume discounts and preferential tax treatment. At the same time, the great estates have experienced a long-term profit squeeze rooted in their economic inefficiency, their weak position in national markets, the barriers to technical progress, and most recently, the development of mass insurgency.

The cornerstone of grower power has been their dominance over the farm workers. Farm worker powerlessness has underwritten the economic growth of the great estates and effectively removed their major antagonist from the political scene. The growers have therefore enjoyed what might be called *structural access* to centers of public policy (Lindblom 1977; Block 1977). Structural access derives from two sources: the structural dependence of policy-makers on particular social institutions, and restrictions on the articulation of antagonistic interests. The tangible product is a general solicitude among policy-makers for the preservation of particular institutions. The rural communities have structurally depended on the prosperity of the large estates and, in the absence of an effective farm worker opposition, public officials have treated grower interests as identical to those of the larger community. The prosperity of the large estates has become the paramount concern in routine policymaking.

The growers have also mobilized to secure specific advantages on the basis of *organized access*. Organized access derives from direct participation or pressure on the formation and implementation of public policy. The major avenues are interest group linkages and electoral politics. The tangible product is a set of specific policy decisions such as exemptions from the acreage limits on public irrigation projects or investments of public funds in the development of new agricultural technology. California growers have supported a wide range of interest organizations, from peak associations like the Farm Bureau to narrowly gauged irrigation associations, labor bureaus, and commodity associations, and have dominated the electoral politics of the rural communities (Goldschmidt 1978:169–85, 344–53; McCune 1943, 1956; Hardin 1952).

Structural access creates a diffuse general orientation among policymakers that reinforces the specific, easily measured policy gains of organized access. The foundation of grower power lies in the rural communities and radiates outward into state and national arenas. In general, interest group linkages are more important than electoral politics. Agricultural policy has been profoundly shaped by the development of what Wolfe (1977) has called the "franchise state." The basic principle is the allocation of exclusive control over governmental programs to narrow, organized interest groups. This franchise state has two basic sources: the use of decentralized or so-called participatory administration in place of bureaucratic structures, and the dominance of narrow-gauged "subsystem" legislative politics over broadly oriented party politics. Both work to weaken broad, less-organized groups and strengthen small, well-organized groups.

The key feature of participatory administration is the allocation of authority over governmental programs to advisory committees and independent governing boards which, in turn, are dominated by representatives of narrow beneficiary groups (Selznick 1949; Martin 1957). The soil conservation program, for example, is basically controlled by special farmer committees in each county, who oversee the details of administration and guide the development of policy changes. Despite the rhetoric of participatory democracy, control is actually centralized in the hands of the more wealthy farmers while less organized general constituencies such as consumers and farm workers are excluded. Agricultural programs represent the most developed form of this participatory administration with grower committees controlling the irrigation projects, major commodity programs, labor bureaus, rural electric cooperatives, farm loan programs, and the entire extension system (McConnell 1953; Benedict 1953; Hardin 1952; Lowi 1979:68–77).

Agricultural policy has also been the major center for "subsystem" politics. The key feature is the development of an insulated policy system controlled by the "triangular alliance" of interest organizations, specialized legislative committees and program administrators (Ripley and Franklin 1978). Political parties are weak "catch-all" coalitions of interest groups (Kirchheimer 1966) that leave elected officials free from any broad-gauged ideology that might limit their responsiveness to the better-organized groups. Seniority rules and legislative specialization insure that the representatives from rural districts dominate the major legislative committees controlling the authority and appropriations for agricultural programs. Farm associations, in turn, finance their electoral campaigns and provide technical information and advice in support of favored programs. Administrators depend on the farm associations for political support and the legislative committees for their resources, channelling program benefits toward the more organized groups and the favored legislative districts. The twin pillars of popular democratic control, coherent parties and bureaucratic administration, are circumvented. As Secretary of Agriculture Charles Hardin once described the agricultural policy system, it is "built upon a network of state and local farmer-elected committees effectively interlocked with influential persons in state and local farm organizations. Such organizations [are] responsible to neither the Secretary of Agriculture nor to any effective general electorate" (1948:905).

The growers have also forged strong alliances with other segments of the capitalist class, especially the industrial and mercantile segments of the agribusiness oligarchy, and supported the shift in emphasis in agricultural policy from a concern with rural institutions to the issues of prices and profitability (Hathaway 1963, 1969). The origins of this alliance date to the early sponsorship of the Farm Bureau Federation by the U.S. Chamber of Commerce in 1919. In California, the strongest ties were forged during the 1930s when the threat of farm worker insurgency prompted the State Chamber of Commerce to fund and organize the vigilante attacks of the Associated Farmers and press for an agribusiness program of irrigation subsidies, tax reforms, and market commodity controls (Chambers 1952:53–55, 135–146; Auerbach 1966). The links have since become more elaborate, including farmer-industrialist policy formation organizations such as the Agricultural Institute and the Farm Foundation (McCune 1956), the joint business ventures of the Farm Bureau Federation (Berger 1971:85–91), and the creation of standing agricultural policy committees in the major business associations.

The structure of agripolitics, then, has furnished growers with a virtually impregnable fortress. As advocates of both small farmer and farm worker interests have found, the growers have used their entrenched political access to advance their claims to cheap labor, public subsidies, and market stabilization while effectively excluding all opposing interests.

3

California Agriculture and Farm Worker Powerlessness

"Farming became industry, and the owners followed Rome. They imported slaves, although they did not call them slaves: Chinese, Japanese, Mexicans, Filipinos. They live on rice and beans, the businessmen said.

And all the time the farms grew larger and the owners fewer. And there were pitifully few farmers on the land any more. And the imported serfs were beaten and frightened and starved. And the farms grew larger and the owners fewer.

And the crops changed. Fruit trees took the place of grain fields and vegetables to feed the world spread out on the bottoms.

And it came about that owners no longer worked on their farms. They farmed on papers, and they forgot the land, the smell, the feel of it, and remembered only that they owned it.

And the great owners, who must lose their land in an upheaval, the great owners with eyes to read history know the great fact: when property accumulates in too few hands, it is taken away. And that companion fact: when a majority of the people are hungry and cold they will take by force what they need."

John Steinbeck (1939)

On September 4, 1875, the *Morning Chronicle* of San Francisco admonished its readers about the evils of the new "farm labor problem" emerging in the Central Valley, declaring the labor system "undoubtedly the worst in the U.S. In many respects it is even worse than old-time slavery. That, at least, enabled the planter to know what labor he could depend upon and made the labourer certain at all times of shelter, clothing, food and fire. Our system does neither. The farmer must take such help as he can get. The labourers themselves, knowing that they cannot be permanently employed, demand high prices, do their work carelessly, and start out on a tramp for another job." Over a century later, California's "peculiar institution" has changed little. As Carey McWilliams (1949:156) described the labor system: "temporary hiring from a mobile pool of unemployed workers . . . [in which] . . . the employers maintain complete control of labor relations." Until the United Farm Worker victories, the foundation of California agriculture has been farm worker powerlessness.

A powerless group is unable to initiate and sustain a concerted challenge to advance its interests. Powerlessness arises from two major sources: obstacles to mobilization, especially disorganization, lack of resources, and strong institutional controls by antagonists; and a weak strategic position, generally due to social marginality. The major problem for farm workers has been their lack of a strong basis for mobilization. The harvest bottleneck and the perishability of specialty crops have provided workers considerable strategic leverage. Although the migratory labor estates are not central to the national economy, they have generated about eight percent of California's postwar economic boom. Major disruptions constitute a significant threat to the California economy. Farm worker disorganization, lack of resources, and grower controls, however, have been major problems. The root of this powerlessness has been the structure of the labor system, that is, the arrangements for recruiting, supervising, and compensating workers as well as dividing up productive tasks. In terms of the economic axes introduced in chapter 2 the labor system lies at the interface between the relations and forces of production. The traditional farm labor system, as we will see, has disorganized farm workers, stripped them of essential resources, and provided significant grower controls.

The Labor System and the Farm Worker Community

The specialty crop revolution rested on the formation of a rural proletariat harnessed to the special requirements of the migratory labor estates. The estates laid down three requirements. First, labor had to be cheap. The profits of the migratory estates depended, as we have seen, on access to labor-power that was paid less than comparable labor-power elsewhere. Second, the workers had to be docile. Harvest strikes threatened investments in standing crops and, at the minimum, reduced flexibility in the marketplace. Third, the technology of specialty crops required large numbers of low-skilled workers amenable to highly erratic, seasonal employment. Mechanization was difficult and the growers could relieve the squeeze on profits by using direct labor-power in preference to underutilized machines.

The labor system created to meet these requirements has posed major obstacles to farm worker mobilization (figure 3.1). The most central has stemmed from the division of labor between two sets of workers: an extremely small internalized labor force with stable employment, some skills, and job rights, known as "permanent" workers, and the vast externalized labor force that is seasonal, low skilled and lacking in job rights, known as "seasonals" (Doeringer and Piore 1971; Burowoy 1979; Friedland, Barton and Thomas 1981). The division is essentially that between the office workers, tractor drivers, irrigators, and foremen who are permanent employees and participate in varying degrees in the management of the production process, and the seasonal field hands who are completely excluded. The permanent workers handle the management, sales, supervision and maintenance activities of the ranch, often switching among these tasks during the course of the season. The seasonal workers carry out the heavy manual labor of planting, harvesting, and packing the crops for shipment.

This division has created two groups of workers with different interests and potentials for mobilization. Despite their greater economic security and commitment to farm work, the permanent workers are resistant to unionization. They constitute the aristocracy of farm labor, enjoying steady employment, better conditions, and a sense of involvement in the management of the enterprise. As well, the growers have developed strong paternalistic controls, offering favors such as cheap housing, emergency loans, small gifts, and a show of personal concern in exchange for personal loyalty. Because they often reside in ranch housing, the permanents also lack independent community ties that might serve as free spaces for organizing. In other words, to use Newby's (1975) characterization, they are deferential workers. They are also a critical link in the control of seasonal workers. Their autonomy in the production system and relative privilege among the farm workers has made them the natural leaders of the farm worker community. The growers have routinely used the

Figure 3.1

The Logic of Farm Worker Powerlessness

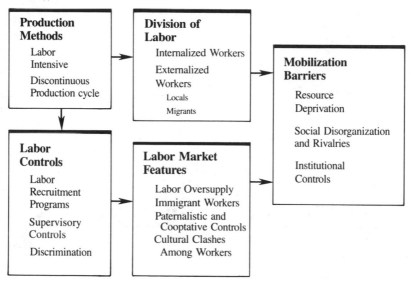

permanent hands to coopt dissidence by sounding workers for grievances, pressing quiescence, mediating individual complaints, and if these
moves fail, using them as labor drummers to recruit new crews of seasonals.

The externalized seasonal workers make up over eighty percent of the
labor force. Figure 3.2 gives some notion of the hiring pattern in the
early 1960s, charting seasonal fluctuations in hiring for particular crops
in Kern County, the major agricultural area in the Central Valley. Another gauge is the rate of monthly labor turnover, that is, the percentage
of workers hired who are then released within the same month. In the
fields, a rate of 250 percent is quite common, while national turnover
rates normally range from 1.4 percent to 2.5 percent and from 6 percent
to 9 percent in the more seasonal industries like construction and for-
estry (Sosnick 1978:175). Job insecurity reduces the independence and
cohesion of the seasonal workers. Yet it is important to note that they
are not as seriously disorganized as those in John Steinbeck's portrait of
destitute migrants roaming about in their Model T jalopies and sleeping
in tent camps. Most of the seasonal workers have stable ties to local
communities or work crews. The seasonals are made up of two groups:

Figure 3.2

Seasonal Fluctuations in Employment: Kern Co., California (1961)

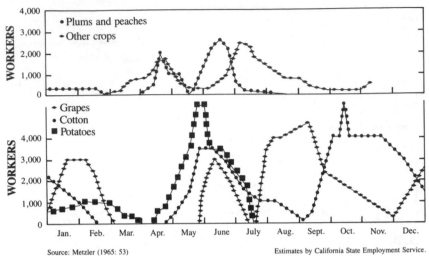

Source: Metzler (1965: 53)   Estimates by California State Employment Service.

the locals who reside permanently in a single area and seek out work on neighboring farms, and the migrants who move from area to area with the crops. Both of these segments are divided into specialized workers who are more skilled and concentrate on particular crops, such as asparagus and grapes, that provide more or less continuous employment, and the unspecialized workers who have no skills other than their strong hands and must continuously shift among crops as well as employers (cf. Friedland 1981).

The major differences in mobilization potential stem from the resources, community attachments, and autonomy of these workers. The local workers are the most promising, enmeshed in small, close-knit, ethnically homogeneous communities that dot the rural backroads. These *colonias*, as the Mexican-Americans call them, provide a powerful basis for worker cohesion and the major free space among the farm workers. Most are small clusters of twenty to thirty houses at a crossroads linked together by casual meetings at a country store. The larger settlements have their own church and schools. Store-front preachers, an occasional priest, and permanent hands who live off-ranch form the indigenous leadership of these small communities. The local workers have their own cars and housing, making them highly independent. In addition they derive their income from multiple farm or industrial jobs, reducing the risk of supporting a strike. However, the unspecialized local workers are only marginally committed to farm work and consider their wages a secondary source of family income. The students and housewives who work only during the seasonal peaks and on crops such as onions that require only brief spurts of unskilled labor have been among the most difficult to organize (Thomas 1982). In general, though, the local workers have the most resources, cohesion, and autonomy from grower controls.

The migrant workers vary immensely in terms of their degree of specialization. The unspecialized migrants or fruit tramps who live in the itinerant slums of the small towns and seek day jobs at the 4 A.M. labor shape-ups lack resources and community ties. Most move from town to town, working erratically, often no longer than necessary to buy a night's loft in a flop house and a "Tokay blanket" of cheap red wine (cf. Friedland and Nelkin 1971). Not only are they impoverished and without strong community ties and job commitments, but they are generally demoralized and under the thumb of a labor contractor. Most of their jobs come from the early morning labor shape-ups that form during the peak season around a lighted street corner outside a restaurant or drugstore in the rural slums. The labor contractors or crew bosses line up their buses in the early hours before dawn and, selecting among the huddled workers, choose the strongest arms and most compliant faces. The rewards of the day-haul are meager, often $10 to $15 per day after charges for the bus ride and food have been subtracted. Although many labor contractors shun the shape-ups, those who participate use them to get workers for a tight squeeze in the harvest or to do undesirable jobs like weeding or the final harvest pass that the other workers avoid.

The specialized migrants are far more promising. Most work in cohesive, stable crews, typically of younger males recruited by a family elder or village leader. These crews specialize in skilled work such as broccoli cutting or grape girdling. Although jobs are short-term, many develop a routine migration cycle and keep employed eight to nine months of the year by moving with the harvest. During the season they live in temporary housing provided by the grower or a labor contractor or sleep in tents and cars along the roadside or in one of the few public labor camps. During the off-season, they winter in the small rural towns or return to their villages in Mexico or Puerto Rico. The growers prefer housing the specialized migrants on their ranches to reinforce their control and insure punctuality. Because migrants perform most of the harvest work in certain crops, their cooperation can be extremely critical.

There have been three systems for recruiting seasonal workers: self-recruitment, labor contractors, and rationalized recruitment through the labor bureaus and the bracero program. Self-recruitment has been the dominant method, especially among the locals and specialized migrants; it gives the workers greater cohesion and autonomy. The work groups are often made up of an extended family or a circle of friends from a small town or neighborhood. A family elder or community leader lines up the jobs and negotiates the work terms. The grower or his foreman supervises, making conflicts of interest highly visible. The labor contractor and rationalized systems provide the growers with better controls and have been more common among the unspecialized workers, especially the migrants. In most cases, the labor contractor is in complete charge of the crew, lining up jobs, providing transporation housing, supervising the work and negotiating the contract with the grower (Hill 1972; Sosnick 1978:286–311). The contractor serves as a buffer between grower and worker, blurring the underlying antagonisms and absorbing much of the worker's hostilities. The workers call them coyotes, scavengers who live off the weak smaller animals of the fields. While contractors have been known to support strikes, most are opposed to unionization. Often they were set up by a protective grower who provided a cheap bus and perhaps shack for temporary housing. Because their future contracts depend on a reputation for reliability, they often prefer a crew of tractable, dependent workers. This insures ability to meet schedules and increases their income. Contractor income comes from two sources: deductions from wages for services, such as transportation, housing and food; and the difference between the wages paid to workers and the contract with the grower that specifies particular tasks, a time schedule, and quality standards. Dependent workers have to purchase more services. Wage boosts come out of the contractors' pockets, cooling their sympathies for the workers. However, contractors leading crews of specialized migrants have been known to organize harvest strikes and bargain for better conditions. Typically this has been where the contractor is tied to the crew by strong ethnic and personal loyalties, as among the Japanese and Filipino immigrants.

Both self-recruitment and labor contracting approximate market processes insofar as workers and growers make independent decisions based on their resources, interests, and past experience. The rationalized systems are quite different, entailing grower organization and long-range planning. The labor bureaus and the bracero program for importing seasonal Mexican workers recruit for all the growers in a district, generally defined by a crop or a county, and use a predefined production schedule and wage rates. In some cases, the labor bureau even supervises the work crews and signs the paychecks.

Rationalized recruitment presents the growers with several advantages. They can schedule their harvest with assurance that sufficient workers will be available. Costs are known in advance and terms do not have to be negotiated with each crew. In times of scarce labor, workers can be recruited from distant places. The greatest advantage, however, comes from the creation of an effective employers cartel. The growers meet months in advance of the harvest, agreeing on a common wage rate and terms. In many cases, the association or crop board even hires fieldmen to enforce the agreement. The workers have little choice but to accept the offered terms. As Fisher (1953:97) argued:

Wage fixing by employers is taken as a matter of course in California and the terms of these agreements are disseminated by the public press or by association bulletins or by the journals of farm organizations and commodity associations.

The division of workers by tenure, skills, and residence has also been overlaid by sharp ethnic cleavages. Different ethnic groups have specialized in particular crops and production tasks. The historical timing of immigration waves, the prominence of self-recruitment, and grower hiring policies have worked to produce a cultural division of labor. The Anglo workers, for example, came from the dustbowl immigration of the 1930s and, by breaking Mexican and Filipino strikes and currying favor with growers, were promoted to permanent positions. The Filipinos, by contrast, specialized in high skilled tasks such as asparagus harvesting and worked in specialized migrant crews composed of single males, typically under a Filipino contractor. The Mexican and Mexican-Americans have shared a language but are otherwise quite diverse. The Mexican-Americans are mostly local workers, concentrating on crops such as grapes that require skills and provide nearly year-round employment. The males often join crews of specialized migrants, working crops such as tree fruits and head lettuce that allow a coherent migration cycle. The Mexican immigrants, both illegals without papers and the "green card" immigrants holding temporary citizen papers, are mostly unspecialized migrants, working crops such as tomatoes and sugar beets that provide the least desirable, short-term jobs. There are also gender- and age-based divisions. Because of their age and family obligations, women and children are concentrated in the most seasonal, low-paid and low-skilled jobs such as onion topping and hoeing while the men dominate the more secure, skilled, and better-paid jobs. None of these divisions, however, is so rigid that workers cannot cross the line from, for example, unspecialized seasonal work to specialized permanent jobs. Strikes supported by any particular segment can readily be broken by workers of different tenure, skill, residence, or ethnicity.

The growers have also followed the policy of systematic overrecruitment of seasonal workers, especially at the harvest peak. As Fisher (1953:7–12) argued, the costs of recruitment are negligible, and a general oversupply of labor holds down wages. This gives the growers protection against crop loss and increases their flexibility in marketing. It also intensifies competition among workers, reinforcing labor discipline and holding wages down. As a result, farm workers have been kept at the bottom of the national income hierarchy, and despite significant unionization since 1970, their average family incomes in the late 1970s still remained below the federal poverty line (Dunbar and Kravitz 1976; Sosnick 1978:21–23; Goldfarb 1981). Like any deprived group, most farm workers lack the economic margin to support a prolonged strike. The more ambitious, talented workers are always on the watch for opportunities to escape. As the barrio from which Cesar Chavez hailed was named, the popular motto was "Sal Si Puedes!" ("Get Out If You Can"). This drains the farm worker community of indigenous leaders and undermines commitment to farm work as an occupation. Not surprisingly, leadership for farm worker insurgencies has tended to come from the outside.

The geographic dispersion and small size of most farm crews also makes organizing difficult. The crews are continually moving from field to field, and there is no factory gate where organizers can catch workers filing in to their jobs. Organizing takes considerable effort simply to maintain contacts and coordinate actions. The workers assemble from multiple points and drive along hidden back roads to fields that change daily. Many reside in private ranch housing. Nor is organizing on the job easy. "Submarines," as the UFW has called them, are promptly fired once discovered, and if a picket team attempts to cajole workers from the roadside, the grower merely orders the crew farther back out of earshot.

The growers have also used direct coercive controls, ranging from firings and harassment to open violence. In the early 1930s, the mass strikes provoked the growers to organize vigilante committees that passed out machine guns and dynamite to suppress the strikes (Chambers 1952; Jamieson 1945). In the post-World War II strikes we will examine, mass violence has been kept at a much lower level. Still, the growers have burned union buildings, hired thugs to beat union organizers, supported sporadic vigilante attacks, used "yellow dog" contracts and company unions, and chased pickets off the roads in their pickup trucks. Farm strikes remain intense, violence-prone affairs.

The Making of an Underclass

The history of farm labor is in large part that of successive immigration waves. The labor market is unstructured in that there are few barriers of skills or customs restricting access to jobs. The market has therefore been open to all comers, regardless of their previous work experience, skills, or citizenship. The growers have also actively recruited immigrant workers, dispatching labor drummers, staging mass advertising campaigns, and setting up rationalized recruitment programs to insure access to international labor markets. In this, they have been favored by world historical developments, especially the projection of U.S. economic and military power into underdeveloped countries such as China and the Philippines and the adoption of development strategies by countries such as Mexico and Japan that have generated large pools of willing emigrants (Portes and Walton 1981).

The initial labor basis was provided by Chinese immigrants, who had originally been imported in the 1860s as indentured laborers for the railway companies and mining operators. With the completion of the transcontinental railways in the late 1870s, the railway companies laid off the Chinese en masse, abandoning them in the rural hinterland. Unable to return to their homeland and excluded by employer prejudice and domestic worker agitation from urban jobs, they gravitated to the farms. By 1880 the Chinese constituted one-third of the labor force and, praised by the grower press as "especially clever in the packing of fruit," soon dominated the fields (Chiu 1967:79–88; Fisher 1953:4–5). They also sparked intense prejudice among the native workers and small farmers. At the peak of the economic crisis of the late 1870s, the small farmers and white workers began agitating for their jobs and, in 1882, secured the Chinese Exclusion Act. During the depression of 1893, unemployed white workers again marched on the rural areas, this time driving the Chinese into the urban slums where they became house servants, launderers, and small entrepreneurs (Lyman 1974).

Although the growers had temporarily lost their "clever workers," they had learned a valuable lesson. The choice seasonal workers were immigrants. Immigrant workers would accept low wages and harsh conditions. Most were economic refugees with low economic expectations and plans for returning to their homeland. Long hours, low pay, and harsh working conditions were a temporary expedient.[1] Additionally, some of the immigrants returned to their homeland during the off-season, relieving the rural community of the burden of supporting unemployed workers and their families. The immigrants were also vulnerable. Without citizenship, they could easily be intimidated and threatened with deportation. Officials looked the other way when natives attacked, and their cultural distinctiveness set them off, discouraging coordination with domestic workers.

Deprived of their Chinese workers, the growers promptly turned to a new pool of immigrant labor, this time the Japanese. Here again, U.S. military power opened the door, and Japanese development strategies created a flood of willing immigrants. By 1920 over 30,000 Japanese were in the fields. The growers praised the Japanese who were skilled and willing to work long hard hours for low pay, often 35 to 40 cents per day. Soon the Japanese dominated the higher-skilled jobs such as asparagus harvesting and working the vineyards and provided the skills for new crops. Again, mass unemployment led to attacks by domestic workers and finally to a relatively weak exclusion act in 1908 and local limits on Japanese employment, residence, and mobility. Then the Japanese shocked the growers, using their skills and strong kinship ties to organize powerful harvest strikes, making themselves the highest paid farm workers and pooling their savings to buy highly successful small farms that economically threatened the large estates (Iwata 1962; Lyman 1974). The growers promptly revised their assessment. "Japanese labor is not cheap labor. The little brown traders [sic] know how to get as much for their product as the traffic will bear" (*Los Angeles Times*, January 17, 1920). Swinging behind the nativist tide, the growers pressed for the Alien Land Acts of 1913 and 1919 in a bid to strip the Japanese of their land and, in 1924, endorsed the Johnson-Reed Act that finally closed the door to further Japanese immigration.

The growers had learned two additional lessons. First, no single ethnic group could be allowed to dominate the labor force as thoroughly as had the Chinese and Japanese. Ethnic solidarity, as in the case of the Japanese, might give rise to rapid and powerful insurgency, and during periods of mass unemployment, native workers would mount attacks, potentially displacing the immigrants. In other words, a mix of diverse groups was preferable. Second, most of the workers should not be deportable. Otherwise, nativist exclusionary agitation might force the growers to accept domestic workers at higher wages.

The next candidates for the sweatshops in the sun became the mainstay for the expansion of the migratory labor estates—the Filipino and Mexican immigrants followed by the depression era dustbowlers. These workers were culturally diverse and, for the most part, could not be deported. The Philippines was a U.S. protectorate, and the dustbowlers were, of course, citizens. The Mexicans were so numerous and close to their homeland that, even when they were deported en masse during the 1930s (Hoffmann 1974), they could later be enticed to return. These workers also fit the general model of the cheap docile laborer amenable to erratic hiring. By 1930, over 30,000 Filipinos were in the fields, dominating the asparagus and lettuce harvest (Fisher 1953:5). Mexican workers began immigrating shortly after the Mexican revolution, and with the construction of the railways in northern Mexico and the squeeze on peasants, the campesinos began journeying northward for the Yankee dollar (Reisler 1976). By 1930, there were over 368,000 Mexican workers in the fields, dominating the field crops in the southern end of the state. The delighted growers had found the perfect solution: "No labor that has ever come to the U.S. is more satisfactory under righteous treatment. He is the result of years of servitude, has always looked upon his employer as his padron, and himself as part of the establishment" (G. P. Clements, President of the Los Angeles Chamber of Commerce, cited in Kushner 1975:18). The "Mexican harvest" was also vulnerable since subject to deportation, and many returned to peasant villages during the off-season.

On the heels of this immigrant invasion came the dustbowl migration. The farm depression of the 1920s created a mass exodus from the southern midwest. By 1940, around 108,000 Okies had made the trek from the midwestern drought to the California fields (Fisher 1953:5). In fact, the influx was so great that by the late 1930s the growers could not fully use the refugees, and to prevent the Okies from collecting county relief, the growers and local businessmen sporadically organized vigilante teams to turn the dustbowlers back at the county line. Because of their small farmer individualism and their general demoralization, the dustbowlers proved ideal strikebreakers, destroying the mass strikes of the Mexicans and Filipinos throughout the tumultuous 1930s (Stein 1973; Kushner 1975:13–17; Daniels 1981).

The most severe test of grower control over the labor market came in the 1940s. The mass unemployment of the 1930s had created a vast labor surplus, but wartime expansion in the early 1940s drained it off and the mass deportations of Mexicans during the late 1930s had cut off the closest supply of cheap labor (Hoffman 1974). The growers confronted a major labor crisis. Their solution was quite novel. Pointing to the importance of agriculture to the war effort, the growers demanded a system of sponsored immigration administered by the federal government. Although they had doubts about direct state controls over labor recruitment, the scope of the "labor emergency" was too great. In 1941 the U.S. State Department and Mexican officials finalized diplomatic agreements creating a rationalized labor recruitment system for importing braceros for seasonal agricultural jobs. The bracero system fit the grower requirements perfectly, providing "cheap" docile labor that vanished during the off-season. Moreover, the system strengthened the employer cartel, making the labor associations the chief contractors of labor. In addition, the braceros provided ideal strike insurance. If they supported a challenge, they could be deported and permanently barred from returning by being labeled an "undesirable worker." Nor could domestic strikes succeed. The growers would simply order up a new crew of braceros and, despite legal bars on bracero hiring during strikes, they would finish out the harvest. And when the season was over, the braceros were simply shipped home to Mexico.

For the growers, the experiment in rationalized recruitment was a fantastic success. The growers could submit orders for their field crews months in advance of the harvest, confident that the braceros would arrive on schedule. Since recruitment costs were negligible, the grower could order up larger crews to complete the harvest quicker. If there were temporary delays because of bad weather or a slow-ripening crop, the braceros could be kept in camp until needed. Moreover, they were efficient "cheap" workers. The typical bracero was a young able-bodied male, 16–25 years of age, seeking a quick return to invest in a small peasant farm at home. Wages were unilaterally set by grower committees meeting months in advance of the harvest and simply inserted in the bracero contracts. "Farmers in northern California were supplied with braceros from contracting centers 800 miles away on forty-eight hours notice. Not a crop was lost. Wages were held in line. The bracero lived up to his reputation as a tractable, obedient, cheerful and eager worker" (Galarza 1964:115).

In fact, the program was such a success that major use came in the 1950s long after any wartime "emergency" had passed. Insurgency was the prime consideration. In the war years, braceros made up only 5–10 percent of the total labor force and were concentrated in the least desirable seasonal jobs. But in 1948 the National Farm Labor Union mounted a challenge, and bracero use expanded rapidly. By the peak of bracero use in 1959, they made up almost one-quarter of the total labor force and dominated most of the field crops, especially lettuce, tomatoes, and sugar beets.[2] Nor were they confined to seasonal jobs. In 1951, provisions were introduced for "specials," workers who remained year-round with a single employer. Soon there were bracero irrigators, mechanics, and tractor drivers, even an occasional foreman. Although the bracero statutes specifically prohibited their use in place of domestics, many growers replaced their troublesome domestics with the new import model. Of course the growers still contended that the "labor emergency" still existed, but now their rationale was that Americans "would not accept the hard stoop labor required." This, of course, ignored the fact that the availability of braceros had made possible the "hard stoop labor" conditions and cheap wages that U.S. citizens shunned (Jones 1965; Salandini 1969). Nor, given their their systematic avoidance of domestics, did the growers make serious efforts to recruit domestic workers (Galarza 1964; Salandini 1969).

The fruit for the workers, especially the domestic workers, was an unmitigated disaster. The program strengthened the employers' cartel, driving wages down to the lowest levels since the 1930s. In 1948, California farm wages were 64.7 percent of average manufacturing wages but, by 1959, the peak bracero year, they had fallen to 46.6 percent.[3] Bracero hiring strengthened labor discipline, allowing speed-ups and longer hours under more difficult field conditions. In addition, the domestic workers faced mass displacements. In cotton, for example, the availability of braceros and new harvest machines produced a mass displacement of around 100,000 black tenant farmers, most of whom fled to teeming slums like Watts. Labor-intensive crops like tomatoes, melons, and lettuce went almost overnight from Mexican-American crews to braceros, forcing the domestics into the urban barrios (Galarza 1964; Glass 1966:52–60). For the domestics who stayed, jobs became increasingly scarce and transitory as growers had less incentive to stabilize their hiring. And, should the workers resist, the growers merely phoned in orders for more braceros. As we will see, braceros became the major strikebreaking force, destroying the National Farm Labor Union and Agricultural Workers Organizing Committee challenges (chapters 4 and 5).

None of this was officially allowed by the bracero legislation. Public Laws 54 and 78 and the various treaties with Mexico charged the public officials with administering the program so as to guarantee no "adverse impact" on domestic workers. But the growers were politically entrenched and dominated the administration of the program. The labor associations served as advisory committees over the bracero offices, effectively controlling the details of the program. Meeting months in advance of the harvest, the growers agreed on a common wage base, officially known as the "prevailing wage," and an estimate of their anticipated "labor shortage." Farm Placement officials simply copied down their request, recruiting the workers and inserting the terms into the bracero labor contracts. Because the supply of braceros was unlimited, the "prevailing wage" effectively became the maximum wage. If domestics resisted, the associations simply filed a request for additional braceros. In fact, domestic workers generally found it necessary to underbid the bracero wage to secure work at all (Sosnick 1978:401–402).

The growers' next major test came in the early 1960s. As we will see in chapter 8, political alignments shifted against the growers in the early 1960s, weakening the farm block and giving farm worker allies a stronger voice. The advantages of the braceros quickly disappeared. First, the Kennedy administration began enforcing the protective statutes, ordering the growers to first offer jobs to citizens, cease hiring "specials," and remove braceros from strike zones. The growers shifted back to the labor contractors and stepped up the hiring of sindocumentos (undocumented workers) or illegal immigrants. The Department of Labor then ordered that growers caught with "mixed crews" (i.e., illegals alongside braceros) could not receive further bracero shipments. The growers retaliated by further withdrawing from the program. Finally, under White House pressure and an intense lobby campaign, Congress abolished the program outright, extending the program through the 1964 season so that an orderly transition could be prepared.

The end of the bracero program brought new life to the labor contractor system and the influx of "green carders" and illegal immigrants. The contractors, of course, could perform many of the same functions—recruiting immigrant workers, fostering ethnic rivalries, providing an oversupply of labor, depressing wages, and providing strong controls over the workers. Moreover, they were especially adept at the recruitment of illegal labor, a commodity that came into great demand as the braceros disappeared.

In a typical operation one contractor was caught by the Border Patrol while directing a convoy of two trucks and a passenger car northward from Tijuana. Seventy men were aboard the trucks, which were preceded by a scout car. The men had crawled through the border fence and were being taken to prearranged employment 500 miles to the north. Occasionally this contractor found his "wetbacks" nearer home. Asked by a government commission where he obtained them, he replied, "From the state employment service." (Galarza 1964:60–61)

By the late 1960s, green carders and illegal immigrants had become the new seasonal labor base, making up over two-thirds of the seasonal labor force (Sosnick 1978:432). The growers encouraged their braceros to file for citizenship papers, sponsoring their re-entry as green card immigrants. Having secured their green card or temporary citizenship document, the workers did not have to actually pursue full citizenship or even reside in the United States. Many of the green carders lived in Mexico and regularly crossed the border on a daily or seasonal basis. Although there are no precise figures on the number of green carders or their role in the border labor markets, available evidence suggests that by the late 1960s they made up as much as a quarter of the total border-area labor force and perhaps as much as a third of the statewide seasonal labor force (North 1970; Fineberg 1971:80–83; Sosnick 1978:411).

Another route has been illegal immigration. Although the mass deportations of the 1930s and "Operation Wetback" in the early 1950s demonstrated the technical feasibility of halting the influx of sindocumentos or undocumented workers (Hoffman 1974; Portes 1977), the Immigration and Naturalization Service has been unable to stem the tide. By the late 1970s, illegal immigration was the major source of population growth in the United States, and the illegal immigrants had begun moving from the fields to urban service and industrial jobs (North and Houstoun 1976). The agency, in large part because of the pressure of Congressional representatives from the rural districts, has long been understaffed and without sufficient authority (Hadley 1956; Greene 1969). At the same time, the growers have pressured the Border Patrol to stay out of the fields during the harvest. In effect, la migra, as the workers call the Border Patrol, has been little more than a device to keep the illegals scared and continually on the move, insuring that they do not become dependents on the rural communities.

The undocumented worker, however, represents a mixed good. The prime virtues are the same as those of the bracero. As the *Associated Farmer*, a prominent grower publication with special concern for labor reltions, claimed, the chief virtue of the "wetback" (or illegal immigrant) is that "he is tractable and will not strike" (April–May 1951:4). They depend on the contractors for jobs, housing, and transportation, and they are also "scared" workers in the sense that they can be deported. In fact, especially avaricious employers have been known to report their illegals to the immigration authorities on payday to avoid paying wages. The illegals also fit the bracero model of an efficient worker—young, male, a temporary immigrant seeking quick earnings to put back into a peasant farm or small business in Mexico (Samora 1971; Goldfarb 1981; Sosnick 1978:96–105). As a California Farm Placement officer explained: "the 'illegal' is a worker that warms the grower's heart" (cited in Wolf 1964:181). Yet, the undocumented worker also regards himself as a *libre* (free worker), not bound to set terms or a named employer.

"Wetbacks" have a way of vanishing from camp overnight singly or in groups, enticed by some runner who leads them to greener pastures. As pirating made the price of "wetbacks" uncertain, so fear made them unpredictable. (Galarza 1964:58).

The United Farm Workers also found that with patience the illegals could be organized, at least enough to encourage them to leave a strike zone.

The growers' overall strategy has been to recruit an oversupply of labor of various types, pitting illegals against braceros, green carders and domestics. The ethnic groups have been kept apart, housed separately, assigned to jobs on the basis of their proven loyalty and supervised by padrone-style labor contractors. Because of short-term jobs and transiency, many workers have week job commitments and community ties. Few have the resources to support prolonged strikes. Given the chance, the ambitious move on to new opportunities, draining off indigenous leadership. Geographic dispersion and small employment units make organizing difficult. Periodically, however, a cohesive group of specialized workers has gotten sufficient hold on a particular crop or set of production tasks to mount strikes. The Filipino asparagus cutters would march out on strike, demanding a wage hike and better field conditions. A few growers might concede. But soon the ethnic rivalries would reemerge. The growers would dispatch labor contractors to bring in the Mexicans or the Okies or phone in an order for an emergency shipment of braceros. If the strikers persisted, the local courts would intervene, taking away their loudspeakers and ordering them twenty yards apart. Sheriff's deputies would harass the pickets and look the other way at grower attacks. Under the cover of darkness, vigilantes might appear. Amid turmoil and recriminations, the strikebreaking crews would cross the picket lines, and when the exhausted strikers ran out of food and money, the battle would draw to another bitter end.

Did Powerlessness Change?

Our major concern is determining the conditions that made for sustained and successful farm worker insurgency. Improved mobilization conditions could have been a significant factor. In the mid-1960s the United Farm Workers initiated a challenge and within a decade had a mass base of support. As we will see in the next two chapters, the National Farm Labor Union and the Agricultural Workers Organizing Committee both failed to mobilize a mass base. Was the UFW success due to more favorable conditions for organizing farm workers?

Although the UFW still faced major barriers—scarce resources, social disorganization and grower controls—it did benefit from more conducive conditions. The change, however, was not dramatic. From the late 1940s through the early 1960s, the influx of braceros and the strengthening of the grower cartel pushed wages steadily downward. In 1965 the braceros disappeared, and uncertainty about the supply of seasonal workers left the growers vulnerable. Farm worker income remained below poverty levels, however, suggesting that the change was less a question of economic resources than greater work independence. There was also a favorable ethnic shift, in broad terms, from Anglos to Mexican workers. The Mexican workers had better organizing facilities and indigenous leadership. This was due to their minority status, which kept potential leaders in the farm worker community, and external sponsorship. In the early 1960s the Catholic Church expanded services to the growing Mexican-American population in the southwest, organizing a lay leadership training program known as the *cursillo* movement and sponsoring mutual benefit associations. Although most of the projects were in the urban barrios, farm workers in small towns were involved (Grebler, Moore and Guzman 1970:453–456). About the same time, the Protestant churches also expanded their mission, supporting the community organizing projects of the National Migrant Ministry that, as we will see, became directly involved in the United Farm Worker struggle. These projects trained indigenous leaders, created networks, and gave greater access to future sponsors.

In addition the workers became more cohesive and autonomous because of changes in the labor market. Increased farm size, mechanization, and crop specialization coupled with the end of the bracero program reduced the degree of ecological dispersion and encouraged a shift from permanent hands, domestic migrants, and braceros to local workers and illegals. During the NFLU challenge in the late 1940s, permanent workers made up about thirty percent of the labor force, locals about two-fifths, and domestic migrants about a third.[4] Braceros and illegals were relatively negligible, probably less than ten percent. The AWOC in the late 1950s faced the least favorable conditions. Permanent hands were almost two-fifths of the labor force, locals were only a third, and domestic migrants had largely been displaced by the braceros. The UFW enjoyed the most favorable context. By the peak of UFW organizing in the late 1960s and early 1970s, the permanents had declined again to about thirty percent, locals had increased to almost two-fifths, and the braceros had completely disappeared, replaced by green carders and illegals. Although comparable figures on crop specialization trends are not available, the increase in local workers and the increasing specialization of districts in particular crops suggest that workers were more specialized (cf. Metzler 1966; Friedland, Thomas and Barton 1981).

Even more favorable was the decline in ethnic diversity. In the late 1940s, the Anglos were three-fourths of the San Joaquin workers, Mexicans around one-sixth, blacks five percent, and Fillipinos around 3 percent (Metzler and Sayin 1948:42).[5] The NFLU quite logically focused its initial organizing on the Anglos and later expanded to the Mexican workers. By the late 1950s, however, the Anglos had declined to about a third of the San Joaquin workers, while Mexican workers increased to almost two-fifths with black-Americans, Filipinos, and Arabian workers making up the rest (Metzler 1965:20). As we will see, the AWOC made a major strategic error by focusing its organizing on the Anglo workers, and it was destroyed by the growing "Mexican harvest." By the late 1960s, the trend was even clearer. The Anglos were less than a third, Mexican workers were almost a half, and the blacks, Filipinos, and Arabian workers were each about six percent of the total labor force (California Assembly 1969:23). The further immigration of green carders and illegals in the 1970s made Mexican-descent workers overwhelmingly dominant, almost two-thirds of the labor force. Althought there have been significant clashes between the settled Mexican-Americans and the newer Mexican immigrants, these workers have shared a common cultural heritage and ethnic solidarity that has been an important theme in UFW organizing.

It should be kept in mind, however, that even in the late 1960s and early 1970s the major barriers to farm work organizing were still intact. The UFW found this out when illegals, green carders, Arabian, Anglo and even Mexican-American workers crossed their picket lines. Farm workers were still impoverished, the ethnic division of labor was intact, and the growers still had their labor contractors and paternalistic controls. More important, as we will see, were the new organizing strategies of the UFW and altered political alignments that created increased sponsorship, a weaker opposition, and increased opportunities for collective action.

4

The Agony of the NFLU (1946–1952)

BALLAD OF THE DI GIORGIO STRIKERS

Pickets standing on the line
Looking down the country road,
Saw a lonesome stranger coming
And he said his name was Joad.

Now the stranger stood beside us
And his face was pale and thin,
Said he'd like to join the Union
So we said we'd let him in.

Thursday night he came to meeting
And he raised his snowy head
With a voice like Resurrection
Spoke, and this is what he said:

"There's a fence around Creation,
There's a mortgage on the sun,
They have put electric meters
Where the rivers used to run.

"God Almighty made the valley
For a land of milk and honey,
But a corporation's got it
For to turn it into money."

Insurgencies are inevitably marked by their political times.
The National Farm Labor Union challenge was decisively shaped by the
political currents of the late 1940s. As World War II came to a close, the
labor movement threw off wartime constraints and mounted a mass strike

wave in a bid to renew the insurgency of the late 1930s. But the political setting had changed dramatically. The "new labor statesmen," as C. Wright Mills (1947) presciently called them, had begun to consolidate their hold over the house of labor, seeking to convert the unions from a mass movement supporting a broad range of social reforms into a narrow special interest group attempting to protect its hold on privileged jobs and economic security. The union leaders had become inseparably wedded to the Democratic party, trading on blue collar votes for access to party leaders. Yet the predictability of blue collar votes meant that the Democratic leaders were less dependent on them and, because of mounting concern about postwar economic recovery, turned towards conservative political programs. In April of 1946, President Truman turned on his political allies, containing the mass strike wave by nationalizing the coal mines, jailing the leaders of United Mine Workers Union, threatening to conscript the railway workers if they carried through a national strike pledge, and purging the Cabinet of Henry Wallace and other left-wing New Dealers. Although the Congress of Industrial Organization's newly created Political Action Committee campaigned heavily for Democratic candidates, the New Deal Democrats suffered a major rout in the November elections, and the Republicans seized control of both Houses of Congress for the first time in a decade and a half (Davis 1980; Foster 1975). In June 1947, the resurgent Congressional conservatives overrode Truman's veto to push through the Taft-Hartley Act, restructuring the terrain of national labor relations. Under the Wagner Act and its NIRA Section 7a predecessor, employers had been compelled to recognize unions and bargain "in good faith" under the supervision of the National Labor Relations Board (NLRB). This meant that they could not sign yellow dog contracts, fire union members, or refuse to negotiate with duly elected union leaders. Although the Wagner Act outlawed recognition strikes and substituted lengthy negotiations for direct action, overall it had facilitated industrial worker insurgency. The Taft-Hartley amendments were far more stifling. The amendments barred the major tools of labor solidarity—secondary boycotts, sympathy strikes, mass picketing, and direct contributions to political campaigns. Union officials had to sign anticommunist disclaimers, thereby breaking the left stronghold in the industrial unions.

In March 1947 the red purges began when President Truman issued his Loyalty Order. Soon afterwards a freshman representative from California named Richard Nixon orchestrated the showcase trials of Alger Hiss and the national leadership of the American Communist Party (Caute 1977). The bitter rivalries and union raiding between the leftist Congress of Industrial Organization and the conservative American Federation of Labor reemerged, effectively destroying the promising new organizing drives in the industrial belt of the South and among the growing white collar proletariat (Galenson 1960; Montgomery 1980). Despite Truman's surprise victory in the November 1948 elections, the labor movement had clearly stalled. Congress was still controlled by the Republicans, and Truman promptly scuttled the campaign pledges to the "Fair Deal," most notably the full employment platform, the repeal of Taft-Hartley, and civil rights reform.

On virtually all levels, it was an unpromising context for a new challenge among farm workers. The mobilization barriers that had undermined the mass strike waves of the 1930s were still intact (Stein 1973; Daniels 1981). Although the wartime economic boom had drained off some of the labor surplus, the farm worker community was still fragmented and without resources. Mexican braceros were beginning to represent a significant force in the fields. Nor was the political environment favorable. The labor movement had stalled, and national labor relations were becoming more restrictive. Although farm workers had been explicitly exempted from the National Labor Relations Act, the Taft-Hartley amendments barred union support through sympathy strikes and secondary boycotts that targeted a firm rather than a particular commodity and sympathy strikes. The political turmoil and center-left government of the late 1930s were being replaced by a conservative drift that later turned into red purges and McCarthyism. The growers, then, were relatively entrenched, and political elites were likely to oppose insurgency.

Yet the intense rivalries between the AFL and the CIO prompted the formation of a new farm worker challenge. The AFL had traditionally been organized around craft unions among the higher skilled occupations, while the CIO was built during the upsurge of the 1930s by industry-wide organizing among the mass production workers (Galenson 1960; Montgomery 1979; Brody 1980). Although the AFL was more conservative, its President, William Green, wanted to outflank the CIO. In particular, Green saw organizing farm workers as an excellent opportunity to outflank the Food, Tobacco and Agricultural Workers Union, a CIO-affiliate, descended from the United Cannery, Agricultural, Packing and Allied Workers of America (UCAPAWA) that had organized mass strikes during the late 1930s. When H. L. Mitchell, the President of the AFL-affiliated Southern Tenant Farmers Union (STFU), approached him at the 1946 convention about rechartering the union to organize California farm workers, Green immediately pledged financial support for a Director of Organizations and promised future support for additional organizers and help in lining up aid from AFL unions.

Mitchell promptly rechristened the union the National Farm Labor Union (NFLU) and recruited Henry ("Hank") Hasiwar, a fellow member of the Socialist party attending the AFL convention, as the new Director of Organizations. Mitchell and Hasiwar were both experienced, resourceful organizers trained by the labor upsurge of the 1930s. H. L. Mitchell, president of the union, had been the secretary and later president of the STFU. A member of the Socialist party, Mitchell had organized tenant farmers out of his dry cleaning shop in Tyron, Arkansas and masterminded the STFU's political defense against the mass displacements of tenant farmers carried out in the late 1930s under the Agricultural Adjustment Act. A personal friend of Eleanor Roosevelt and prominent leftist New Dealers, Mitchell was well known in labor circles and brought important political connections to the new challenger. While a student at Columbia University in the early 1930s, Hasiwar had been involved in socialist student organizations, organizing demonstrations against President Nicholas Murray Butler's speaking invitations to university officials from Nazi Germany. After he graduated in 1936, he became involved in union organizing drives among New York hotel and restaurant workers and New Jersey auto workers and kept up his affiliations with the Socialist party. After service in World War II, he served briefly as the chief military liaison between the Japanese unions and the American occupation forces, but after political disputes with General MacArthur, the head of the American occupation, he resigned and returned to New York. Through his friend Bill Becker, then labor secretary for the Socialist party, Hasiwar learned of the newly chartered union and eagerly signed on as the union's main organizer.[1]

Although the NFLU still claimed STFU chapters in the South, Mitchell and Hasiwar decided that the migratory labor estates in California offered a better target. A fellow Socialist, Carey McWilliams, had recently written about the battles of the 1930s, and the LaFollette hearings in 1940–42 had riveted attention on California farm workers. In addition, the large estates more closely resembled the restaurants and auto factories that Hasiwar had organized in the 1930s. The California project also offered their sponsor, the AFL, the opportunity to contest a CIO competitor that still claimed jurisdiction over the fields. Organizing farm workers would also build off the recent Teamsters victories over the United Packinghouse Workers (CIO) in the California packingsheds.

The Initial Strategy

Hasiwar and Mitchell arrived in Stockton, California in early March 1947, surveying the area and making contacts among the local labor councils. The initial strategy flowed directly from Hasiwar's organizing experience in the industrial unions. Instead of organizing mass area strikes of migrant workers at the harvest, as had the International Workers of the World in the 1910s and the United Cannery Workers in the 1930s, they decided the NFLU should pick out a few large firms and build a stable union membership among the permanent and local seasonal workers before striking. According to this analysis, the area strikes had failed because the migrants were disorganized and the organizers had not developed extensive contacts among the workers prior to strikes. As Hasiwar argued: "the area-wide operation of organizing these people is impossible. There is no way of controlling the big flow of people coming in" (Mitchell and Hasiwar 1974:I, 22–23). Moreover, the area strikes were, in effect, general strikes and therefore inevitably political. Although the union would eventually take on all of the growers, mass strikes would undoubtedly provoke wholesale repression. In this vein, Hasiwar and Mitchell decided to keep their involvement in the Socialist party under wraps to reduce their vulnerability to grower repression. As well, this would probably maximize their support among the politically conservative Anglo farm workers and potential liberal allies. All strikes would first be cleared through the local AFL labor councils to insure greater credibility and external support. Unfortunately, however, the councils in the rural towns were largely controlled by the politically conservative building trade unions.[2]

Over the spring and summer of 1947 Hasiwar, accompanied by several volunteer organizers, crisscrossed the Valley, organizing a half dozen small union locals. Because the "Okie" workers, as all the Anglo workers were derogatorily called, held most of the permanent jobs and were more likely to live in one of the small towns, they were the major organizing focus. The small shanty settlements of local seasonal workers and permanent hands knit together by a storefront church, a weekly auction, and a few ramshackle "smokehouses" and general stores were the best organizing contexts. Many of the workers had supported the strikes of the 1930s and were well aware of the dangers of grower repression. In fact, many had gotten their jobs by crossing picket lines in the late 1930s, a fact that made Hasiwar wary of his first union meetings:

We put it (a truck) back of the beer joint called the "Smokehouse." They strung up some lights for us, on a cord with bare bulbs. I was sitting on the platform of the truck. Then cars started coming, parking, switching off the lights, and I got up on the truck bed. There was no public address system. I spoke. I read a little from that story "Heartless Harvest" (about migrant workers). Then I asked them to come up and sign with the union. I told them it cost a dollar to join, and dues would be $1.00 a month. I told them if they were going to join, to pay the $2.00. I was amazed. Everyone in that big field joined that night, and they paid. Mitchell 1980:252)

To Hasiwar's surprise, the workers flocked to the union. By July the NFLU held membership cards on over 2000 workers. The most important recruits were "jack leg" preachers such as Phineas Parks and Jim Harron who worked in the fields during the week and held forth among their church congregations on Sundays. The preachers instantly became grass-roots organizers enlisting their congregations and pushing the organizing campaign at every opportunity. The first strike target was the Zaninovich ranch near Earlimart in the southern end of the San Joaquin Valley. The ranch's major crop was grapes, an ideal organizing target. Not only was the harvest highly perishable, but grape production was labor-intensive, required relatively skilled workers, and provided more or less continuous employment for most of the workers. About 200 of the 300 workers were local workers who lived in their own private houses. There was, however, an important ethnic split. About 50 to 60 Mexican migrants lived in temporary housing on the ranch while the permanent Anglo workers lived in the neighboring town of Orange Cove. Although Hasiwar tried to organize both groups, he was able to make contacts only with the Anglos. The Mexican workers did not speak English, and at that time, the union lacked a Spanish-speaking organizer. They were also off-limits in the private ranch housing (Mitchell and Hasiwar 1974:I, 20).

When Zaninovich heard of the organizing drive, he immediately fired all workers suspected of being union members. The union was caught unprepared. Since they lacked coverage by the NLRA, there were no legal remedies. The only choice was to strike. On June 13, Hasiwar called a hasty meeting. Angered by the firings, the workers voted unanimously to strike, demanding grievance procedures, union recognition, and a wage hike. The next morning they threw up a picket line, the central target being the packingshed where most of the permanent hands worked. Because all production had to pass through the shed, it was the most strategic point for disrupting the ranch. Strike support followed the ethnic split. Most of the 200 Anglo hands who were permanent or local workers marched out, while the Mexican migrants reported to work. The strike closed down the packingshed, but the field harvest continued with the Mexican hands.

Hasiwar had cleared the strike with the local labor council, and on the second day, members of the Fresno Ironworkers Union local who were building a water tower on the ranch marched out on sympathy strike. But by the end of the week, the ironworkers were grumbling about the lost work and, pointing to the failure to pull out the Mexican workers, argued that the strike could not succeed. Under pressure from the Fresno Labor Council, Hasiwar reluctantly urged the strikers to accept Zaninovich's offer of a token wage gain and back down. The first strike, lasting only a few days, had hardly tested the union's mettle, but the growers were now on notice.[3]

The DiGiorgio Strike

Shortly afterwards Hasiwar received a promising letter forwarded through Mitchell, who had returned to the STFU's old headquarters in Memphis, Tennessee. Robert Lee Whatley, a veteran labor organizer and socialist out of Oklahoma, was requesting "a good speaker and some literature" to organize farm workers in Lamont, California. Since Lamont and nearby Arvin had been the main scene for John Steinbeck's *The Grapes of Wrath* and the most ferocious vigilante actions in the late 1930s, Hasiwar decided to first firm up his support from the Kern County Labor Council. As he said, "I did not want to get involved, or to involve the people, if we were going to get stabbed in the back by the building tradesmen again" (Mitchell 1980:252). Secretly meeting with the council leaders in a hotel restaurant in nearby Bakersfield, Hasiwar was firmly assured by the council head Fred West, the business agent for the Hotel and Restaurant Employees and a former "Wobbly" (IWW) organizer, that the local unions would help the strikers (Mitchell and Hasiwar 1974:I, 26). Neil Haggerty, secretary of the California Federation of Labor, offered financing for two full-time organizers, and Hasiwar and Whatley set off walking the streets of Arvin and Lamont, holding meetings and signing up members. On July 10, Whatley set up a rally of 1200 workers in Lamont, and soon the local had over 1000 members.[4]

The small town of Lamont contained about 3,000 Anglo farm workers and was the principal labor pool for the nearby DiGiorgio ranch, the largest estate in the Central Valley. The ranch contained 12,000 acres of specialty crops and hired around 2,500 workers at the harvest peak. Three-fourths of the workers were Anglos who lived off-ranch in the tents, ramshackle houses, and cardboard shacks of nearby Lamont and Arvin. About five hundred Mexican migrants lived on-ranch, and there were a handful of Filipino migrants who lived off-ranch in contractor housing. Because the ranch had a winery and packingshed in addition to several fruit and vegetable crops, about half of the workers were permanent hands, and the rest were either local seasonals or migrants specialized in particular crops. If the largest ranch in the Central Valley could be broken, the door was opened for major changes.[5]

Hasiwar had planned to organize a base of support throughout the fall and winter, holding back on strikes until the spring plum harvest, rumored to be the ranch's most profitable and perishable crop (Mitchell and Hasiwar 1974:I, 33). But DiGiorgio struck first, firing Hasiwar's volunteer organizers, James Price, the President of Local 218 and foreman of the packingshed, and Phineas Parks, the preacher-organizer with the largest following. With a signed-up membership of slightly over 1,200, most of whom were DiGiorgio employees, Hasiwar phoned the DiGiorgio ranch and demanded a meeting. Receiving no answer, he forwarded a certified letter demanding a meeting but was again stonewalled. It was late September, near the end of the grape harvest, and it was the last chance for a major confrontation. Hasiwar called a hasty strike meeting, attended by 800–900 workers in the Weedpatch Grange Hall, who unanimously voted to strike. The strike demands were grievance procedures, seniority, union recognition, and a wage increase of 10 cents per hour on top of the current pay of 75–80 cents (Mitchell and Hasiwar 1974:I, 31).

As dawn broke on October 1, over 100 pickets marched outside the ranch gates. Although the support was not complete, the strike closed the shed and seriously crippled the field operations. Of 1100 workers currently employed, the union pulled out over 900. Of the 200 left, 130 were braceros who had been threatened with deportation, and there were about 75 Mexican-American and Filipino migrants.[6] The contention immediately riveted on the Mexican workers, especially the braceros who were legally barred from working in strike zones. Hasiwar hired Louis DeAnda, a Mexican-American recently released from the Air Force, to reach the Mexican workers, and put him on the picket line with a loud speaker that a sympathetic lawyer had donated. DeAnda managed to pull out several of the Mexican migrants and after some initial wavering, the braceros marched back to their barracks. DiGiorgio had only a skeleton workforce.

Since it was past the harvest peak, DiGiorgio decided to stonewall recruit a new labor force, and hope that the strike would collapse. The walk-out by the braceros was the key. Joseph DiGiorgio called on the Mexican consul for the southwestern states and the Department of Agriculture officials overseeing the braceros. The Counsul and the bracero officials, escorted by Kern County Sheriff John Lousalot, immediately drove out and instructed the braceros to "fulfill their contracts" or be terminated, which meant deportation.[7] When Hasiwar asked the Mexican consul to advise the braceros of their rights and enforce the regulations barring their employment as strikebreakers, the consul replied that the workers were "happy," were not involved in American "labor troubles," and the matter was for U.S. officials to resolve (Galarza 1977:104). The braceros returned to the grape harvest.

After a month of protests and threatened legal suits, the braceros were finally removed, but by then the grape harvest had been completed. In late October, AFL President Green upbraided U.S. Secretary of State George Marshall, then attending the AFL convention, for strikebreaking. Marshall had his aides check into the charge but did little else. Finally, after NFLU pickets rallied around the bracero barracks, the Mexican Ambassador decided that the braceros might become the target of violent attacks and passed a diplomatic note to Secretary Marshall requesting they be withdrawn. On November 11, a month and a half after the strike had begun, the 130 braceros were finally loaded on buses bound for Mexico.[8]

By this time, the ethnic rivalries and sagging morale had become a major problem. In early October, DiGiorgio had dispatched his foremen to round up workers from the Los Angeles barrios, and sent several to south Texas and across the Mexican border. On October 23, the pickets turned back a train load of Mexican illegals being shipped in by the DiGiorgio labor drummers (*San Francisco Chronicle*, October 24, 1947). In early November, DiGiorgio bought advertising time on several radio stations along the border and began hiring workers through the Bakersfield Farm Placement Office. Although the pickets finally closed the Placement Office, the labor recruiters had come up with around 600 workers, enough to finish pruning the grape vines.[9]

By this point the strike was effectively defeated. The root problem was the poverty of the farm workers, their lack of skills, controls over the braceros, and the multiple rivalries. Most of the workers lived on the margin of existence. The union had only about $2800 in strike funds at the outset and, despite extensive early support from other unions, support for the strikers was meager. When the braceros returned to work, a few strikers decided they could not hold out and returned to their jobs. There were also too many options for recruiting strikebreakers. There were no insurmountable skill barriers preventing the hiring of untrained workers, and there were several pools available. If it were not braceros, then it was migrants from other crops who were delighted by an opportunity for more stable work. Or it was unemployed barrio dwellers from Los Angeles or a crew of illegal immigrants looking for quick cash, always watching out for the Border Patrol. By the conservative estimate of the Immigration and Naturalization Service, DiGiorgio hired over 350 sindocumentos over the fall.[10] A labor surplus, the ethnic rivalries rooted in the cultural division of labor, and a general climate of economic desperation made prolonged strikes virtually impossible.

The strike was also weakened by the NFLU's mobilizing approach. Although Hasiwar and his organizers had made use of bloc recruitment tactics, working through the preachers and crew foremen, they had not developed a solution to the collective goods problem. Although he was sensitive to broader political issues, Hasiwar did not make these central in the meetings. The major topics in the union meetings were the collective economic benefits of a union and redressing DiGiorgio's paternalistic attitude that irritated the independent-minded Anglo workers. The Union conducted training programs, but the focus was on technical skills like keeping membership records and how to conduct a public meeting. There were no selective incentive projects, like the United Farm Worker's cooperative gas station or burial insurance program. Nor was there an overriding vision to an alternative way of life or a pervasive sense of solidarity. Of course, the individualistic culture of the Anglo workers worked against this, but the organizers did little to directly confront the incentive problem. Collective material benefits might be sufficient to organize the permanent local workers who were enmeshed in the local community and committed to their jobs, but the migrants, especially the short-term workers recruited from outside the area, could not be mobilized by these concerns.

The local political environment was also unfavorable. DiGiorgio enjoyed the automatic support of local officials. Acting on the basis of a noise ordinance originally passed by the Kern County Board of Supervisors the week after Hasiwar's arrival, Sheriff Lousalot ordered the loudspeakers off the picket line. As the Sheriff argued before the board, the equipment was a "dangerous thing."[11] Dangerous it was, for it had helped convince many workers to put down their tools. On January 16, 1948 Justice of the Peace Parrish, a personal friend of Joseph DiGiorgio, ordered the Sheriff to evict the strikers who still resided in company housing.[12] Although police harassment was minimal, the Sheriff did order pickets to the side of the roads and shielded strikebreakers from picket agitation.

Still the strikers did receive significant financial help. Without the backing of the AFL unions, the strike would probably have collapsed within the first week. The union entered the strike with only $2,800. Picketing and legal expenses immediately exhausted the treasury. Around 100 pickets were needed to keep the entrances covered, and the Union relief list ran to over 200 families. In October, the union collected over $6,700 from union sympathizers and $16,000 the next month, totaling $43,000 before the end of the year.[13]

The union also mounted a general publicity campaign to generate external support. Although most of the support was symbolic, it boosted the strike morale and legitimized the strikers' demands. On November 3, U.S. Representative Helen Douglas visited the picket line, accompanied by news reporters, and condemned the bracero strikebreaking. Shortly before Christmas, a group of Protestant ministers from the Los Angeles Ecumenical Council visited the strikers, pressuring DiGiorgio to recognize the union. About the same time, Harold Ickles, former Secretary of the Interior under President Roosevelt, and a national newspaper columnist, attacked DiGiorgio in his national column for holding his workers under conditions of "chattel, slavery and serfdom."[14] But by the end of the third month, the picket line was no longer a direct threat, serving more to publicize the strike and raise funds. As Mitchell instructed Hasiwar:

"As long as there is a picket line we can raise money and get publicity; once it's pulled off, both stop. So keep that line on whatever you do, even if Jim [Price] has to stand down there with a sign day in and day out."[15]

Although DiGiorgio had lost money on the grapes and prunes, he had recruited sufficient crew to get most of the work done. By late December 1947, over 350 pruners were at work in the grape vineyards.[16] The strike had become a war of attrition, a battle in which the corporation's superior resources would eventually prevail.

With strike morale at an ebb and several of the core supporters drifting away, DiGiorgio set out to crush remaining support. On January 7, 1948, four pickets were arrested on trumped-up charges of cutting trees on ranch property. After being held at bail of $1,500 apiece, the Judge dropped the charges when the DiGiorgio foreman admitted that the trees had been cut by company workers because they were diseased.[17] DiGiorgio then launched a public relations attack on the strikers, hiring a public relations firm to put out a slick pamphlet entitled "A Community Aroused" that portrayed the strikers as "outside agitators, crack-pots and left-wingers and associates of known Communists."[18] On February 9, Joseph DiGiorgio bought a full page ad in the *Los Angeles Times* charging that the union was an "obvious Communist maneuver," prompting the California Senate Fact-finding Committee on Un-American Activities then holding hearings in Los Angeles to subpoena Hasiwar and Mitchell for interrogation (*Los Angeles Examiner*, February 9, 1948). The investigation, however, failed to find useful evidence, and despite additional investigations by the House Un-American Activities Committee, nothing could be pinned on the union. (*San Francisco Chronicle*, June 16, 1948; Galanza 1968:26).

Despite the dim prospects for a settlement, the union leaders decided to hold out, appealing for strike relief to supporters of the National Sharecroppers Fund and the unions. On February 6, 1948, a 300–car caravan arrived from the Los Angeles trade unions with an estimated $20,000 of supplies and cash. The next month, the San Francisco Labor Council sent a second caravan. This kept the 200–300 remaining pickets and their families in basic necessities. DiGiorgio organized a counter-caravan of strikebreakers to bait the pickets, hoping to create an incident that would justify more severe measures.[19] The critical break came four days later. A crowd of forty strikebreakers led by the ranch general supervisor and a foreman and armed with chains and farm tools suddenly attacked the pickets parading at the ranch entrance. Three pickets were hospitalized, and in the ensuing riot, a crowd of about 1,000 union supporters armed with axe handles and rifles menaced the Sheriff's deputies and State Highway Patrolmen blocking the main entrance. When Hasiwar arrived he found that:

about ninety percent of our folks had rifles. As soon as I came up, I was surrounded. They began saying to me: "Hank, this is going to be it. We are going to settle this strike here and now." Then John Lousalot, the Sheriff, came up to me and said: "Hank, you are the only one who can do anything." I said: "John, dammit, you are the one who caused this. You should have kept that caravan from coming out of the ranch. You know who beat up the pickets. You should have arrested them." One of the younger fellows walked up, looked straight at the Sheriff, and said: "John Lousalot, we are going to kill you first. We are going to shoot you dead." The Sheriff had been arresting our people right and left. With the help of the older heads, we got things calmed down, but there was still a division. The real militants, who had done a real job in organizing, blamed me. This was the turning of the DiGiorgio strike. If the people had gone in on the DiGiorgio ranch, it would have been a wild one. I can still see those little old ladies with their glasses on. They were unafraid. They had clubs in their hands, and maybe guns too. After this march, the younger people drifted off. (Hasiwar, cited in Mitchell 1980:261).

Sheriff Lousalot refused to arrest the DiGiorgio attackers, claiming that the union was responsible for the violence. As he later testified in hearings before the House Committee on Labor and Public Welfare, the picketing "smack(ed) of old time IWW methods."[20]

The strike was now thoroughly broken. The picket line dwindled to less than fifty as the most militant supporters drifted off. The corporation stepped up its recruitment efforts, bringing in Mexican workers from Los Angeles, Texas, and across the border as well as a crew of skilled workers from the Borregos Valley Ranch, another DiGiorgio operation in the south, to handle the more difficult tasks. Since the packingshed was still closed by the strike, the grapes had to be shipped to a nearby winery.[21] Although the union had some success in clearing the fields of illegals by calling on the Border Patrol, the picket line was clearly collapsing.[22] Even the most committed members began to doubt the effort, "look[ing] with alarm upon the increasing number of Mexicans who passed the picket line along with their own kinsmen."[23]

With strike morale at an ebb and the picket line reduced to less than fifty determined supporters, two organizers from the Food, Tobacco and Agricultural Workers (CIO) appeared, challenging the pickets to join a "real militant union."[24] Then out of nowhere came a surprise vigilante attack. On the evening of May 17, union leaders were holding a strike meeting in the cottage that served as strike headquarters. Suddenly out of the dark came a fusillade of bullets fired out of a passing car. As the vigilantes roared off into the darkness, James Price, the President of the local, lay critically wounded on the floor. When Mitchell arrived on the scene, he immediately issued a press release charging both the rival FTA and the Associated Farmers with the shooting.[25] The California Federation of Labor offered a $1000 reward and Governor Earl Warren ordered a full-scale investigation, but the vigilantes had left no clues. No official identification of the gunmen was ever made. Hasiwar, at least, was convinced that the gunmen had missed their mark, that he, sitting next to Price, had been the intended victim.[26]

The union had only one option left—to focus its efforts to exert external leverage by organizing a boycott. DiGiorgio Corporation had developed several prominent trade brands—"Treesweet," "Blue Flag," and "We Grow the Best." Although these were already on the California AFL "unfair lists," a primary or consumer boycott had little leverage. In early March, James Price and a crew of pickets had followed a truckload of scab potatoes into the Los Angeles Safeway shipping terminal where the Teamster warehousemen dumped them out the windows. For a week the pickets sealed off the largest fruit terminal in Los Angeles and then visited neighboring grocery stores where sympathetic Teamsters, Retail Clerks, and Butcher Workmen members refused to handle DiGiorgio products. Hasiwar dispatched other picket teams to San Francisco where they received solid support.[27]

The boycott was a serious threat. Robert DiGiorgio, having taken the helm after his father's recent death, opened exploratory talks through the California Mediation Service.[28] At the same time, he ordered his lawyers to file suit against the boycotters in Los Angeles, claiming that the recently passed Taft-Hartley amendments to the National Labor Relations Act barred the secondary boycott. Although the NLRA clearly did not cover production agriculture, Judge Hall promptly issued an injunction against the Teamsters, Winery Workers, Retail Clerks, Butchers Union, and the NFLU to halt all boycott activity. The NFLU then filed counter charges with the NLRB, charging DiGiorgio with unfair labor practices and demanding a union recognition election. To the union's surprise, an NLRA examiner upheld the boycott prohibition while incongruously setting aside the petition for an election for later review.[29]

Though the injunction was eventually overturned, the case served its purpose. The NLRB did not resolve the case until nine months later, long after the union's supporters had dropped the boycott. The legal defense consumed much of Hasiwar's time and diverted the union from its major aims. It also soured relations with the California Federation of Labor. In November 1948, the President of the Federation notified Hasiwar that there would be no more strike relief, forcing the union to further trim the beleaguered picket line to a lone marcher.[30] Within a few weeks, DiGiorgio administered the final blow, filing a multi-million dollar libel suit against the Federation, the NFLU, and Paramount Pictures for airing the film "Poverty in the Midst of Plenty" that had been donated the previous fall by the Hollywood Film Council. The union had used the documentary of the DiGiorgio strike to raise funds and create support for the boycott by showing it to church groups, student organizations and chapters of the Democratic Clubs and Civil Liberties Union across the state. Instead of challenging the hastily filed suit, the State Federation accepted an out-of-court settlement that put all the penalties on the NFLU. The NFLU accepted technical guilt for libel and promised to destroy all copies of the disputed film. The lone picket at the DiGiorgio gate would come down. In exchange, the damage claims were reduced to $1. Against his better judgment, Mitchell reluctantly instructed Hasiwar to pull down the lone picket, bringing the longest strike in the history of farm labor organizing to an inglorious conclusion.[31]

The NFLU's difficulties were major. DiGiorgio was politically well connected. The local police and courts blocked critical actions and raised the costs of insurgency. Federal bracero officials provided strikebreakers, and the NLRB had halted the boycott. Nor were the workers easily mobilized. Ethnic rivalries, weak community ties, scarce resources, and grower controls led to widespread strikebreaking. The union also had strategic problems. Although the plan had been to organize before striking, DiGiorgio hit first by firing suspected supporters. The focus on permanent and local workers and use of bloc recruitment tactics generated sufficient support for an initially powerful strike, but the strike momentum could not be sustained. There were no incentives beyond collective economic benefits and the cadre failed to develop links to the migrants. The campaign was also hindered by weak sponsorship. As one of the growers commented: "Hasiwar was sent with a pop-gun to shoot elephants."[32] Although early support was significant, the unions backed away at critical points, refusing to challenge the boycott injunction and caving in to the libel suit. When the initial drive did not produce immediate results, the State Federation cancelled its backing altogether.

The Wage Strikes

The union cadre came out of the DiGiorgio campaign convinced that a new strategy was needed. The union had to enlist the support of the Mexican migrants who had broken the DiGiorgio strike and get the braceros removed as quickly as possible. This led to three new tacks. The cadre shifted the organizing focus from the local and permanent workers on the largest ranches to the migrants in the major "row" crops. This led to a change in strategy. Strikes were now area-wide, challenging the growers throughout a crop region rather than a single large employer. Strike demands were also narrowed. Instead of union recognition, the major demands centered on wages and working conditions, especially cheating on weights and poor field conditions that trimmed the day's earnings. The assumption was that the migrants would not respond immediately to unionization, but by playing on traditions of passive resistance, by encouraging "wildcatting, staying at home or quiet migration out of the area" (Galarza 1977:127), the cadre could demonstrate the collective gains of wage strikes and gradually build up union solidarity and consciousness. The third tack—removing the braceros— was yet to be worked out. Since it depended on political pressure, the first step was better publicity about the nature of the problem.

The new strategy required three things: a larger organizing team to cover the 5000 to 10,000 workers that might be in the harvest at one time, increased ability to work with the Mexican workers, and a director of public relations to write up and disseminate reports on the grower abuses, especially of the bracero system. All three were met by adding a new organizer that Mitchell had discovered—Ernesto Galarza.

The son of an immigrant Mexican family, Galarza had shown great academic promise and, by tenacity and luck, had received a Masters degree from Stanford University and his Ph.D. in economics and Latin American affairs from Columbia University. During seven years' service with the Pan American Union (later known as the Organization for American States), Galarza rose to become director of labor relations and traveled extensively throughout Latin America as a unofficial liasion for American unions and an adviser for U.S. policy makers. After the Department of State supported the brutal repression of a miners strike in Bolivia in the winter of 1947, Galarza resigned in protest. Looking for a new avenue to advance Mexican-American interests, he heard of the NFLU's first convention. Speaking unannounced from the floor, he challenged Mitchell and Hasiwar to organize Mexican-American farm workers. Mitchell immediately cornered him, offering a position as an organizer if funds could be turned up. Although he had no direct organizing experience, he was experienced at writing reports and arousing the attention of policy makers. When Mitchell notified him in early March of support from the Robert Marshall Civil Liberties Fund for conducting research on the status of civil liberties of Mexican-Americans, he immediately signed on. What this meant to the Marshall Fund was not clear but its meaning to Mitchell, Hasiwar, and Galarza was certain. "Research" meant organizing, and "Mexican-Americans" meant farm workers (Mitchell 1980:272–274).

Galarza arrived as the DiGiorgio strike collapsed. Setting out on a survey of the Mexican-American colonias in the southern end of the Central Valley, Galarza found it necessary to be "cautious" about straight "union talk." Despite using sympathetic clergy and social workers as initial contacts, the Mexican migrants had strong memories of the Okie strikebreaking, and the word union was associated with the mass deportations of the 1930s and the pervasive corruption in the Mexican trade unions. After six months of making contacts, Galarza had a box full of index cards with names and addresses of willing supporters and half a dozen promising union locals.[33]

The time was ripe for testing the growers' nerve. On the morning of September 2, 1949, Hasiwar forced his way into the annual wage conference of the San Joaquin Valley Agricultural Labor Bureau being held in Fresno. Demanding that workers have a voice in their wages, Hasiwar charged the growers with price-fixing and demanded they negotiate with the union. The growers could not ignore a clear challenge. Voting to cut the wage offering for the upcoming cotton harvest from the previous year's $3 to $2.50 per hundred weight, they accepted the challenge. Encouraged by word that 5000 braceros would be available, several growers even decided to undercut the Bureau by offering $2.25 per hundred.[34]

The three organizers—Hasiwar, Galarza, and Bill Becker (Hasiwar's friend)—immediately fanned out, driving up and down the back roads distributing a wage ballot to the cotton pickers. Stamped with the union's address, the ballots asked: "What do you think would be a fair wage?" About 5000 replies from the more than 10,000 ballots distributed indicated overwhelming support for a $3 per hundred weight minimum. Although Hasiwar was still involved in the DiGiorgio strike, he helped organize rallies and distribute leaflets asking the workers to walk out until the growers gave in to the $3 demand. The major tactic was to organize a car caravan of a dozen or more jalopies which, stuffed with shouting farm workers, drove around the farm roads distributing leaflets and bidding support for the strike. At the minimum, the workers were asked to work outside the strike zone. The more enthusiastic tagged along at the end of the caravan with the promise that the union would pay for their gasoline. After three weeks, the union had over two dozen caravans roving the back roads looking for crews and covering an area roughly 150 by 80 miles square: "To the beating of fists on truck panels and the clang of tire irons, the strikers shouted invitations to those in the field to join them. The measure of success was the number of pickers who folded their sacks and left or swung their own cars to the rear of the column as it moved on" (Galarza 1977:124).

The growers struck back, getting the county authorities to pass noise ordinances and bidding one another to hold out against the strikers. Despite dozens of arrests for violating the noise ordinances, and the exhaustion of the union's gasoline fund, the growers finally caved in. As the harvest came to a close, the State Conciliation Service surveyor found that most of the growers had ended up paying the union wage. As the strike moved northward with the harvest, the growers dropped their wage cut without a fight. On October 18, after six weeks of picketing and with the cotton harvest completed, an exhausted cadre called off the strike.[35]

The key test was whether the strike paved the way for more durable organizing. In a short-term economic sense, the strike was a great success, generating an estimated five million dollars for the workers. But organizationally it was a clear defeat. Although over 10,000 workers were mobilized, the campaign generated only 300 dues-paying members organized into ten locals. The reason was quite simple. The strikers gladly accepted the free ride, withdrawing temporarily from the strike zone to neighboring fields and returning once the wage had been forced up. But commitments ran skin deep. In fact, several growers demonstrated the thinness of worker support by hiring for $3.50 per hundred contingent on a signed repudiation of the nefarious union. Many workers eagerly signed. The strike was also limited to field hands, leaving the permanent workers untouched (Galarza 1977:126).

Over the next year and a half the organizers redoubled their efforts but held to the same strategy. In the spring of 1950, they tried a slightly new tactic, organizing the labor contractors in the potato harvest. The major demand was an end to "short weights," paying the pickers for 53 pounds when they brought in 60-pound "stubs." Since the contractors were paid on a weight basis, they shared an interest in fair scales. Although several contractors signed on, most steered clear. Yet the union eventually prevailed by sending supporters to the fields armed with accurate scales. If the grower or contractor resisted, a "spot rest" usually cleared up the dispute. But as an organizing venture, the campaign was no more successful. Although widely known among the farm workers, the union still had a paper membership of less than 1,000 members scattered among ten to fifteen locals with no certainty that these would support a prolonged strike (Galarza 1977:120).

The following September the organizers decided to make one last challenge in the tomato harvest. Tomatoes were highly perishable and were worked exclusively by migrants, most of whom were Mexican-Americans who wintered in the Imperial Valley. The previous year the picking rate had been 18 cents per fifty-pound lug with a "bonus" of 2 cents. The bonus was widely hated by the workers. Instead of being an increment, it was actually a pay deduction withheld by the grower until the last of the crop was harvested. Because the picking rate dropped near the end of the harvest, the workers tended to disappear for better fields.

The growers withheld the bonus to keep them available. This year, the growers decided to cut the rate to 12 cents per lug with a 2 cent bonus. The three organizers immediately toured the migrant camps, informing the workers of the wage cut and asking each camp to send a representative to a strike meeting at the union headquarters. On the first of September, over 250 representatives showed up, only a handful of whom held union cards. They responded enthusiastically to the wage ballot, demanding 18 cents and the abolition of the bonus system. On September 5, the delegates posted bulletins throughout the area and organized roving picket teams with maps indicating the initial strike zone (Galarza 1977:122–123). Because there were no strike funds, car caravans were limited and workers were to simply remain in camp and demand their legal thirty-days eviction notice if threatened with removal. A sit-in also reduced the danger of being arrested. The strike rapidly spread north with the harvest, over 300 pickets touring the area in caravans armed with handpainted signs demanding: "18 Cents—No Bones" (sic) and "Down With The Bonus!" Despite threats, numerous arrests, and mass importing of strikebreakers, the strikers eventually prevailed:

The dawn patrols of the strikers could see the scraggles of crews and smell the sour bouquet of tomatoes that would never be picked. At the height of the action there were over three hundred pickets on duty, all of them at campgates, none at the ranches. Foremen paced the rows with pistols at their belts, racing between fields with hunting rifles and shotguns on the gunracks of their pickup trucks. (Galarza 1977:141)

In short-range terms, the strike was a fabulous success, mobilizing over 5000 workers and generating a total wage gain of more than $300,000 and an end to the bonus system. As the NFLU leaflets proclaimed: "The Bonus is Dead. Ganamous la huelga!" But still there was no durable basis for renewed insurgency. The next season the growers would reinstitute the bonus and the wage cut. Local 300 had only twenty members, mostly local workers from the small town of Tracy.[36] The central problem was lack of incentives for more durable support. As Galarza concluded, surveying two years of wage strikes: "As soon as we organize new locals, old ones go to pieces."[37] The wages gains failed to create more than transitory commitments, one sign of which was the refusal to pay dues. This, of course, left the organizers unsupported. "As the union had outwitted the growers, so had the workers outbargained the union."[38]

Death in the Imperial Valley

If the DiGiorgio strike had taught the cadre that only large-scale area strikes supported by the migrants as well as the permanent local workers could succeed, then the area-wide wage strikes had taught another lesson. Migrants could not be organized into stable union locals on the basis of short-term involvement and collective economic benefits. The strike victory had hardly been announced before Hasiwar and Galarza called a strategy meeting of the most loyal supporters. Having outlined the nature of the problem, Hasiwar called for suggestions. After a day's debate, the meeting endorsed three changes. The union would no longer support strikes unless a local with a stable membership was involved. Second, a bonafide membership required paying dues and regular participation in local meetings. Third, the cadre would again return to preparatory organizing, building locals before venturing into harvest strikes.

The last was the most important, for it meant a shift in the organizing focus. The migrants were most accessible during the winter off-season. Since most lived in the southern valleys during the winter, the union had to move its operations. Hasiwar and Galarza were therefore delighted to receive a letter from a Mexican-American worker in El Centro, a small town in the Imperial Valley, bidding help in organizing a union. Over 10,000 migrants wintered in the Imperial Valley, making it the major target for migrant organizing. Beginning with the melon harvest in late May, the workers moved northward, working several different crops and returning in the late fall. By playing on the local community ties and cohesion of the migrant crews, the organizers hoped to build a stable base of migrant supporters.[39] The move also afforded a challenge to the expanding bracero system, potentially opening it to public scrutiny. In fact, the migrants' chief complaint was the loss of their jobs to braceros. Since it was right on the border, the Imperial Valley was known as the gateway to alien labor. Although Mexican immigrants had always been present, the bracero build-up was creating an increase in illegal immigrants as well as braceros. By the early 1950s, the labor force had become half immigrant.[40]

In early January 1951 Hasiwar visited the Valley, surveying the situation and making contacts with the Labor Council. Since the workers spoke little English, Galarza was put in charge of the organizing campaign, supported occasionally by Hasiwar, DeAnda, Becker, and Carl Lara, a Spanish-speaking electrical union organizer from Salinas. Because the workers were idle during February and March, the organizers had ample opportunity to make contacts, build locals, train local leaders, and instill a sense of union solidarity. By late April as the harvest began, the NFLU had local chapters in virtually every colonia in the Valley, published a regular bulletin that was distributed to over 1500 households, and under Galarza's prompting, had decided to adopt the novel approach of acting as a general service organization to the workers, offering citizenship counseling and legal aid as well as standard union activities (Galarza 1977:158).

With the strongest base of support to date, Hasiwar notified the Imperial Valley Farmers Association that the NFLU claimed two-thirds of the Valley farm workers as members and was prepared for negotiations. The chief demands were limited: domestic workers would receive preference in hiring. Wages would be raised to $1 an hour. Melon-picking rates would rise from 20 to 25 cents a crate. There would be no discrimination against union members. No illegals would be hired. Significantly, the growers did not have to recognize the union. The Farmers Association was the target because it, rather than the individual growers, handled the bracero contracts for the entire Valley. Seven large operators held forty percent of the cropland and, in turn, controlled the Association and county politics, appointing their Secretary-Treasurer, B. A. Harrigan, as Agricultural Commissioner, Sealer of Weights and Measures, and President of the Board of Trade. The Imperial growers were also powerful in the larger political arena, holding key seats on the State Agricultural Commission and the U.S. Ambassadorship to Mexico (Galarza 1977:147–148).

In a bid for international solidarity, Galarza contacted the Mexican unions, and after an abortive meeting with the corrupt Association de Braceros, signed mutual aid pacts with two other unions—the Union de Trabajaodores Agricoles del Valle de Mexicali and the Alianza de Braceros. The unions were pledged to respect each other's strikes, and in the event of an NFLU strike, the Mexican union would help close the border by picketing.[41]

The growers retaliated by purging their crews of domestic workers, tripling their order for braceros, and sending out labor scouts to entice illegals. Since the four largest growers also controlled all of the pack-

ingsheds, they had little difficulty convincing the smaller farmers to follow their lead. On May 23, the American Fruit Company, the largest
employer, suddenly fired the domestic workers. That evening the workers assembled in Hidalgo Hall in Brawley and, after an intense discussion, voted to strike. The next day 500 pickets covered the packingsheds
and the Association's bracero camp in El Centro. Their sole demand was
domestic hiring preference.[42] This time the outrage at being displaced
by both the braceros and the new programs mobilized virtually all of the
domestic workers. Women and children who normally left economic issues to the paterfamilias joined the picket lines, and several Catholic
priests sent to minister to the Spanish-speaking workers found themselves drawn into the conflict. "It seemed as if the whole social fabric of
the *locales* had tightened in an effort to preserve itself" (Galarza 1977:161).

Strike success depended on blocking two sources of scab labor—the
green carders and illegals who would cross the border, and the braceros—and closing down the packingsheds. Closing the border crossings
proved easier. Hasiwar and DeAnda raced around the Valley sporting
goods stores, buying every baseball bat in sight. Armed with the bats,
three hundred pickets spread out across the border zone in teams of a
dozen or so, covering every major crossing point:

They stationed guys at every hole in the whole area from Mexicali to Calexico.
There are a lot of holes. Our Union boys just stood there with the ball bats. If
they insisted on coming, they used the ball bats. (Mitchell and Hasiwar 1974:
III, 7)

In one dramatic clash, a truck driver hauling illegals for the Farmers Association ran over a picket and was mauled by the picket teams. The
pickets generally held the line. The Mexican unions held their side of
the bargain, marching with the NFLU pickets and helping to turn thousands of workers back. The next line was clearing the fields of illegals
and green carders already across the border. Shortly after the vigilante
attack on the DiGiorgio strikers, the unions volunteer lawyer Alex
Schulman told Hasiwar of a California statute that authorized citizen's
arrests of anyone violating federal or state laws. The solution was obvious. Since the police could not be counted on to enforce the laws barring green card hiring and illegal entry, the union would have to take
matters into its own hands. The union pickets began arresting green car-

ders and illegals, turning them over to the Border Patrol. Within a few days, the Immigration Service holding pens and local jails were teeming with over 5000 prisoners.[43]

The attack then shifted to the packingsheds. Initially the shed workers and truck drivers marched out, but then the union was caught in a jurisdictional dispute. The sheds were organized by the United Packinghouse Workers (CIO) but the truck drivers were Teamsters (AFL). The Teamster drivers were pledged to support the strike, but the packingshed leaders were unsympathetic because of rumors that the Teamsters were about to move on their territory. A sympathy strike would give them an opportunity. Nor were the Teamster leaders anxious for a prolonged strike. They were locked in a legislative battle over a "hot cargo" bill that would have weakened their favored organizing weapon—"hot cargo" actions (i.e., secondary boycotts against employers). In exchange dropping the bill, the regional Teamster leadership secretly promised conservative California Senators that they would destroy the NFLU strike. Only two days into the strike, the Teamster President, David Beck, wired the Teamster local ordering them back to work. The trucks should roll "regardless of any labor interferences or other alibis" (Mitchell and Hasiwar 1974: III, 4–5). The next day, the United Packinghouse Workers local marched back to work. Then came a major blow; the Mexican unions stalked off the border picket line claiming that the NFLU owed them strike relief (Wolf 1964:328–330; Galarza 1977:162).

Yet the strike was still solid. Melon shipments were off by over three-fourths. A grower committee headed by one of the larger operators, United Fruits Distributors, put out tentative feelers to the union.[44] With the excitement of prospective victory in the air, the strikers redoubled their efforts. The key contention was the roughly 4000 braceros still at work. In April, Mitchell had contacted Department of Labor officials in Washington, who were now responsible for overseeing the program, forewarning them of the impending strike. They assured him that the braceros would be removed in a strike.[45] The question, however, was whether the local officials would follow the rule. The first step was formal strike certification. The second day of the strike, a representative from the California Mediation Service arrived, followed Hasiwar to the struck fields, and certified the strike. The local bracero officials, however, claimed that they had to make their own determination. Carefully selecting the fields, the Labor Department officials claimed that only 100 domestic workers had struck.[46] Hasiwar promptly dispatched a picket team to harass the Mexican consulate in Calexico and sent protest telegrams to the Secretary of Labor and the State Department. The Mexican Embassy replied that there was no strike according to the Department of Labor. Getting no response from the Department of Labor, the union filed suit against Secretary of Labor James Tobin, a Democratic machine politician and former Mayor of New York and telegraphed a list of the growers still hiring braceros.[47]

The solution at this point was for the union to turn its citizen's arrest tactic against the braceros, but naively hoping that the Secretary would follow through on his commitments, Hasiwar waited patiently for the expected withdrawal. Finally, after a two-week delay, Secretary Tobin sent out an investigator to report on the strike. Convinced that there was a strike, he then claimed formal agreements would first have to be worked out with the Mexican government. Individual fields would have to be certified one-by-one before braceros would actually be withdrawn. Since the legal employer was the Association and the strike target was all of the Association members, this made no legal sense. As the Secretary confided to a friendly Congressman, the actual strategy was to delay the withdrawal until the completion of the harvest or until the Mexican government demanded a pullout.[48] Meanwhile, the President of the Imperial Valley Farmers Association, Keith Mets, phoned the Mexican consul to assure him that the braceros were happily at work and that further shipments were needed. The U.S. Ambassador to Mexico William O'Dwyer, the brother of Frank O'Dwyer who was a ranch partner with Mets, sidetracked a diplomatic note from the Secretary of State inquiring about the Mexican government's position. When Mexican officials in Mexico City finally learned of the strike, the message had been altered to a simple assurance that the braceros were protected.[49]

Only in the third week did the Labor Department officials finally arrive. To protect their hindflank, the grower committee continued to negotiate, finally agreeing to the union's basic demands for domestic hiring preference and a restoration of the wage cut.[50] The next day the Mexican government, presumably having finally learned of the strike, lodged a diplomatic protest with the State Department, claiming that Mexican citizens were endangered and that the braceros should be removed immediately from the strike zone.[51] Even this did not get an immediate response, for the Secretary of Labor waited a full week before ordering the braceros' removal (Craig 1971:68). By then the melon harvest was three-fourths completed. If a short harvest gave strikers leverage, it also shortened the required strikebreaking. The Labor officials proceeded on a field by field basis, leaving the growers free to move braceros from field to field to complete the harvest. Checking the union authorization cards against employer payrolls took a week. Nor could the Union select the fields to be certified. Of course, the first fields were those which had already been harvested. Nor did the braceros have to go home to Mexico. They could work in other fields, at least until these were strike certified. The entire investigation took three weeks, at the end of which the issue was virtually moot.[52]

Still the union held onto one reed of hope. If the braceros scheduled for the upcoming tomato harvest could be blocked, the growers would have to honor their verbal agreement. The union had solid domestic support. The question was forcing the growers to hire domestics instead of braceros. The President of the Farmers Association fired off a telegram to Ambassador O'Dwyer to confirm that the melon strike would not compromise the tomato braceros. On receiving confirmation, he called on the Association, recommending that all contacts with the union be suspended. The verbal agreement promptly dissolved.

The next day, the new braceros began to arrive in bus loads, shipped in under the cover of darkness:

The guy from El Centro . . . woke me up on the cot the next morning and told me that the *bracero* camps were full. . . . We called our people together. We checked everything out. We saw the camps. We saw the people [braceros] there, and man, the camps were loaded! So we decided to call off the strike. There was no way of fighting it any more.[53]

On Saturday, June 26, 1951, Hasiwar called off the pickets. Strong worker support was not enough without strong political allies. The dramatic and solidly supported strike of the Imperial Valley farm workers had been broken by the Department of Labor.

After the Imperial Valley defeat the NFLU essentially ceased organizing California farm workers. Hasiwar moved temporarily to southern Louisiana to organize sugar cane workers and cooperatives among small strawberry farmers and, after a year's frustration, returned to New York to make a living. Galarza became the sole organizer, since the Marshall Fund grant and local labor support had dried up, and shifted the attack to the bracero program. Since the bracero program gave the growers a guaranteed strikebreaking force, Galarza held back from open strikes, organizing walkouts that demanded domestic preference and staging protests at the Farm Labor Placement offices. Although he scored a few small victories, including one verbal agreement with Schenley Industries, a mammoth liquor corporation, to honor the domestic preference rule, bracero hiring steadily increased and the union lost even its token handful of members.[54] In 1952, Congress strengthened the growers' hand by passing the "Texas proviso" explicitly exempting growers from possible prosecution for harboring illegal aliens and what Galarza jokingly called the "Hasiwar proviso" barring anyone but Immigration officers from arresting illegal entrants (Craig 1971: ch. 3; Hawley 1966:159–160, Galarza 1977:185). Reluctantly, Galarza concluded that he could no longer ask workers to support strikes when the only benefit would be losing their jobs to braceros or illegals. The only route left was to focus on publicity work, attempting to stir up public sentiment against the abuses of the bracero program. For the next decade, Galarza subsisted on a half salary donated by the Butcher Workmen's Union, while keeping up his pamphleteering and barbed attacks on culpable public officials and what he called the "labor fakirs" in Washington who talked proudly but ignored the plight of the farm workers.

The key to the NFLU defeat was the political environment. Initially the cadre failed to generate sufficient farm worker support but, after two years of trial and error, finally developed an effective mobilization strategy. By organizing in advance of strikes, using bloc recruitment and collective incentives, training grass roots organizers, pyramiding actions, and appealing for external support, the cadre organized a powerful strike. A transition to sustained insurgency was not guaranteed, but the promise was there. The problem was that the growers were too powerful, using their political ties to bring in sufficient bracero strikebreakers. Moreover, the movement's sponsors readily withdrew. Both of these developments were, in turn, linked to unfavorable political trends. As the comparisons with the UFW experience will highlight, the early 1950s was a period of conservative political realignment. The Republicans strengthened their hold on Congress and, in 1952, seized the White

House. The loyalty oaths, purges, showcase trials, and general attacks on insurgents grew more intense, peaking with Senator McCarthy's censure in the Senate in 1954. Organized labor and liberal reformers were thrown on the defensive, leaving few opportunities for sponsoring new causes. The forces of social reform went temporarily underground, waiting for a more promising time.

5

The Flawed Strategy:
The AWOC (1959–1965)

The point of union-building is to organize people into lasting structures. This the AWOC never did, although it spent far more money than any organizing drive in American agriculture. It was bankrupted by too much money. The assumption was that money is the answer to all organizing problems; that one did not need a rational plan; if only the right amount of money were spent, farm workers would automatically fall into line. In its own way this attitude was as paternalistic and contemptuous of farm workers as the attitude of the growers. And it killed the AWOC.

Joan London and Henry Anderson (1969)

If the NFLU had demonstrated that a sustained challenge could not be mounted by a powerless group with weak sponsorship against a politically entrenched antagonist, then the Agricultural Workers Organizing Committee (AWOC) showed that strategic decisions could destroy a challenge. Over a six-year period, the AWOC received extensive support from organized labor—over $1 million in direct financial aid—but failed to mobilize a base of farm workers. The AWOC leaders concentrated their energies on the least promising farm workers, the declining group of casual labor Anglo fruit tramps in the northern San Joaquin Valley. Despite contrary advice, they limited incentives to the collective benefits of a union contract. Nor did they invest in preparatory mobilization, resorting instead to ad hoc strikes organized by "flying squads" of pickets at the harvest peak. When the opportunity arose for mobilizing external support through protests, the AWOC leaders declared that theirs was a union campaign, not a social movement. The challenge was also hindered by changes in the labor market. Mexican immigration sharpened ethnic rivalries. The growth of the bracero program undercut strikes, and increased migrancy made organizing more difficult. Although the political environment had begun to change—the union eventually succeeded in getting braceros withdrawn—the environment was not as favorable as during the UFW challenge. Even if it had been, it would have made little difference. The AWOC leadership was unprepared to make use of a supportive political environment.

The Agricultural Workers Organizing Committee was launched in the winter of 1959 under the leadership of Norman Smith, a veteran organizer of southern auto plants for the United Auto Workers during the 1930s. With an annual budget of $250,000 provided by the AFL–CIO, Smith kept a team of ten to seventeen full-time organizers in the field, creating the impression of a serious organizing campaign. As the *Western Fruit Grower* warned: "The [organizing] campaign is being conducted in a very hardheaded and businesslike way. You can count on them for a maximum effort to prove it" (October 1959). From a different quarter, the Communist Party's *People's World*, came the judgment that this was to be the "most concerted drive to organize America's farm workers since the 30's" (June 6, 1959). The *San Francisco News* prophesied: "The Central Valley is about to become a battlefield" (June 15, 1959).

The greatest strength of the challenge was the size and durability of the labor sponsorship. In 1956, H. L. Mitchell, still president of the moribund NFLU, convinced the executive board of the National Sharecroppers Fund to create a National Advisory Committee on Farm Labor to organize support for the farm worker cause among liberal reform associations, unions, and churches and to lobby Congress and the White House for an end to the bracero program. By enlisting prominent figures such as Eleanor Roosevelt, A. Phillip Randolph, and James Vizzard, head of the Catholic Rural Life Conference, Mitchell created a wide range of contacts. Despite a meager budget and no paid staff, the Committee published a series of influential pamphlets that attacked the bracero program and the lack of protective legislation for farm labor and pressured labor leaders to support a new organizing campaign.[1]

The pleas also found a receptive hearing. Organized labor faced an internal crisis. The unions had steadily lost membership and political standing since the late 1940s. Despite the merger of the AFL and CIO, the Taft-Hartley Act discouraged unionization, the revelations of union corruption created cynicism about union leadership, and the growth of the labor force in the south and in white collar occupations made for a difficult terrain. Union membership fell from 29 percent of the labor force in 1946 to 24 percent in 1960 (U.S. Department of Labor 1976:23). Meanwhile, labor "voluntarism" regained ground, with the AFL in control of the newly merged AFL–CIO and the Committee on Political Education, the reorganized PAC, failing to make a political mark except in the closest elections. The AFL–CIO Executive Council decided to meet this deadline by new organizing campaigns centered on the rapidly expanding white collar workers and unorganized industrial workers. Although several on the Executive Council, most prominently George Meany, President of the AFL–CIO, favored concentrating on the white collar drive because it promised quicker returns than groups such as farm workers, the proponents of a more diverse strategy won out. In part, this was because of the increasing rivalry within the Executive Council between Walter Reuther, President of the United Auto Workers, the largest former CIO union and the natural heir to leadership of industrial unionism, and George Meany, the former head of the craft union AFL. The labor conservatives were dominant, holding 64 percent of union membership and seventeen of the twenty-seven seats on the Executive Council, but Reuther controlled the Industrial Union Department (IUD) through which he funded several organizing efforts, including Ernesto Galarza's publicity campaign against the bracero program. The rivalry stemmed from different visions of the labor movement as well as a personal clash. Reuther had designs on the AFL–CIO Presidency and offered a broad vision of the role of the labor unions, supporting the civil rights movement and several reform associations like the National Advisory Committee on Farm Labor, the League for Industrial Democracy, and the Students for a Democratic Society. Fortunately for the AWOC, the ideological-cum-personality rivalry spurred competition in supporting the fledgling campaign.

There was also the threat that the International Longshoremans Union, which had been expelled from the AFL–CIO in the early 1950s because its leader, Harry Bridges, refused to disavow his Communist membership, might renew the "march inland" that had been tried in the 1930s (Meister and Loftis 1977:59–70). They had recently organized the Hawaiian plantation workers, playing off their control of shipping. Although they did not have the same leverage in California, the rumor was that they would set up a joint organizing venture with the recently expelled Teamsters Union to strengthen their combined hold over the food and fibre industry.[2] In addition, the United Packinghouse Workers of America (UPWA) was attempting to reseize packingshed contracts recently lost to the bracero program and had made claims to the jurisdiction over the field workers (London and Anderson 1970:46).

In February 1957, Reuther announced an IUD grant of $25,000 to the National Agricultural Workers Union (NAWU), the renamed skeleton of the NFLU being held together by Ernesto Galarza. Galarza embarked on further protests against the bracero program, helping domestics file legal suits and launching a public speaking campaign. When Galarza returned at the end of the year with a petition for $40,000, Reuther replied that he was more interested in an organizing campaign.[3] But rather than turn the request down outright, Reuther promised to press for major organizing support from the AFL–CIO. Reinforced by the lobbying of Vizzard and Eleanor Roosevelt and the jurisdictional threats by non-AFL–CIO unions, the Executive Council decided to support the campaign. In February 1959, the AFL–CIO announced support for a major organizing campaign by the AWOC. In a novel twist, the AWOC would organize both field and packingshed workers, funnelling members to both NAWU and the UPWA.

The selection of Norman Smith, a former Reuther ally and a close friend of Jack Livingston, Director of Organizations for the AFL–CIO, resolved several problems. Galarza had many enemies in the labor unions because of his bitter attacks on what he called the "labor fakirs" and his focus on the bracero program instead of worker organizing. Reuther also wanted to sidestep the jurisdictional dispute between the NAWU and the UPWA, both of which were AFL–CIO affiliates and previous recipients of IUD assistance. But, to preserve peace, Galarza was to become Director of Training and the AWOC was to be strictly an organizing committee, turning dues and organized locals over to the NAWU and UPWA. The bargain quickly fell apart, however. Smith ignored Galarza's organizing advice, assigned him no duties, and refused to turn over membership lists. Encouraged by Reuther's frequent suggestion that the NAWU merge with the UPWA, Smith began consulting Clive Knowles, President of the UPWA, about a joint organizing campaign.

117

Mitchell and Galarza rebelled, but they had little influence. If only to save face, they formally merged the NAWU with the Amalgamated Meat Cutters and Butcher Workmen, which had helped the NFLU help in the past and held a lone contract on fieldworkers at Campbell Soup's Seabrook Farms in New Jersey (Galarza 1977:328–337; Mitchell 1980:290–295). The Butchers Union, however, was not about to support an organizing campaign, so Mitchell returned to his political activities and Galarza turned to writing and anti-bracero attacks.

The Mobilization Strategy

The AWOC campaign centered initially on the fruit workers around Stockton in the northern San Joaquin Valley. Smith did follow Galarza's advice on one issue, selecting Stockton because it was the major winter home for farm workers in the northern Valley. His openness stopped at that point, however. Rather than organizing the rapidly increasing Mexican-American workers, Smith decided to concentrate on the migrant Anglo fruit tramps who worked the nearby tree harvests. Since he did not speak Spanish and had little empathy for the Mexicans, the Anglos seemed to him a better target. Smith also thought that the Anglos were skilled aristocracy of the farm workers and would therefore be the easiest to organize. In fact, they were the most casual, disorganized workers in the industry, and their importance was rapidly declining. Many of the Anglos worked on a casual basis, showing up at the shape-ups only when completely destitute. They offered little basis for bloc recruitment or the development of indigenous leaders. Although they would support a wage strike, they could not be organized for more sustained campaigns.

In making this choice, Smith spurned one of the most promising bases for the new drive—the Agricultural Workers Association, a community service association of local Mexican workers organized by Father Thomas McCullough, a Catholic priest with the Spanish Mission Band. In the winter of 1958, Father McCullough had convinced his church superiors that pastoral support to the Mexican farm workers required building a sense of community. Founded in 1951 by Archbishop Mitty of San Francisco, the Spanish Mission Band had traditionally been restricted to two traveling priests ministering sacramental functions to Mexican farm workers. In the late 1950s, the Catholic hierarchy became concerned about the weak support of the nominally Catholic Mexican-Americans of the southwest and initiated new ministries, built new parochial schools, and sponsored the revivalistic cursillo movement and various community organizing projects (Grebler, Guzman and Moore 1970). Father McCullough's petition for a community organizing project found a receptive hearing. He immediately teamed up with Fred Ross and Cesar Chavez, the directors of the Community Service Organization (CSO), a state-wide service association of urban Mexican-Americans, and began organizing the Agricultural Workers Association among the Stockton farm workers. Borrowing on the CSO strategy, McCullough assumed that the basic need of the farm workers was for a sense of community and economic security. The first step was to create projects that pooled indigenous resources and gradually built solidarities that could later be harnessed to the battle for a union. By holding house meetings, the Association avoided the need for elaborate meeting facilities and built on existing social ties. Early recruits invited friends and relatives to their homes and, guided by McCullough's prodding, set up their own projects to deal with such problems as exclusion from commerical credit, poor schools, low voter participation, and difficulties in securing citizenship. Within a year, the Association had 500 families and operated a cooperative credit union, a consumer co-op, and language-training programs. Ernesto Galarza attended several meetings, encouraging support for a unionization effort. The service programs not only provided selective incentives but gradually built solidarity and a set of community ties (London and Anderson 1970: 91–96; Meister and Loftis 1977:92–93).

When the AWOC was created, McCullough immediately contacted Norman Smith and offered the Association as an initial basis for organizing. His ultimate aim had been to start a union drive, but the Church would not sanction his direct involvement, so McCullough left Dolores Huerta, the treasurer, in charge of the Association. Huerta's mother owned a Stockton boardinghouse for farm workers and had sent many tenants to the AWA meetings. Huerta had a college degree and later would become a key leader in the United Farm Workers. At McCullough's prodding, Smith hired her to do office work for the AWOC.

It soon became obvious, however, that Smith had little interest in the AWA's community benefit approach or the Mexican-American farm workers. In his vision, a farm worker union was essentially an economic bargaining unit with little concern for credit discrimination, racism in the public schools, or the problems of immigrants. Nor was it necessary to invest extensively in preparatory organizing. Presumably the workers were already cohesive and resourceful. All that was needed was to send organizers into the fields at the harvest. Moreover, Smith was infatuated with the Anglo fruit tramps. Gradually the organizing efforts of Mc-Cullough and Huerta were shunted aside (Thompson 1963:87).

Over the next two years, the AWOC organizers, seventeen strong at their peak, scoured the northern end of the Central Valley, recruiting farm workers and organizing wage strikes. Most of the union offices were located in former NFLU strongholds: Lodi, Tracy, Corchoran, Porterville, and Stockton. But rejecting the advice of Galarza and Mc-Cullough, Smith decided that a geographically-fixed organization was unnecessary, that an effective labor union had to conform to the fluidity of the labor market. Instead of house meetings, the organizers focused on the early morning shape-ups in the slums of small rural towns. Smith saw these as the closest approximation to the factory gates of the auto plants, giving the broadest access to the workers. The problem, of course, was that the shape-ups attracted the most seasonal, undisciplined workers and, at most, supplied no more than ten to fifteen percent of the harvest labor force. Bloc recruitment tactics and the training of indigenous leaders were difficult, and instead of building solidarity and insurgent consciousness, the organizers specialized in lightning wage strikes that flickered across the Valley but never set fires. The campaign repeated almost ever tragic mistake of the NFLU wage strikes, but this time as a farce.

The Wage Strikes

The AWOC strike wave was on the surface impressive. Between the spring of 1960 and the winter of 1961, the AWOC was involved in over 150 strikes, 90 percent of which received sufficient support to be certified by the California Department of Employment (Thompson 1963:87–88). The campaign, however, failed to generate a sustained base of farm worker support. The problem clearly was not organizing resources. Smith controlled a large pool of funds, more than ever invested before, and kept a dozen or more organizers in the field. Nor was the problem support for the wage strikes. Most received sufficient support to compel wage concessions. Nor were braceros an insurmountable obstacle. Generally they were withdrawn. The major problem lay in the narrow economic goals and the organizing tactics.

The first test came in the spring cherry harvest at the Podesta Ranch. In early May 1960, six AWOC organizers infiltrated the Anglo fruit crews by joining the shape-up. After three days' organizing on the job they called a strike and pulled three-fourths of the 800 workers. The sole demand was a wage hike, but Podesta refused to negotiate, sending off labor contractors and appealing to the Cherry Growers Association. The Association announced a publicity campaign over the airwaves to "save the cherries" and recruited local growers, housewives, and students to complete the harvest. Although he managed to avoid contacts with the union, Podesta lost most of his $100,000 crop and finally had to raise wages to get enough strikebreakers (Thompson 1963:103–108).

The growers to the south began preparing for the organizing drive. The Council of California Growers announced an agreement to pool strikebreakers, and the growers doubled their bracero orders, claiming labor scarcity (*San Francisco Chronicle*, June 15, 1960). But the 1958 election of Edmund Brown, a liberal Democrat, to the governor's mansion spoiled their plan. Brown had received strong labor support, and one of his key pledges was to enforce the state's labor laws. in the middle of the campaign, Galarza stirred public controversy by charging the director of Farm Placement Service with accepting kick-backs for providing overorders of braceros. The Director and several assistants had to resign, and Brown ordered a wholesale clean-up of the Placement Service (*San Francisco Chronicle*, August 9, 1959; Galarza 1977:256–274). The new Director announced that he would not authorize braceros as strikebreakers and would fully enforce the statutes on housing, hours, and safety conditions.

The AWOC organizers decided to test the new Director by organizing a strike on the DiGiorgio ranch at the Dantoni and New England orchards. On the morning of July 14, 132 out of 184 workers marched out. DiGiorgio secured a court injunction to keep referrals coming from the local Farm Placement Office and the scheduled braceros. The local sheriff provided protection, and at least half of the 700 workers referred to the DiGiorgio orchards crossed the picket line. The AFL–CIO lobbyists in Washington pressured Secretary of Labor James Mitchell, a liberal Republican in the second Eisenhower administration, to block shipment of additional braceros, and to their surprise, he ordered it. Bruce Sanborn, Vice-President of the Corporation, sputtered that Mitchell had "an inordinate interest in unionizing farm workers (*San Francisco Chronicle,* July 13, 1960). The next week Mitchell violated another tradition, ordering that all braceros on the struck ranches had to be removed. Three days later, the Corporation caved in to the strikers' aims, granting pay raises and reinstating all the strikers (Thompson 1963:111–114).

The DiGiorgios were not to be taken easily. On May 18, two months before the strike, DiGiorgio had filed a libel suit against the AWOC, the NAWU, Ernesto Galarza, and H. L. Mitchell. Louis Krainnock, Director of Training after Galarza's resignation, had discovered an intact copy of the old film *Poverty in the Midst of Plenty* that the NFLU had used. Ignorant of the previous libel suit, Krainnock had been showing the film at recruitment meetings. DiGiorgio promptly filed libel charges and, after discovering that Galarza and Mitchell were no longer associated with the AWOC, upped the suit to $2 million damages against the AFL–CIO and the AWOC. A year and a half later, the court granted DiGiorgio $150,000 in damages based primarily on the previous acknowledgement of guilt. The AFL–CIO paid a high price for refusing to fight the earlier suit (Galarza 1970:93–116).

Meanwhile, the strike campaign spread. On August 1, the AWOC pulled out 149 workers from a 300-acre peach orchard near Gridley and pressured the Placement Service to pull out the braceros still in the orchards. When the strikers assaulted several braceros, the Mexican government demanded their immediate withdrawal. The growers had to concede and announced a wage hike. The AWOC then turned to nearby orchards and over the rest of the month conducted over a dozen small wage strikes, most of which gained wage hikes (Thompson 1963:111–119).

In September, the AWOC shifted their base of operations to the tomato harvest near Tracy, the scene of the NFLU wage strikes. Infiltrating the 890-acre Corchoran Ranch through the shape-up, the organizers pointed to their past successes and enlisted most of the Anglo and Mexican-American workers. The Conciliation Service certified the strike, but seventy braceros remained in the fields. Supported by the California Employment Office, the union filed suit to have the braceros removed, but on September 23, the local judge ruled that the case was irrelevant. Although the union was correct, the grower had now finished the first pick, and since the second pick was a new operation, the braceros could stay. For the first time, the AWOC had failed to get the braceros re-moved (Thompson 1963:124–128).

Over the next month and a half, the AWOC expanded the drive to the Lodi grape workers and the neighboring crops. Although they scored impressive wage victories, the union still lacked a stable base of mem-bers and had trained virtually no grass-roots organizers. It was a purely professional campaign, run by the paid organizers and focusing solely on short-range economic gains. Few of the workers paid dues, which meant that the professional organizers were living off the patience of the AFL–CIO. The enthusiasm and missionary zeal of a grass-roots campaign was conspicuously absent. If the organizers lost their sponsorship, the cam-paign would end immediately and the growers would rescind the pay hikes. The most promising sign was getting the braceros removed.

Fiasco in the Imperial Valley

Smith and his assistants gradually decided that Galarza had also been right about the importance of challenging the bracero pro-gram. The braceros had been a problem even in the tree crops where they were less than five percent of the labor force. In the row crops like tomatoes and lettuce, they were over half. In addition, the election of John Kennedy as President promised an even more favorable regime in the Department of Labor. The bracero program also offered a tempting short-cut to organizing. If they could be consistently withdrawn, the AWOC would not have to organize more than a handful of workers. In other words, the most—not the least—favorable settings were ranches dominated by the braceros. Smith had also tied his campaign to the United Packinghouse Workers, which had recently lost the contract on the mammoth Bud Antle lettuce ranch to braceros. When the UPWA tried to de-authorize the braceros by mass picketing, Antle signed a sweet-heart contract with the Teamsters local that held a contract on his truck drivers, giving the Teamster leaders dues without genuine gains for the workers. The other lettuce growers adopted the same strategy, shifting to mechanized field packing with braceros and, in a fit of pique, threw Antle out of the Salinas Valley Growers Association (Glass 1966:105–107). Clive Knowles, President of the UPWA, decided that the top priority was halting the bracero traffic. Since the Imperial Valley contained the largest concentration and the UPWA had lost several packingshed contracts there, he pressed Smith to join forces against the Imperial Valley lettuce growers.

They did not need to organize large numbers of workers. Since most of the lettuce workers were braceros, all they had to organize were a handful of domestic workers and a few green card commuters. Nor were large sacrifices required. If the bracero withdrawal came, the strike would only last a few days. Once these domestics struck, the union would demand removal of the braceros. What happened then, however, was not clear because neither union had sufficient members to supply the harvest force.

In late November the two unions moved to Brawley and rented a storefront as an organizing office. Within three weeks they had contacts throughout the 1500 domestic and green carder lettuce workers (Thompson 1963:136–137; Paige 1968:15–18). On January 3, the AWOC–UPWA notified the Imperial Valley Farmers Association they represented the workers and demanded a wage increase, union recognition, and domestic preference. The next day they organized a demonstration of 500 workers, calling for a strike vote and a one-day work stop. When the growers ignored the rally, the AWOC–UPWA committee sent the strike threat to the Imperial Valley Lettuce Growers and Shippers Association, adding a demand for gate hiring to insure domestic preference. The growers kept silent (Paige 1968:17–18).

The unions also notified Secretary of Labor Arthur Goldberg, Kennedy's new appointee in the Department of Labor, of their organizing and demanded that domestic preference be honored. Satisfied that it would be, the unions called a strike and pulled sixty-three domestic workers out of the Bruce Church ranch. When Department of Labor and Farm Placement officials visited the ranch, they found mixed crews of illegals and braceros working side by side. Under pressure from the Mexican government to eliminate the practice, the USDL officials ordered the braceros removed. Church secured a temporary injunction from a local judge on the pretext that strikes could be certified only for a field, not an entire ranch. The braceros in adjoining fields returned to work. As for the struck fields, Church sold the standing crop to another grower who still held bracero authorizations. The Mexican officials were still irritated by the mixed crews and, on January 31, demanded all braceros be pulled from the Church ranch. In frustration, Church hired the domestics back at a big wage boost (*Imperial Valley Press*, January 13, 1961; Thompson 1963:136–138).

The battle spread rapidly throughout the Valley. On January 16, the unions struck the Freedman Farm as eighteen out of twenty-four domestic workers walked out. The next week the organizers became involved in eighteen more strikes, several of which were spontaneously initiated. A total of 367 workers walked out, forcing the removal of another 2000 braceros. The Growers Association filed suit, asking for a permanent injunction against the picketing on the ground that the union's intent was to subvert Federal law, namely the diplomatic agreements underlying the bracero program. The major evidence was a letter purloined from the AWOC files that outlined the plan of striking to force bracero withdrawals. Judge Heald agreed and ordered the injunction (*Imperial Valley Press*, January 27 and 31, 1961; Thompson 1963:139).

The ruling made sense only by the most twisted logic. While it was true that the unions were challenging the bracero program, they had organized the domestic workers and their objective in striking the major bracero hirers was to force compliance with the domestic hiring rules. More relevant was the fact that neither union had enough domestic supporters to fill the bracero positions. The growers had simply displaced too many domestics with braceros.

The unions decided to defie the injunction and provoke a diplomatic crisis by holding demonstrations at the bracero camps. This would force the Mexican government to either demand the withdrawal of the braceros or perhaps even abrogate the agreements. Smith and Knowles sent a joint telegram to Secretary of Labor Goldberg, warning him that "in the present explosive situation" there was considerable danger "to the health and safety of the Mexican workers" (Paige 1968:20). On February 2, 1961, the AWOC and UPWA forces assembled at the gates of the Dannenberg Labor Camp, then occupied by over 300 braceros. The braceros were boarding buses to go to the fields. After forcing the buses back inside the compound, the demonstrators held a sit-in inside the camp gate. Someone started a fight, and in the ensuing melee, several braceros were badly beaten. The demonstrators then moved outside the camp gates and continued chanting and shouting threats for over an hour. Sheriff's deputies soon arrived, arresting thirteen of the demonstrators and several AWOC–UPWA organizers, including Clive Knowles, for violating the court injunction, trespassing, and assault. However, the strategem worked. The Mexican consul demanded the braceros be removed (*Imperial Valley Press*, February 2, 1961; Thompson 1963:142–143; Paige 1968:20–21).

The Mexican intervention spurred the Department of Labor to investigate. Three days later Assistant Secretary of Labor Willard Wirtz arrived to mediate the dispute. The Farmers Association called a meeting to determine their response. After an acrimonious debate, they decided to scrap plans for vigilante actions against the unions. This would only provoke Mexican officials and produce more bracero removals (Thompson 1963:143). Meeting separately with Keith Mets, President of the Farmers Association, and the union leaders, Wirtz hammered out an agreement to insure domestic priority hiring. All hiring would begin at the gate with braceros brought in only to fill vacancies. Wirtz also recommended to Secretary of Labor Goldberg that the 1700 braceros in the fields that had been strike-certified be returned to Mexico rather than transferred to unstruck fields. The Mexican government concurred, requesting all the braceros removed. Three days later the braceros boarded buses for Mexico (*Imperial Valley Press*, February 7 and 8, 1961; Thompson 1963:149; Paige 1963:20–21).

The unions smelled victory and stepped up the demonstrations. There were still about 500 braceros on ranches that had not yet been struck, and although the injunction was still in effect, another attack might bring complete removal. The next day a team of pickets met the braceros returning to the Corona Labor Camp. But this time they overplayed their hand. The pickets attacked the camp manager and several of the braceros, raced into the camp, and set fire to the camp barracks. That night the Sheriff raided the El Centro Labor Temple, arresting the rest of the union leaders on charges of trespassing and destruction of property (*Imperial Valley Press*, February 9 and 10, 1961; Paige 1963:21).

Again, the violence worked. The Mexican government pressed for removal of the remaining braceros. But this time the Department of Labor delayed, waiting until the lettuce harvest was complete. After all, the union leaders were in jail and could not organize any more demonstrations. The growers transferred another 1000 braceros from unstruck fields to complete the harvest, and as the trucks pulled out with the last of the lettuce, the USDL finally ordered the removals (*Imperial Valley Press*, February 26, 1961; *San Francisco Examiner*, March 4, 1961; Thompson 1963:152).

The AWOC campaign was in shambles. Although they had succeeded in getting protections on domestic hiring and a ruling against the field-by-field method of removal, the leaders were in jail and the union treasury was bankrupted (*Imperial Valley Press*, February 8 and 26, 1961; Thompson 1963:151–152; Paige 1968:21–33). Court costs and fines ran over $50,000. Then came the negative ruling in the DiGiorgio libel suit. President Meany of the AFL–CIO sent in investigators to seize the AWOC records and bail the organizers out of jail. Looking over the records, they found that the membership had been systematically inflated, that there were actually only about 2500 paid members rather than the 15,000 that Smith had claimed. The scenario confirmed Meany's belief that farm workers could not be organized. If the drive did not pay for itself in a short period in terms of dues returned to the AFL–CIO, then the workers simply could not be organized. As Smith informed a news interviewer: "Mr. Meany is a very practical businessman" (Meister and Loftis 1977:103–104; Thompson 1963:152–157). The AFL–CIO Executive Council voted to terminate the organizing drive and seized the AWOC books and treasury.

The Imperial Valley fiasco also destroyed the Spanish Mission Band. The two priests with the Mission Band, Fathers McCullough and McDonnell, had decided to follow the organizers to the Imperial Valley. Although authorized to organize farm workers into community associations, they were prohibited from becoming directly involved in a union conflict. The problem stemmed from their appearance at several union meetings, prompting the local priests to charge that they were organizing the union and had condoned the violence at the labor camps. The situation was complicated by the fact that they were outside Bishop Mitty's territory, and to make matters worse, Mitty was terminally ill. The San Diego Archibishop demanded their ouster and eventually convinced Church superiors to completely disband the Mission.[4]

With the AFL–CIO funds cut off, Smith fired the rest of the organizers and began operating off the trust fund of dues that he had kept out of the AFL–CIO's control. Henry Anderson, the AWOC's Director of Research reactivated the volunteer AWA organizers and began organizing area councils to keep the effort alive. The councils sent representatives to public hearings and grower wage conferences, protesting the wage-fixing and the hiring of braceros, and filed suits to secure access to private labor camps. Several volunteers even tried organizing the bra-

ceros. In December 1961, the AWOC volunteers held a statewide conference in Strathmore to debate future strategy and Anderson proposed
that they send representatives to the AFL–CIO annual meeting then being
held in Miami Beach, Florida. Each conference participant chipped in
$2 to pay the bus ticket for the delegates and off they went, certain that
they could not be turned away:

> Their plea was addressed to a packed, emotional session of the AFL–CIO con-
> vention by Maria Moreno, a farm worker who described near-starvation condi-
> tions that were a daily fact of life for her and her twelve children in the citrus
> groves of Tulare County. She told of boiling greens to make meals, of entire days
> in which the family lived on soup made from potato peelings, of a nineteen-year-
> old son who passed up this pitiful fare so his younger brothers and sisters could
> have more. (London and Anderson 1970:56–60; Meister and Loftis 1977:104–
> 105)

Reuther renewed his pressure and several Catholic leaders attending the convention chimed in, pushing for another chance. Reluctantly, President Meany succumbed, promising to refund the AWOC with
"as much money as needed" (cited in London and Anderson 1970:60).

This time, however, Meany overruled the Reuther faction and appointed C. Al Green, a former officer of the Plasterers Union in rural
California and currently working for the California Committee on Political Education, as Director. Smith became second-in-command, and Maria
Moreno was hired as an organizer. But Henry Anderson, who had started
the new effort, was fired and the volunteers disbanded. This was to be
a professional, businesslike campaign. The ties to the church, student,
and liberal associations that Anderson had cultivated atrophied. Later in
the midst of the UFW boycott, Green would point proudly to his avoidance of protest tactics and volunteer support, claiming that his was a union
campaign, not a social movement. But instead of organizing farm workers, Green concentrated on getting out the vote for Edmund Brown, then
running for a second term as governor (Meister and Loftis 1977:105–106).

The organizing campaign finally began in earnest in early spring of 1963.
Again Ernesto Galarza and Henry Anderson were ignored, and Green
turned to Norman Smith's strategy of focusing on the shape-up and the
Anglo migrants. There was, however, one modification. Rather than organizing workers directly, Green decided that it would be more efficient
to organize the labor contractors. In the building trades, the subcontrac-
tors who recruited and supervised the workers were the organizational

backbone of the union. Because of the high skill levels, the work crews were cohesive and the contractors honored workers' interests. The parallel with the farm labor contractors was irresistible to Green. But the farm labor contractors were quite different, with weak ties to their crews and little interest in any genuine changes. This was especially true of the contractors specializing in the most casual labor, the segment to which Green and Smith gave most of their attention. There was, however, one significant exception—the Filipino labor contractors who supervised specialized crews of Filipino grape pickers and broccoli cutters. Because of their loyalties and dependence on the crews, the Filipino contractors would support strikes and economic demands. Yet the Filipino contractors represented no more than a token share of the labor contractors. This, however, did not block Green. It was easy to force the contractors to join the union. They could easily deduct the dues, along with charges for transportation and food, and from the day-haul workers' pay. They did not have to support strikes or attend meetings. And for those who balked, Green's organizers quickly surrounded their buses, turning workers away to another waiting contractor. All in all, it was a cozy arrangement. The AWOC collected its dues, the AFL–CIO was assured that a union was being organized, and the contractors were freed of any hassle from pickets. The loser was the worker who received nothing in return and had to pay union dues or get off the contractor's bus (Meister and Loftis 1977:106–107).

The strategy did, however, inadvertently mobilize several crews of Filipinos. Green hired two Filipino organizers—Larry Itliong and Andy Imutan—both of whom had previously been involved in union drives among Filipino workers in the west coast fisheries industry. Although Green viewed the Filipino effort as a sideline and kept his attentions focused on the other contractors, Itliong and Imutan hit a responsive cord. The Filipino contractors responded enthusiastically, enlisting their entire crews and helping to organize strikes. Here, among the workers to whom Green had the least commitment, was a genuine base of worker support that would eventually ignite the strikes that gave rise to the Delano grape strike of 1965 and launched the United Farm Worker (Meister and Loftis 1977:107).

Meanwhile, Green spent most of his time lobbying in Sacramento. The contractors furnished a steady income of dues and the appearance of a union. But Governor Brown, having secured his second and last term in office, ignored Green and flew to Washington to support a renewal of the bracero program (cited in Meister and Loftis 1977:108). While Green and the AFL–CIO were pleased with their new pseudo-union, the real organizing was going on elsewhere in the National Farm Workers Association set up by Cesar Chavez and by Itliong and Imutan among the Filipino crews.

The AWOC experience highlights the importance of competent leaders with an effective strategy. Despite massive sponsorship, the AWOC leaders had little understanding of the farm labor market and the obstacles to organizing an effective challenge. They concentrated on the most disorganized workers, limited the campaign to bread-and-butter unionism, trained few indigenous leaders, skipped preparatory efforts, and confronted with difficulties, turned to the pseudo-organizing of labor contractors. Although organizing contractors did work among the Filipinos, this was because of the solidary ties among these crews that could not be extended to the rest of the farm workers. Nor were the AWOC leaders alert to the possibilities of tapping external support.

The AWOC campaign did, however, indicate significant political changes. Organized labor provided extensive sponsorship, especially compared to the NFLU challenge. The general political environment was also more favorable, as the activities of the liberal reformers and the success in getting braceros removed indicated. The growers were still politically entrenched, but governmental officials did not automatically take their side. As the next chapter will show, the late 1950s and early 1960s represented the beginning of a period of reform. Liberal reformers became more active, the Democratic party won a series of electoral victories, and the civil rights and student movement emerged. As the UFW would soon demonstrate, these changes created opportunities for the development of sustained farm worker insurgency.

6

La Causa Ascendant: Building the United Farm Worker Challenge (1962–1970)

VIVA LA HUELGA EN GENERAL

(LONG LIVE THE GENERAL STRIKE!

El dia 8 de septiembre
De los campos de Delano
Salieron los filipinos.

On the 8th of September
From the camps of Delano
Came the Filipinos.

Y despues de dos semanas
Para unirse a la batalla
Salieron los mexicanos.

And then after two weeks
To unite in the battle
Out came the Chicanos.

Y juntos vamos cumpliendo
Don la marcha de la historia
Para liberar el pueblo.

And together we're fulfilling
The march of history
To liberate our people.

Coro:

Chorus:

Viva la huelga en el fil!
Viva la causa en la historia!
La raza llena de gloria!
La victoria va cumplir!

Long live the farm strike!
Long live our historic cause!
Our people crowned with glory!
Will achieve the victory!)

In December 1961, Cesar Estrada Chavez, Executive Director of the Community Service Organization (CSO), a civil rights organization of urban Mexican-Americans, made a fateful decision. For two years he had tried to get the CSO executive board to support an organizing project among Mexican-American farm workers but had been turned down. In frustration, Chavez finally resigned and set out single-handedly on the seemingly impossible task of organizing farm workers into an insurgent movement that would eventually transform rural California. Loading his family into an old dilapidated car, Chavez set out with life savings of a few hundred dollars for Delano in the heart of the southern San Joaquin Valley. He chose Delano for two reasons. His brother Richard worked there as a carpenter. At least he would not starve. He also knew that Delano was a major residential center for Mexican-American farm workers and would provide an excellent starting point. Although his plan was to eventually organize a farm workers union, his initial aims were far more modest. The farm workers were too disorganized and the growers too powerful. A direct challenge would be quickly crushed. The first step was to organize a community benefit association that would train grass-roots organizers and create solidarity and experience with pooling resources. Perhaps in ten years, thought Chavez, his Farm Workers Association could turn into a union and directly battle the growers.

His initial approach drew heavily on a decade's experience with the CSO. In 1952 Fred Ross, the principal organizer for the Alinsky-sponsored CSO, began working in a San Jose barrio known as "Sal Si Puedes" ("Get out if you can"). Ross had been a civil rights worker in east Los Angeles for the American Council on Race Relations in the 1930s, defending Mexican-Americans against the "zoot suit" riots and illegal deportations. After World War II he took a position with Saul Alinsky's Industrial Areas Foundation to organize the Community Service Organization as a Mexican-American civil rights organization. The CSO focused on two issues: police brutality against the pachuco gangs in east Los Angeles and school discrimination problems. In 1951 the Industrial Areas grant dried up, and Ross became a fund raiser for the American Friends Service Committee with the understanding that he could still work half-time with the CSO. After moving to San Jose, he discovered the newly formed Spanish Mission Band and, asking Father McDonnell about possible volunteer organizers for the CSO, was directed to Cesar Chavez.[1]

Chavez was initially skeptical, but Ross was determined. After avoiding the meeting, Chavez finally decided to invite a group of friends to give the intruding do-gooder a bad time. But Chavez was so impressed with Ross that he immediately volunteered as an organizer. Two years later Ross found funding to hire Chavez as the CSO's sole full-time organizer. By the late 1950s, Chavez had built the CSO into the largest

Mexican-American organization in California and was made director in charge of a paid staff of six. Many of the United Farm Workers original cadre were trained in this school: Dolores Huerta, who resigned from the AWOC in 1959; Gilbert Padilla, who became a volunteer organizer in 1957 and later served on the CSO staff; and Antonio Orendain, who helped as a volunteer in the Oxnard anti-bracero campaign. At the same time, Chavez developed useful ties to civil rights leaders, liberal politicians, social workers, and leaders of the church agencies and labor unions throughout the state.[2]

The Community Service Organization was an urban organization. Yet Chavez knew from personal experience, having been a son of a migrant worker and a supporter of the NFLU Tracy tomato strike in 1950, and from Father McDonnell's continued reminders that farm workers also needed an organization. The chance to move back to the fields came in 1958. The United Packinghouse Workers had launched a campaign to organize California packingshed workers and, allied with Saul Alinsky's Back of the Yards movement in Chicago, offered support for an organizer to organize field workers. Their target was Oxnard, a southern coastal town sheltering the canneries for nearby vegetable and fruit farms. Chavez quickly decided that braceros were the biggest problem and, over the summer and spring of 1958, organized a campaign among the domestic workers, contesting the hiring of braceros in preference to domestic workers. After several mass rallies secured gate-hiring and promises by the Farm Placement Office to abide by the domestic preference laws, Chavez approached the CSO board with a proposal to make Oxnard the center for a full-scale organizing campaign. But the CSO board felt that their focus was on urban problems and turned him down (Taylor 1975:93–96).

Chavez decided to stay with the CSO for the time being, contenting himself lobbying against the bracero program and for the extension of minimum wage laws to agriculture. He had little hope, however, of using the CSO as the launching pad for farm worker organizing. At the 1962 CSO convention, coming directly on the heels of the AWOC debacle in the Imperial Valley, Chavez renewed his plea. When the board again turned it down, he resigned and set out to organize farm workers. His two lieutenants, Huerta and Padilla, stayed with the CSO temporarily, planning to join him as soon as he lined up funding for their positions (Levy 1975:138–50).

The Mobilization Strategy

The strategy for mobilizing the Farm Workers Association drew on the two organizing traditions in which Chavez had been schooled: the multi-issue community organizing model developed by Saul Alinsky and Fred Ross, who had founded the CSO; and the mutual benefit associations of the Catholic Church, most directly represented by the Spanish Mission Band's Agricultural Workers Association. Chavez drew selectively on both, borrowing organizing tactics from the former and programs from the latter. Of these, Ross was the most important influence. Although trained by Alinsky, Ross had developed a slightly different organizing approach. Alinksy had organized the Back of the Yards Movement in settled working class neighborhoods surrounding the old stockyards in Chicago on the assumption that the neighborhoods had sufficient resources and indigenous organization to support a challenge. The key problem was creating an awareness that the neighborhoods were excluded from city politics and that urban elites were exploiting their exclusion. Organizing was primarily a question of building formal associations, typically by forming alliances among existing groups, and using confrontation tactics to reveal elite exploitativeness. The organizer was purely a catalyst, initiating the challenge and then withdrawing to allow the community to direct its own fate (Alinsky 1947, 1971; Bailey 1974). In contrast, Ross contended that the Mexican immigrants were sufficiently disorganized and without leaders that an open challenge would immediately collapse. First, they had to develop solidarity ties, indigenous leaders, and a tradition of pooling resources. Organizing was a question of developing solidarity, training indigenous leaders, and creating new organizations. The organizer had to make a long-term commitment, investing years and perhaps a decade before open challenges would be possible (Friedland 1981).

The organizing tactics that flowed from this approach proved extremely effective. Because solidarity was so central, Chavez held house meetings at which supporters invited friends and neighbors to their homes to discuss solutions to local problems. Organizing automatically zeroed in on the more settled, cohesive farm workers and made use of bloc recruitment. Chavez also tried to be a friend to all the workers, Association members or not, taking personal interest in their lives and any problems they brought to his attention. "Once you helped people, most became loyal. The people who helped us back when we wanted volunteers were the people we had helped."[3] Friendship was a selective solidarity incentive that helped create networks of solidarity and, at least until the Association became too large, strong ties to Chavez himself. The Association also held festivals and parades on religious and civic holidays and used Catholic and Mexican symbols to stir the workers. If anything could generate instant solidarity among the Mexican immigrants, it was the Virgin de Guadalupe at the head of a procession or a festival on Cinco de Mayo, the anniversary of Mexican independence. Chavez also insisted that the workers had to be willing to sacrifice for the collectivity, and he deliberately set Association dues high, at $3.50 a month, with little tolerance for late dues. "If things are done with sacrifice, they are more lasting. If they cost more, then we will value them more" (Levy 1975:92). The point was to instill a morale of sacrifice and commitment to la causa. Throughout the initial organizing, there was no talk of a union or strikes. Not only might this intimidate the workers, but it would alert the growers and prompt the attention of local police and courts. The strategy was to prepare a basis for a union, not organize a union outright. Chavez also followed Ross' advice on staff. Professional organizers had to make a long-term commitment, and since the aim was to create indigenous leadership, volunteer organizers would come only from the farm workers. He also borrowed the Catholic vow of voluntary poverty, requiring professional staff to accept a subsistence salary of housing and food plus $5 per week for personal spending. Commitment was total, often requiring 80–100 hours' work a week and, as the organization grew, communal living arrangements.

Chavez also drew on the mutual benefit associations of the Catholic Church. The basic notion here was solving immediate life problems and generating a sense of community. By providing selective incentives like low cost credit, health services, and cooperative buying and collective incentives through festivals and celebrations, the Association solved the farm workers' most immediate problems and created a sense of solidarity. Once immediate problems had been addressed and a base of solidarity created, the farm workers would be prepared to deal with larger problems.

The choice of Delano was more fortunate than Chavez imagined. Delano was the center of the table grape industry, probably the most favorable organizing setting in the entire state. With a population of around

135

5,000 farm workers, it was also the major residential center for recent Mexican immigrants in the southern San Joaquin Valley. Most of the grape workers were also local workers, employed eight to nine months of the year within the local area. The grape workers were also highly skilled, girdling grape vines and pruning as well as handling the delicate harvest. Table grapes were far more demanding than raisin or wine grapes, allowing only a few days' leeway at the harvest and considerable care in handling. Harvest strikes, then, would be extremely threatening.

There were two groups of Delano grape growers: the large corporate farmers such as Schenley Corporation, the nation's largest liquor conglomerate, and the DiGiorgio Corporation, which had diversified into canning, fruit sales, and shipping; and the smaller growers involved solely in field production, most of whom were of Italian and Yugoslav descent. The smaller growers operated farms of 500 to 1,000 acres and were also immigrants; they had come to California in the 1920s and built up their farms by frugality and hard work. They proved the most intransigent, having invested their lives in their farms and depending completely on field operations. Ethnic clannishness and stubborn determination reinforced their intransigence. The table grape industry was also a relatively centralized target. In the mid-1960s, thirty of these growers produced 75 percent of all California table grapes, or about two-thirds of the national total (Dunne 1967:9–12; Matthiessen 1969:135–138; Brown 1972:111–112).

Chavez spent the winter and summer of 1962 making contacts throughout the Valley under the pretext of conducting a social survey of the colonias. By leaving postcards to be filled out on which the workers could express their desires, Chavez identified potential supporters and learned more about the workers' immediate concerns. He later followed up these leads with house meetings at which he revealed the plans for a benefit association. Soon he had a long list of small-scale projects that could address immediate concerns. If a family member died, few of the workers had sufficient savings for a funeral. The Association would offer a funeral benefit fund. Most had trouble getting by during the winter and could not secure credit at the local banks to buy cars or houses. The Association would organize a credit union. Because the workers had to drive long distances to work, keeping a car in repair was a major expense. The Association would organize a gasoline co-op and buy tires and supplies cooperatively. Many workers were trying to obtain citizenship and clearance for a relative to move to the United States or to collect welfare payments. The Association would provide immigration counseling, set up citizenship classes, and intervene with welfare agencies.[4]

By September 1962, the FWA had a membership of 300 families and several thousand contacts. Chavez decided to call a founding convention in Fresno for September 30. Around 250 supporters showed up, ratifying the proposal to create the Farm Workers Association and Richard Chavez's Aztec black eagle flag as the Association symbol. Benefits were initially limited to a burial insurance plan and a credit union, with plans for a gasoline co-op, counseling services, and eventually a health care center. Over the next two years, Chavez patiently kept organizing, living off donations by members, his brother's support, and a small salary. By 1964 the Association had over 1,000 members and a well-established credit union administered by Helen Chavez with $25,000 in assets. Yet the Association was still an extremely limited operation, with only Chavez as full-time professional staff and fewer than a dozen volunteer organizers.

The New Sponsors

The transformation of this fledgling community organization into a full-scale insurgency was made possible by new sources of sponsorship. The most important was that from the National Migrant Ministry, a missionary agency of the National Council of Churches. In the fall of 1964, Chris Hartmire, the Director of the California Migrant Ministry, asked Cesar Chavez and Fred Ross to serve as trainers for a new community organizing project in nearby Porterville to be sponsored by the Ministry, the Rosenberg Foundation in San Francisco, and two local churches. The Tulare Community Development Project was to build a countywide organization of farm workers that would be "primarily responsive to the aspirations of the low-income farm workers" and, by forging coalitions among existing organizations, eventually "transform the structure of political power."[5] When Reverend James Drake and David Hazen, the two new organizers, arrived, they of course found no indigenous farm worker organizations and immediately set out to organize a new organization, the Farm Workers Organization, modelled on Chavez's Farm Workers Association. Over the spring of 1965, they used the Organization to launch a voter registration campaign, lend credibility to their testimony at public hearings against the bracero program, and organize a new chapter of the Mexican American Political Association. By the spring, Hazen and Drake decided to combine forces with Chavez and, despite resistance by some of the older members, merged the Organization with the Farm Workers Association. Shortly afterwards, Hazen and Drake became involved in the NFWA's strikes and, amidst the publicity and internal debate over the Migrant Ministry's new role, supported Hartmire's proposal to formally ally the Migrant Ministry with the new insurgency.[6]

The new direction for the Migrant Ministry was the culmination of a series of organizational changes that began in the late 1950s in the parent organization, the National Council of Churches. Originally organized as a domestic mission for the dustbowl migrant workers of the late 1930s, the Migrant Ministry had long been guided by the "social gospel" philosophy that evangelical work first required addressing social problems. Through the 1950s, the major programs were day schools for migrant children, medical services, free emergency meals, and assistance in securing aid from public welfare agencies. The program depended almost entirely on volunteer labor from local congregations.[7] In 1955, the National Council of Churches hired John Regier, a minister and social worker trained by Saul Alinsky, as director of the newly created Home Missions Division, under which the Migrant Ministry was housed. Regier had a new vision for the agencies, especially those with excluded constituencies, arguing that they should serve as the "general interest representative" of the migrants, Indians, and southern blacks who had traditionally been objects of missionary work. This required expanded funding and increased reliance on a new professional staff (Pratt 1972:38–39; Kelley 1957).

Over the next decade, Regier guided the development of new projects, getting the Division involved in the civil rights movement (Hilton 1969), community organizing in the ghettos (Fry 1964; Lee and Galloway 1969; Martin 1972), and lobbying in Washington for major policy reforms (Adams 1970; Pratt 1972). In 1959 Regier convinced the Migrant Ministry board to hold a series of state conferences to discuss new programs and, under his patient prodding, secured a broad endorsement of voting rights and unionization for the migrants and opposition to the bracero program. With a $112,000 grant from the Schwartzhaupt Foundation in Chicago, a major supporter of Saul Alinsky, he reorganized the Ministry to include community organizing for the migrants.

Because California had the largest concentration of migrants and the most affluent and liberal State Council of Churches, it was the logical site for the new program of "fringe ministries" that were to organize the local workers who had settled out of the migrant stream. Bill Koch, another minister with social work training, spent three months at the Industrial Areas Foundation with Saul Alinsky before setting out to organize self-help projects that included voter registration and assistance in securing citizenship papers as well as counseling and traditional evangelical work.[8] When Koch had to resign in 1961 because of illness, the California Migrant Ministry, which had been reorganized as a semi-autonomous agency of the California Council of Churches, hired Chris Hartmire, then a minister at the East Harlem Protestant Parish in New York who had been actively involved in civil rights work and community organizing. Hartmire promptly pushed for a more activist program, securing a grant from the Rosenberg Foundation to support a series of nine "fringe missions" of which the Tulare Community Development Project was the most activist.

The major force underlying this dramatic change from service work to community organizing and political advocacy was the increasing autonomy of the professional staff and their growing involvement in social problems. As Pratt (1972) has argued, the 1950s witnessed a major increase in the funding, administrative autonomy, and professionalism of National Council of Churches staff. Agency positions, as opposed to traditional clerical roles, attracted the most reform-minded ministers who, given the opportunity, put their new professional training in solving social problems to work addressing the causes rather than the symptoms of poverty and powerlessness. In effect, the most politically conservative segment of the American population—upper and upper-middle class white Protestants—had indirectly become financiers of insurgency.[9]

The key test for the Migrant Ministry came when Drake and Hazen joined the picket line in the Delano grape strike in late September 1965. The Ministry had already lost support from several large donors, such as J. G. Boswell, a millionaire rancher who took offense at Hartmire's testimony against the bracero program, and most of the local congregations, who opposed the voter registration campaigns.[10] But Hartmire convinced the emergency meeting of the Migrant Ministry Commission, the oversight committee for the Northern Council of Churches, that the projects fulfilled the goal of service through self-help. Shortly afterwards, the Commission authorized him to phase out the volunteer projects and center the entire program around worker priests who would devote their efforts full-time to the nascent insurgency. Padilla and Orendain were hired as worker priests, along with Hazen and Drake. The die was cast. The next year the Commission endorsed Hartmire's proposal that the Ministry consider itself "the servant of the farm worker movement," and in 1969 the Ministry was renamed the National Farm Worker Ministry in recognition of its role as a "related movement" whose major program was twenty-six worker priests who served as union organizers for the United Farm Workers Union.[11]

The Ministry's sponsorship came at a critical point. In the fall of 1964, when Drake and Hazen began working with Chavez, the Farm Worker Association was a small community organization of around 1,000 farm workers with only Chavez as full-time staff; it had not yet discussed, much less endorsed, the idea of supporting an open challenge. The ministers' support legitimated the union drive in the eyes of both the workers and other outside supporters and, as the Ministry became increasingly tied to the farm worker struggle, provided most of the budget for hiring new professional organizers. By the summer of 1965, the Ministry supported three worker priests (Drake, Hazen, and Padilla), who made up over half the NFWA's professional staff. The Ministry support, unlike labor support, was also sustained and did not depend on immediate tangible results. Organizing farm workers was a long-term project that, even with effective recruitment strategies, would take five to six years. The NFLU and AWOC had been limited by the short-range calculus underlying labor sponsorship. The Migrant Ministry defined its involvement in terms of humanitarian commitment to a moral cause and therefore imposed no criteria for immediate victory or a quid pro quo. As Chavez explained: "The church is the one group that isn't expecting anything from us. All the other groups, the unions, the civil rights groups, they all want something in return. . . . Not the church" (Chavez 1969:8). Without Ministry support, the challenge probably would not have weathered the first Delano grape strike.

The challenge also received critical sponsorship from organized labor, several private foundations, the Catholic Church, governmental agen-

Table 6.1
United Farm Workers Union Income

	Membership Dues	External Sources Contributions	External Sources Loans	External % of Total
1966 (Oct.–Dec.)	$ 10,147	$ 103,187		91
1967	84,424	436,783		84
1968	91,959	533,581		85
1969	238,551	442,264		65
1970	425,166	596,558		58
1971	1,109,453	448,981		29
1972	1,161,346	503,111		30
1973	787,796	2,948,568	$125,000	80
1974	515,281	2,332,375		82
1975	565,713	1,913,590		66
1976	877,035	1,581,127		59
1977	1,100,406	1,564,394	15,655	59
1978	1,477,348	588,442		29

Source: *Annual Reports to Office of Management Services*, U.S. Department of Labor.

cies such as the Office of Economic Opportunity and the National Health Services Administration, liberal politicians, and several of the other social movements of the period. Support came most directly in the form of cash contributions (see table 6.1) but also in volunteer work on boycotts, donated meals and housing for cadres, political and legal advice, and not least, political protection for organizing and support for major public policy changes. Although these sources were less critical in the initial campaign, their scale and diversity guaranteed the UFW's independence vis-à-vis any single sponsor and allowed the challenge to survive several major disasters. Table 6.1 gives some notion of the scale of support, looking solely at financial contributions and breaking down the UFW revenues into dues and contributions. In the first five years, roughly the time it took to establish a sustained challenge, the UFW received over $2 million in external contributions, or more than twice that received by the AWOC and ten times that by the NFLU during comparable periods. The contributions allowed the UFW to hire professional organizers, purchase space for offices and meetings, carry out major publicity efforts, and on an unprecedented scale, offer service programs that mobilized farm workers.

It took an extremely adept and alert leadership to mobilize this support and put it to effective use. In many respects, this was the feature that most distinguished the UFW cadre from its predecessors. From his community organizing experience, Chavez was aware of the importance of political alliances and soliciting external support. The civil rights movement also provided a model, demonstrating the potentials for organizing outside support through dramatic protests and boycotts. The political context was also extremely conducive. The new reformism of private social service agencies like the National Council of Churches and the Catholic Campaign for Human Development created a new set of sponsors. While limited in terms of legislative accomplishments, the Kennedy administration aroused aspirations and awareness of persisting social problems like poverty. The Democratic sweep in the 1964 elections strengthened the often divisive coalition of liberal reformers and organized labor and created a vast outpouring of private and governmental support for social reform.

The Association seized these opportunities. In August 1965, only a few days before the Delano grape strike was to begin, Chavez received word that the Office of Economic Opportunity (OEO) had authorized a grant of $260,000 for citizen training and economic assistance to the Association. Although the strike forced him to turn the grant down, it was a sign of the new political opportunities.[12] In December, Walter Reuther of the United Auto Workers arrived, pledging $5,000 monthly and bringing the news media and invaluable political contacts. Shortly afterwards, Bill Kircher, Director of Organizations for the AFL–CIO, decided that the NFWA offered more promise for building a farm workers union than the AWOC, and began pressuring for a merger with the AWOC, eventually firing Al Green and his organizers and offering the political and financial support of the AFL–CIO. This stimulated an internal battle over the union's autonomy and the departure of several student radical volunteers, but rechristened in August 1967 as the United Farm Worker Organizing Committee (UFWOC), the union doubled its monthly income and secured invaluable tactical advice and political support.[13]

The previously unknown Cesar Chavez and his Farm Workers Association quickly became the new cause celebre among political activists. Jack Conway, the new Director of the Ford Foundation-funded Center for Community Change in Washington, D.C., and a former UAW lobbyist and Reuther aide, phoned Chavez, asking him to contribute to the development of what he called a community union model of organizing poor people and become one of the Center's projects.[14] The first boycott teams, which were dispatched in the spring of 1966, enlisted an important supporter in Ann Israel (later Puharich), the staff director of radical philanthropist Stewart Mott's Spectamur Agendo Foundation. Israel became so involved in boycott work that she resigned her position, turned over her Manhattan townhouse as a boycott house, and volunteered as a fund raiser, lining up grants from liberal New York philanthropists.[15] La Causa also drew on the at first gingerly support of the Catholic Church. Two priests—Mark Day, a Franciscan, and Victor Salandini, a local parish priest who had supported the AWOC—volunteered for the picket lines, but unlike the Protestant Migrant Ministry, the limits were sharper. Day had to take a leave of absence, and Salandini was formally rebuked then took a leave of absence to finish a Ph.D. in economics at Catholic University, where he simultaneously served as the union's lobbyist. Beyond boycott endorsements, major Catholic support did not come until the 1970s, when the teaching orders and sympathetic bishops began authorizing priests and nuns to take temporary leaves of absence to serve full-time in la causa.[16]

The challenge also mobilized directly off the other insurgencies of the time, especially the student and civil rights movements. When the Delano grape strike made the headlines, student activists at Berkeley who had been involved in the Free Speech Movement and the civil rights organizing in Mississippi in the summer of 1964 immediately flocked to Delano. The union recruited several cadres, such as Marshall Ganz and Eugene Nelson, who used their organizing experience from campus chapters of CORE, SNCC, and SDS to launch the initial boycott. In addition to Chavez's appeal, the white student radicals were also being pushed out of the black militant organizations and some were opposed to the SDS turn from community organizing to resisting the Vietnam War.[17] In the spring of 1966, the Migrant Ministry decided to organize another "summer of '64" event and recruited teams of student radicals to Delano to serve as union staff, organizers, and boycott workers. Although most of the student volunteers, who were derisively called gabachos (or green-horns) by the workers, stayed only a brief time, several stayed as full-time cadres on the standard subsistence-plus-$5 per week (every other week) salary while others returned home to become boycott organizers. Although the student radicals were a persistent source of controversy and several poorly concealed attempts to take over the union, they made up the backbone of administration at least until the early 1970s.

In short, the external support was unprecedented. The union was able to continually add new staff, hire lawyers and physicians for the health clinic, field twenty organizers to mount strikes, and simultaneously launch a nationwide boycott, all without the luxuries of union contracts and, at least initially, a stable mass membership. It also allowed the union to keep up the struggle despite a series of dramatic and initially supported but ultimately ineffective strikes.

The Delano Grape Strike

Although Chavez had vowed to stay out of direct challenges to growers, he soon led the Association into several skirmishes. By the spring of 1965, the Association had over 1,500 families and had several small successes to its credit, having doubled the registration of Mexican-American voters and initiated complaints against a racist teacher and several growers for payroll abuses. In early April, several Association members who worked in the Mt. Arbor rose nursery near McFarland got embroiled in a pay dispute with the manager. There were also Mexican green carders from the village of Tangansequora, known as "Tangues," and several Filipinos and Puerto Ricans. The Tangues and the Puerto Ricans agreed to meet with the Association members one Sunday morning at Delano. To Chavez's surprise, the workers voted to strike, deciding that the best move was to stay in their camps and simply refuse to work. Chavez would contact the owner and ask for the back pay. At dawn the next day, the Association leaders, joined by James Drake of the Migrant Ministry, held what they called the "breakfast club." Visiting each of the workers' homes, the club knocked on the doors to insure that no one was going to work. At one house, Dolores Huerta, convinced that the workers were planning to work, blocked off the driveway. For two days the workers stayed home. Chris Hartmire phoned the owner of the rose nursery in Iowa but to no avail. The next day the manager fired the strikers. The next morning, a local labor contractor brought in a crew of fifteen Filipinos. The Tangues, fearing that they might lose their jobs, secretly settled with the manager. When Chavez got wind of the negotiations, he asked them to wait for a joint meeting

144

the next day. They promised to do so and then marched back to work the next morning.

When the P.R.s [Puerto Ricans] learned of this treachery, they were furious. The last weapon was used Wednesday P.M. Dolores Huerta and Helen Chavez went to the dormitory of Los Tangues and called them women, cowards, and traitors. The men agreed; they were women, cowards and traitors, and that they were going back to work tomorrow. . . . The last bit of organizational work was in convincting the P.R.s not to murder the Tangues. . . . We had to follow a couple around town until we finally saw them go to bed.

Challenged at the gate by the Puerto Ricans, the Tangues shouted back: "We are Mexican citizens. This isn't our fight."[18] The end of the bracero program did not mean an end to immigrant strikebreaking.

The next month the workers living in the Linnell and Woodville Farm Labor Camps near Porterville asked Gil Padilla for help. The camp had been built in the late 1930s by the Farm Security Administration to house the dust bowlers. The Tulare County Housing Authority claimed to operate it at cost but had accumulated a surplus of $80,000. In late May, the Authority announced a fifty percent rent hike, purportedly to finance new construction. Padilla organized camp councils to represent the residents and, aided by a lawyer from the California Rural Legal Assistance Project, called a rent strike. The strikers put their rent into an escrow account, and by June 15, the strike was eighty percent solid. The rent strike grabbed the attention of the student radicals at Berkeley and Stanford, who immediately descended on the Valley. The FWA, desperate for support, gladly accepted the volunteers, asking them to run the mimeo machines and to phone solicitations for strike support.[19]

The rent strike was still in progress in August, when another dispute emerged. Several rent strikers who worked on the J. D. Martin ranch were irritated by pay irregularities and working conditions. On August 25 they voted to strike and asked Chavez to negotiate for $1.40 per hour to match the newly announced bracero wage and restitution of back wages. A local labor contractor immediately brought in a crew from an American Friends Service Committee sponsored labor co-op, and the strike collapsed. Chavez vowed to stay out of strikes for at least three years. The FWA needed a stronger membership base before strikes could succeed.[20]

Fate had other plans. In early May several crews of Filipino grape harvesters organized by the four AWOC Filipino organizers—Larry It-liong, Philip Vera Cruz, Andy Imutan, and Ben Gines—struck in the Coachella grape harvest, demanding the bracero minimum of $1.40. The phasing out of the bracero program created an opportunity. The Coachella growers were worried about their labor supply and also had plans for handsome profits, since their grapes were the first of the season. Rather than fight, the growers caved in. When the Filipino crews moved north to the Arvin harvest in mid-June, they demanded the same wage hike. The Arvin growers, however, were ready for a fight and dispatched labor contractors to bring in Mexican workers who broke the strike. The AWOC organizers then decided to wait until the September grape harvest in Delano. For many of them, this was their home base, and they hoped to organize stronger support.[21]

When the AWOC called a strike on the morning of September 8, there was little to suggest the dawning of a new era in farm labor. The FWA had lost two strikes and was embroiled in a protracted rent strike. Nor was the AWOC in a strong position, since the Filipino crews were the only active element. Indicating his interest, Al Green moved to the Stanislaus County citrus groves to organize field worker support for the Teamsters (*Los Angeles Times*, March 15, 1965; R. Taylor 1975:124). In fact, the Filipino strike only held solid for the first two days. Around a thousand Filipinos stayed in their camps. Then the growers ordered strikers living in ranch housing out of their bunkhouses, infuriating the Filipinos. They immediately organized picket teams, concentrating on the packing sheds that had recently been reopened with Mexican labor.[22]

The Association confronted a dilemma. If it joined the strike, it risked three years of preparatory organizational work. On the other hand, if it ignored the strike, it violated its commitment to the farm workers. At first Chavez temporized, running stories in the Association paper *El Malcriado* ("the bad boy") urging members to respect the AWOC picket lines. But the Mexican strikebreakers continued to walk across the lines. When FWA members began to join the parade, Chavez called on Itliong to discuss possible cooperation, and after considerable staff debate, Chavez announced a meeting to discuss joining the strike.

On Thursday evening, September 16, 1965, Mexican Independence Day, an enthusiastic crowd of over 1,200 overflowed the parish hall of Our Lady of Guadalupe Church. While Chavez was still skeptical about

146

the strike, the crowd was enthusiastic, and the staff and student radicals supporting the strike carried the day. They decorated the walls with posters of Emiliano Zapata, the Mexican revolutionary hero, and Jack London's definition of a strikebreaker as "a two-legged animal with a corkscrew soul, a water-logged brain and combination backbone made of jelly and glue." A huge huelga ("strike") banner graced the rostrum with the Association's black eagle in the center. Speaker after speaker roused the crowd, reminding them of their Mexican revolutionary heritage. "Viva la Huelga! Viva la Causa! Viva Cesar Chavez!" came the reply. When Chavez finally asked for a strike vote, the hall broke out in a unanimous "Huelga! Huelga! Huelga!" The FWA would join the AWOC (R. Taylor 1975:124 125; Nelson 1966:24; Dunne 1971: ch. 7; London and Anderson 1970:150–151).

Chavez asked the members to wait until the following Monday, the 20th, so that the Association could contact the growers, organize picket teams, and finalize their alliance with the AWOC. Reflecting the new aspirations, the Association also adopted a new name: the National Farm Workers Association. The next day Chavez and Drake met with Green to discuss cooperation. While accepting the support, Green was not particularly interested in the Filipino AWOCs and even less in an alliance with the NFWA. Turning aside offers to establish a common strike fund, a strategy committee under AWOC control, and a no-raiding agreement, Green decided to pursue his own separate course and returned to his citrus organizing while leaving Itliong virtually unsupported.[23]

The enthusiasm that had filled the hall had largely melted away by the following Monday morning. Chavez's pessimistic assessment was correct: the NFWA was not organizationally prepared for a strike. By relying on nationalistic revolutionary sentiments generated by September 16, the NFWA staff had managed to muster 1,200 to support a strike vote. While the student radicals had worked hard to create a huelga spirit, this would not sustain a strike that would cost the workers their income, their jobs, perhaps even their lives. Only 100 workers showed up at the 3 A.M. meeting scheduled for Monday morning to organize picketing. crippling the strike at the outset. By 4 A.M. Chavez decided that they had waited long enough. The leaders organized picket teams and assigned them to fields that they knew would be worked (R. Taylor 1975:130–131).

The strike quickly turned into a war of attrition centered on the picket lines. Shortly before dawn, the pickets assembled at headquarters and loaded into cars, forming a caravan with the picket captain at the head. The first target was the farm entrance gates. As the workers began to arrive, the pickets lined up with their signs and began to chant: "Huelga! Huelga! Huelga!" If a car stopped, the pickets filled the air with the argument of the strike. They could work elsewhere. This farm was under a strike vote. The workers had to stand up against the growers and demand their rights. Some of the workers turned away because they supported the strike, others because they didn't want any trouble. Still others drove through the picket lines. By mid-morning the gate picketing had made its impact and the caravans began scouting the backroads, looking for crews at work in the fields. When they spotted a crew, the cars pulled to the side, careful not to cross onto private property where they could be arrested for trespassing. Armed with bullhorns and balloons with "HUELGA" scrolled across them, the picket lines re-formed. Carrying handpainted signs, black and white with "HUELGA" or "ESQUIROL AFUERA" ("Scab stand aside") in dripping paint, the pickets resumed their parade. The pickets waved the signs and chanted "Huelga! Huelga! Huelga" and "Hay huegla aqui." If the workers were near the roadway, the huelgistas urged them out of the fields. If, as was more typical, they were far back, the pickets simply chanted "Huelga!" and motioned for the esquirols to come closer to hear the argument of the strike.

If the grower discovered the pickets, the scene was set for high drama. The grower would come barreling down the farm road, boiling dust up on the pickets, skid to a stop, leap out of the truck, and menacingly confront the picket line. Occasionally a grower would pull his rifle from the gun rack in the back of his pickup truck and threaten the pickets, pointing at the sign posted on the fence: "No Trespassing! Survivors Will Be Prosecuted!" The foreman hurled insults at the pickets, calling them traitors and cowards, and drowned out their shouting with car radios. Some pickets returned the insults, while others seethed quietly in anger. Others were intimidated, realizing that they had made an aggressive move and that someplace someone was recording their actions in a little black book. When the workers in the vineyards heard the shouts, they would stop and look up, returning to work only to look up again. Conferring among themselves in whispers, they were obviously ill at ease. The pickets picked up such signs, intensifying the pressure. Meanwhile the foreman would move between the pickets and the fields, ordering the workers to speed their pace and challenging the pickets to cross the fence line to deliver their message.[24]

The roving picket teams patrolled an area roughly fifteen miles square, containing all fifteen ranches struck by the AWOC and the thirty targeted by the NFWA. The pickets passed out maps showing the strike boundaries and a special *Huelga* issue of *El Malcriado*. But, despite intense picketing, probably no more than half of the 2,000 workers then in the fields walked out.[25] Many went to work Monday morning, planning to walk out if a picket team materialized. Apprehensive and uncertain, the workers hesitated in the fields, weighing their immediate pocketbook against the moral pressure of the pickets. When the pickets first appeared, some would quietly slip out of the fields in ones and twos. A few would boldly throw down their tools and march out. Pickets jubilantly thrust NFWA authorization cards into their hands and invited them to join the picket team. And many who voted for huelga on the 16th became steadfast esquirols on the 20th. Still others waited for nightfall, quietly rejoining the NFWA ranks at the nightly meetings, returning to work in the fields by day so long as no pickets appeared at the gates to turn them away (R. Taylor 1975:146).

The major problem was the workers' poverty. Many sympathized with the strike but felt they could not afford to pass up the harvest wages. The NFWA had only a few hundred dollars in the treasury and could not pay strike relief. The Association called on members to donate food and housing, but they could not handle the entire load. Over 2,000 individuals, workers and their families, passed through the Delano headquarters during the first week (*Valley Labor Citizen*, October 1, 1966). Soon the pickets began asking new supporters to simply move on to jobs outside the strike zone. The AWOC paid strike relief and the Filipinos gave solid support, but they were only a third of the normal workforce.

Then Chavez had a stroke of genius. The growers had secured a court injunction restricting picket teams to five at each ranch gate and bans on any disturbance of the peace. The sheriff had told his deputies that any mention of "huelga" or use of loudspeakers constituted a disturbance. Chavez decided to turn adversity to an advantage, using the restrictions on their freedom of speech to appeal for outside support and renew sagging strike morale. David Havens volunteered to test the injunction by reading Jack London's famous definition of a strikebreaker for the enjoyment of the sheriff's deputies. The deputies immediately arrested Havens, providing the strikers with a protest issue (R. Taylor 1975:141–142; Nelson 1966:96–100). Drake phoned Chris Hartmire, asking for more volunteers to go to jail, preferably with clerical collars.

On the morning of October 29, the NFWA phoned the Kern County Sheriff's office, notifying them that they would again defy the injunction. Then began the strangest strike caravan in the history of farm labor. Forty-four pickets, thirty-one volunteers and thirteen workers, loaded up. Obediently trailing behind were several sheriff's cars and a paddy wagon to cart away the arrested and the press. The caravan had no particular destination, spending nearly an hour crisscrossing the back roads to find a working crew. Finally a crew was spotted. The procession pulled off. Everyone piled out. The forty-four pickets lined up, held up their signs, and chanted in unison: "Huelga! Huelga! Huelga!" The cameramen scrambled around, taking every conceivable shot. After ten minutes a deputy declared the assembly unlawful, ordering the pickets to disperse or face arrest. The pickets then quietly lined up while the deputies took down their names, then herded them gently into the waiting paddy wagon. The workers in the field had hardly even looked up. Brought before the local judge, the pickets were charged with unlawful assembly and disturbing the peace, with bail set at $276 each (R. Taylor 1975:142–143; Nelson 1966:100–104; *People's World*, October 23, 1965).

The arrests gave Chavez the needed ammunition. Speaking that afternoon on the steps of Sproul Hall at Berkeley, he described the arrests and appealed for contributions and volunteers. The outpouring was overwhelming. The students chipped in $2,000, and several student organizations promised more. That weekend carloads of students showed up in Delano to volunteer for the new cause (*People's World*, November 6, 1975). The NFWA immediately appealed for more outside support, receiving delegations from the Northern California Council of Churches, the Mexican-American Political Association, and the CSO and a food caravan from the San Francisco AFL–CIO Labor Council. Anne Draper, the head of the AFL–CIO trade-label office in San Francisco, immediately phoned Paul Shrade, the western director for the United Auto Workers, who organized another food caravan. Significantly, the labor supporters decided to split their contributions equally between the AWOC and NFWA.[26] Chris Hartmire made appeals to sympathetic clergy and began a speaking tour, asking for donations of food, clothing, and money for the strikers.[27] Still the economic situation was so desperate that the unions decided to keep the strike zone restricted so that loyal supporters could work unstruck fields to earn enough to keep body and soul together. Several ardent supporters who otherwise would have been hired as full-time organizers had to take jobs with nearby poverty projects such as the California Center for Community Development.[28]

The growers also played on the fluidity of the labor market, hiring labor contractors who brought in migrants from the outside who had never harvested grapes before.[29] Although they were less efficient, this was better than losing the harvest. Besides, enough experienced workers crossed the picket lines to help train the new recruits. Meanwhile, the deputies kept up the pressure, arresting those who crossed into private property and trailing the picket teams.

By early November it was clear that the growers had won the first round. They managed to harvest a record crop with only small losses. As Harry Bernstein, veteran labor reporter for the *Loss Angeles Times*, exclaimed: "It is one of the strangest strikes in years (R. Taylor 1975:140–141; Harry Bernstein, *Los Angeles Times*, October 17 and December 26, 1965). Teams of pickets, scraggly students in faded overalls alongside leather-skinned workers, marched up and down the dusty roads while workers labored in the fields, trying to ignore the commotion on the roadway. Still, the NFWA and AWOC managed to get a formal strike certification from the state Department of Employment on all but a couple of the original strike targets.[30] Both organizations were still active. The NFWA benefit programs kept up contacts among the Mexican workers, and external support insured the organization's financial survival. Similarly, the AFL–CIO supported the AWOC organizers, and most of the Filipinos decided to stick out the winter in Delano.

The picket teams were beginning to grumble, and as the last truckloads of grapes were hauled off, they had no more fields to picket. To give them something to do, Chavez ordered two workers and a student volunteer to trail a shipment of Schenley grapes to the Oakland docks in hopes of keeping it from being loaded. Al Green had earlier asked for Teamster support, but Delano was a non-union town and the bid had little impact. To everyone's amazement, the pickets persuaded the longshoremen at the dock to refuse to handle the hot cargo. Schenley Corporation immediately demanded an injunction, but before the labor arbitrators could make a decision, the ship had to depart. Over 1,000 tenton cases of grapes sat rotting on the Oakland wharves.[31]

The strikers were electrified. Chavez put Jim Drake in charge of organizing a serious boycott and assigned him the student volunteers and a dozen workers. Since they were not certain of their labor support, the cadre decided to try a primary boycott by asking consumers to shun particular commodities. A more ambitious secondary boycott that would attempt to close off the entire market or retailer carrying the offensive goods was restricted by the National Labor Relations Act (Derenshinsky 1972). Local activists from CORE and SNCC, who had organized civil rights boycotts, volunteered advice and support. The targets were the two largest corporations—Schenley Industries and DiGiorgio. Both had been strike certified and both were likely to give in since they had highly visible trade-brands (I. W. Harper, J. W. Dant, and Cutty Sark liquors for Schenley; S & W and Treesweet canned goods for DiGiorgio) and made little from their vineyards.[32] Because it was near the Christmas buying season, Schenley was the prime target.

The boycott was a rag-tag affair. The boycott teams lived off the land, appealing to local labor temples and churches for food and housing. They passed out leaflets, organized picket teams that closed off store entrances, and harassed liquor store owners. Unions, SNCC and CORE chapters, church leaders, and SDS chapters rallied around the boycott. In no time, the boycott had caught hold.

Dateline: Los Angeles.	Sympathetic students leaflet liquor stores and clear the shelves.
Dateline: San Francisco.	Retail Clerks and Teamsters demand that management pull Schenley off the shelves.
Dateline: New York.	Government workers, 5,000 strong, pledge to boycott Schenley liquor. Union leaders picket Schenley headquarters.
Dateline: Boston.	Civil rights militants hold a Boston Grape Party to spread the boycott.
Dateline: Oklahoma City.	Local priests picket liquor stores, demanding Schenley be removed.

The boycotters also organized actions against the table grapes. Student volunteers followed shipments of "scab" grapes leaving the strike area for distant markets. Sympathetic railwaymen recorded the destinations

of cars, giving the pickets an opportunity to catch up with the shipments. In the neighboring Roseville switching yard, the NFWA pickets
surrounded a carload of grapes, and sympathetic railwaymen sidetracked
the shipment for several days while it rotted under the broiling sun.[33]
Longshoremen and Teamster truck drivers refused to handle shipments
of "scab" grapes. DiGiorgio promptly sued, securing an injunction that
barred further hot cargo actions unless the union contract specifically allowed it or it was purely spontaneous—that is, not encouraged or ordered by union representatives. Meanwhile chapters of the Mexican-
American Political Association and the GI Forum pitched in to help the
consumer boycott (*Valley Labor Citizen,* December 28 and 31, 1964,
January 7, and February 4, 1965).

The boycott campaign also attracted broader support. Anne Draper,
who had been organizing boycott support in San Francisco, pressed Paul
Shrade for stronger support from the United Auto Workers. On December 15, Walter Reuther, President of the UAW, flew to Delano to announce a pledge of $5,000 to be split equally between the NFWA and
AWOC. The Delano city council passed an ordinance barring a planned
AWOC–NFWA parade. With the television cameramen trailing, Reuther
headed up the march, challenging the police: "Let's march. Let them
arrest us."[34] The move forced the AFL–CIO's hand, and President Meany
ordered closer support for the unaffiliated NFWA. Over the winter, the
California AFL–CIO organized monthly food caravans, and actor Steve
Allen, a member of the Citizens Advisory Committee, held a benefit party
to raise funds for the strikers (Matthiessen 1969:68–73).

Still the challenge did not have teeth. Morale was low, and although
the boycott was still on, there were no signs of a breakthrough. With no
crop activity, there was not even anything to picket. Someone suggested
a mass march across the country to imitate the 1963 March on Washington. Scaling the suggestion down to size, Chavez suggested an Easter
perigrinacion, a Catholic procession of Lenten penitence. The march was
to begin in Delano, with the destination Sacramento on Easter morning.
By pressuring Governor Brown, then beginning his campaign for the fall
election, he might be made to intervene, About the same time, Reuther,
Kircher at the AFL–CIO, and the National Council of Churches began
pressing Congressional allies for public hearings to vault the strike into
a national issue and pave the way for national labor legislation for farm
workers. Senator Williams of New Jersey, head of the Senate Subcom-

mittee on Migratory Labor, was considering migrant welfare legislation and decided to hold public hearings. Along with the Congressional delegation came a new member of the subcommittee, Senator Robert Kennedy.

The hearings were uneventful, other than a heated exchange between Senator Kennedy and the Delano police chief who had blocked strike activities and the surprise strike endorsement by Bishop Hugh Donohoe of the Fresno Diocese, speaking for the California bishops. Previously only individual priests and mavericks like Father Vizzard of the Catholic Rural Life Conference had supported the strikers. The growers, who dominated the Valley collection plates, were outraged. More important was the legitimacy the hearings lent the strikers and the stage they provided for the next round of protests. As the hearings closed, the march on Sacramento pulled out under the grinding television cameras. For the next three weeks the seventy-five marchers carrying U.S., Mexican, and the black eagle union flags, headed by a staff bearing the Virgin of Guadalupe, crisscrossed the Central Valley, bringing the NFWA back into contact with its scattered membership. When the Delano strike had begun, Chavez had abandoned the plan to build a statewide organization. The march created an opportunity to renew contacts and assure supporters that it was only a question of time before la huelga would come to their area too. As the procession neared each town, runners were sent ahead to prepare for a festival. When the marchers entered towns, they were met by a local delegation who furnished food and housing for the night. Each night a rally was held for the workers, and each morning the march began with a Mass. Bill Kircher of the AFL–CIO was impressed:

The march was an organizing tool. New. Radical. Different. A crew of our people walking along the highway carrying the banner of Our Lady, calling meetings at night which attracted farm workers out of the fields and towns, opening with "De Colores" [a song used by the lay Catholic Cursillo movement that spoke of the colors of spring in the fields], maybe a prayer. The whole thing had a strong cultural, religious thing, yet it was organizing people. (Levy 1975:206–208)

The 300-mile march gave sympathizers a rallying point. Priests, Protestant clergy, students, and radical unionists flocked to the closing days. As the procession advanced on Sacramento, it swelled from seventy-five originales to over 5,000 (cited in R. Taylor 1975:168–169).

The Sacramento march also highlighted the contrast between the

NFWA and the AWOC. Green had ordered the Filipinos to keep off the march, but several ignored his orders and did so anyway. Kircher chided him for his absence, to which Green replied his was a union, but the NFWA was "a civil rights movement . . . run by ministers."[35] The AWOC leadership still lacked the imagination to mobilize around cultural issues and solidarity, much less appeal to outside support. Kircher decided to ease Green out of the directorship of the AWOC and replace him with Chavez. Meanwhile, he ordered Green to make certain that the trade unionists in every town showed up to welcome the marchers.[36]

At the last moment, Drake realized the opportunity for boycott organizing created by the television camera crews following the marchers. After considerable resistance by Chavez and the march leaders, Drake got authorization for the marchers to carry signs. Hastily they painted boycott signs. That evening, three days out of Sacramento, "Boycott I. W. Harper" flickered across the evening television news screen.[37] Behind the scenes "Blackie" Leavitt, head of the San Francisco Bartenders Union, put the squeeze on Schenley. Leavitt's secretary had attended the NFWA rally, coming away determined to see if the bartenders could do something to help. Leavitt met with Chavez and decided without authorization from either the international or the local membership to draw up a letter recommending that union bartenders throughout San Francisco quietly put Schenley liquors under the counter. Leavitt actually made no effort to circulate the memo among members but surreptitiously made sure it fell into Schenley hands.

Schenley reacted immediately. Sidney Korshak, lawyer for the company, phoned Leavitt, pointing out that a boycott was illegal. Leavitt replied that what individual bartenders did was their own business. Korshak then phoned Lewis Rosenteil, chairman of the Schenley board of directors. The liquor industry had an informal understanding dating from the prohibition days that one should stay out of the news. On learning about the march and hearing that the dispute involved only 5,000 acres of vines, Rosenteil ordered Korshak to sell the farm. Korshak suggested instead that the company recognize the NFWA as bargaining agent for the workers, clearing the company and getting the Schenley name out of the news. Rosenteil agreed and ordered Korshak to settle the issue as he saw fit. Without actually applying serious leverage, the NFWA had broken through the barrier, securing the first genuine field contract in the history of California labor organizing.[38]

The Schenley announcement sent an electric shock through the farm workers and the Delano growers. O. W. Fillerup, director of the Council of California Growers, replied for the grape industry:

While the NFWA and its religious cohorts were righteously preaching democratic processes and marching to Sacramento, the leaders were closeted elsewhere, working out a deal that denied workers any voice in the proceedings. . . . Schenley Industries, whose farm operations are incidental to their basic whiskey-making business, is not representative of California Agriculture, where growers steadfastly refuse to sell out their employees and force them into a union which does not represent them.[39]

The next day, as the jubilant marchers covered the last miles into Sacramento, the signs were switched to read: "Boycott S & W" and "Boycott Treesweet." DiGiorgio responded immediately. Calling a special press conference, Robert DiGiorgio announced that the State Mediation and Conciliation Service would conduct a secret ballot election on DiGiorgio properties. Furthermore, he urged the extension of the National Labor Relations Act to farm workers (R. Taylor 1975:178). The grower ranks were now broken. At least one grower had discovered the boycott protections of the Act.

On Easter morning the ragtag marchers triumphantly moved on the state capitol in Sacramento. At the head of the swelling column was a Mexican worker, his sombrero bent against the sun, brandishing a velvet and silk tapestry depicting Our Lady of Guadalupe, the patron saint of Mexico. Behind him marched over 5,000 workers, students, unionists, priests, and ministers. Some bore scarlet and white banners, their black thunderbird emblems snapping in the dusty breeze. Others waved signs: "JUSTICE FOR FARM WORKERS! GRAPES OF WRATH 1936–1966! VIVA LA HUELGA!" Dolores Huerta was the principal speaker, reminding the workers of the themes that had initiated their march— "Pilgrimage, Penance and Revolution!"—and warning Governor Brown pointedly that the Mexican-American vote "is not in the Democrats' hip pocket. . . . We will be counted as your supporters only when we can count you among ours." Reading the "Plan of Delano" drafted by poet Luis Valdez, modeled on Emiliano Zapata's revolutionary draft of the "Plan of Ayala," Huerta proclaimed to the cheering audience that the sun was about to shine:

The workers are on the rise. There will be strikes all over the state, and throughout the nation, because Delano has shown what can be done, and the workers know now, they are no longer alone. (R. Taylor 1975:180).

156

The initial enthusiasm of the victories had hardly passed before the unions discovered traps in the DiGiorgio offer. DiGiorgio intended to allow only current employees to vote—in other words, the strikebreakers. There would be no boycott or strike actions during negotiations, and if the union got a recognition vote, it would sign a no-strike clause for the duration of the contract. Then, a new union, the Kern-Tulare Independent Farm Workers Union, materialized, secretly sponsored by DiGiorgio. It too would be on the ballot, along with both the AWOC and NFWA. The union rejected the terms and called for a fair election. Meanwhile Chavez asked Fred Ross to help organize workers for the campaign against DiGiorgio, and Kircher lined up a pressure campaign on both Governor Brown and Robert DiGiorgio to amend the election terms.[40]

Then came a surprise. On May 13 a sympathetic crew boss on the DiGiorgio Sierra Vista Ranch walked into the NFWA office with a Teamster authorization card that had been passed out by a ranch supervisor. Joint Council 38, which had previously helped the strikers with hot cargo actions, was signing up DiGiorgio workers. Though the Teamsters had in the past made jurisdictional claims to field workers and held a sweetheart contract on the Bud Antle lettuce ranch, they had never seriously pressed the claim. DiGiorgio had invited them in to head off the NFWA, offering another sweetheart contract. In addition to the easy dues, the Teamsters also wanted to protect their flanks. A fifth of the Teamsters were in packingsheds, canneries, frozen food plants, and agricultural trucking. An independent union in the fields was a threat.

The move was also prompted by Kircher's reorganization of the AWOC. Kircher had come with instructions to revitalize the campaign. Despite a $1 million investment, the AWOC had achieved little. Kircher opposed the alliance with the Teamsters, which had produced contracts for the Teamsters but left the AWOC emptyhanded, and was troubled by Green's weak support for the Filipinos and his avoidance of the NFWA. Finally, he fired Green and put Larry Itliong, leader of the Filipino organizers, in charge. Several of the Filipino organizers resigned in protest and signed on as Teamster organizers. By working through the Filipino labor contractors, the Teamsters could hope to lure the Filipinos away from the AWOC. The clash was aggravated by the cultural differences between the Filipinos and the Mexican-Americans. The Filipino contractors generally protected their stable Filipino crews while the Mexican-American contractors worked temporary crews and tended to take advantage of them. The AWOC had worked with the contractors, while the NFWA was adamantly opposed to the contractor system. The Filipinos also viewed the conflict more narrowly as a "private fight" rather than a "social revolution" (Taylor 1975:183–184).

Chavez and Kircher began negotiating new election terms with Robert DiGiorgio and had worked out the major planks when DiGiorgio made another surprise announcement. The election would be held in three days with the AWOC, the Tulare-Kern IFWU, the NFWA, and the Teamsters all on the ballots. The Corporation's accounting firm would officiate. The NFWA and AWOC asked the workers to boycott the elections, attacked them as a fraud, and petitioned Governor Brown to intervene. On June 23, they got a court injunction removing their names from the ballots. Although the voters had been strikebreakers, the NFWA was still the victor. Of 732 eligible workers, only 385 cast ballots, and of these only 201 followed company instructions to vote for Teamsters, while 41 cast blank ballots.[41] The next week, Brown appeared for a speech at the Mexican-American Political Association Convention, when to his surprise he found himself shaking hands with Cesar Chavez. Quickly recovering, Brown immediately proclaimed the meeting long overdue, and after the speech, the two retired for a long talk. Brown had only narrowly won renomination, and facing an aggressive campaign by Ronald Reagan, could not afford to lose endorsements or Mexican-American support. The following day, he called his personal friend, Robert DiGiorgio, asking for cooperation with an investigation into the election by the American Arbitration Association.[42]

The Arbitration Association sent a top arbitrator, Ronald Haughton, who soon recommended that a new election should be held. Haughton and Sam Kagel, an arbitrator who had the confidence of the Teamsters, would officiate, with the election scheduled for late August. Any worker employed on the DiGiorgio ranch for fifteen days or more, starting the day before the strike, was declared eligible to vote. Although all of the unions and "no union" would be listed on the ballot, the Kern-Tulare IFWU promptly disappeared, leaving the runoff to the NFWA, the AWOC, and the Teamsters. The field workers would vote as a separate unit from the packingshed workers.

DiGiorgio accepted the ruling. The Corporation had relations with other AFL–CIO unions to preserve. The NFWA was also keeping up the boycott pressure, and rejecting the arbitration ruling would only give the cause more publicity. Trade brands, such as S & W, were highly vulnerable because they were visible, and retailers had to accept lower profit margins than on unadvertised brands. If the boycotters could get customers to buy an unadvertised brand, the retailer would make more money and the trade brand might permanently lose shelf space (R. Taylor 1975:194).

In the new election context, Kircher decided to make an open bid to merge the AWOC with the NFWA. There were several advantages for the AFL–CIO. The AWOC campaign clearly needed new leadership. Most of the workers were also Mexican. Because ethnicity was decisive in organizing, the union needed Mexican leadership. A merger would also simplify the upcoming DiGiorgio election. Kircher was also impressed by Chavez's imaginative use of protest tactics and the mix of Mexican culture with religious imagery to mobilize the workers. The Schenley contract convinced President Meany that the campaign might go somewhere.[43] Chavez, however, initially held back, afraid that affiliation would hinder his freedom of action. The NFWA clearly needed the AFL–CIO's financial backing, but Chavez had already seen how the AWOC could be ordered around.

The organizational advantages ultimately prevailed. By late June Chavez and Kircher had quietly worked out an agreement. The NFWA was to retain its autonomy yet enjoy extensive AFL–CIO support. Chavez would be in command with Itliong second. The NFWA staff would hold two-thirds of the spots on the council, reflecting their membership. The AFL–CIO would increase financial support to $150,000 per year, and Kircher's staff would be available for assistance. Although the membership was not consulted, the only opposition came from the student radicals who ideologically opposed any sell-out to the AFL–CIO and any limits on their experiment in participatory democracy.[44] To hold onto the volunteers, who were still needed to organize for the election, the merger was not announced until the week before the election. On August 22, the Executive Committee of the AFL–CIO finally passed the resolution, christening the new unit the United Farm Workers Organizing Committee (UFWOC).[45]

Many of the student volunteers felt betrayed. They had worked feverishly the entire summer contacting all the workers on the DiGiorgio employee list. Using $50,000 donated by the UAW and AFL–CIO, they wrote letters, made phone calls, and personally visited almost all the

159

workers on the list. In their eyes, the AFL–CIO was part of the "establishment" that had betrayed the Mississippi Freedom Democratic Party at the Democratic Party convention in 1964 and would now do the same to la causa. Many volunteers resigned in protest, charging Chavez and the NFWA leadership with "opportunism" (*New York Times*, August 24, 1966).

The election battle was intense. Both sides cranked out reams of leaflets, the NFWA distributing a "Family Portrait" album donated by the Communications Workers Union that contained portraits of Teamsters leaders with their reported gangster connections. The Teamsters "red baited" the NFWA and, pointing to the long hair and scrubby look of the student volunteers, claimed that "beatniks, out-of-town agitators and do-gooders" were running the NFWA. DiGiorgio even asked the California Senate's Fact-Finding Committee on Agriculture to investigate the NFWA as a "Communist front" but could not find anything. UFWOC handily won. Last minute efforts to bring in workers from afar, including several busloads from Mexico, paid off. The vote among the field workers was UFWOC 530, Teamsters 331. The Teamsters won the packingshed vote, 94 to 43. A few weeks later the UFWOC handily won the second DiGiorgio ranch near Arvin, 285 to 82 votes.[46]

Although the DiGiorgio contract was a major breakthrough, conquering a veteran opponent of farm unionism and offering better terms than the Schenley contract, DiGiorgio soon announced that it would sell the vineyards because of the ten-year rule on excess holdings under Bureau of Reclamation projects. There was no successor clause in the contract, giving the union only two years to use its new base (R. Taylor 1975:202–203).

The union immediately shifted the attack to the other wine growers. Early in the spring, the Christian Brothers Winery, owned by the Christian Brothers order, had indicated willingness to negotiate. Bishop Donohoe's endorsement and the boycott threat had softened the winery managers. As soon as the DiGiorgio election was over, the UFWOC asked for negotiations. The winery officials demanded a card check to prove worker support. Then suddenly the winery announced that an election would be necessary. The UFWOC, preoccupied with a new boycott against Perelli-Minetti, reluctantly agreed, and with the assistance of the State Mediation Service, the election was set for late February 1967. At the last minute Chavez decided to boycott the election, charging the winery officials with coercing workers to vote "no union." Leroy Chatfield, a former Christian Brother and a new cadre, met with Bishop Donohoe and Brother West, a Franciscan elder who promised help. The Catholic leaders threatened to boycott the Church's own winery if the election could not be held without anti-union pressure. On March 13, the UFWOC handily won another contract.[47]

After the DiGiorgio election, the UFWOC leaders had mistakenly thought that the rivalry with the Teamsters had been settled. The UFWOC struck the Perelli-Minetti vineyards on August 11. Previously the union had used the Perelli-Minetti vineyards to recycle pickets and had gained a solid base of support. At first Perelli-Minetti was willing to negotiate, but suddenly one morning a busload of strikebreakers passed through the main gate dropping papers out the windows. When one of the pickets retrieved one, he was shocked to find it was a copy of a contract between Perelli-Minetti and the Teamsters signed over the weekend. The UFWOC immediately mounted a nationwide boycott.[48]

The Perelli-Minetti boycott was important because it marked the first time that the union actually demonstrated the full potential of a boycott. The earlier contracts had come from negative publicity and threats to boycott firms with minimal investments in the vineyard and major investments in highly vulnerable trade labels. Perelli-Minetti was heavily committed to grape growing as well as to its premium wines and a special vermouth, marketed under the Tribuno label. Although the liquors were vulnerable, the Perelli family decided to hold out. The UFWOC organized a massive picketing campaign in Los Angeles, the firm's major market. Instead of student volunteers, farm workers would staff permanent boycott teams who would organize local coalitions of students, civil rights workers, and labor activists. With help from AFL–CIO unions, the boycotters infiltrated the Perelli-Minetti shipping system, sending picket teams to great arriving shipments and asking for "hot cargo" actions. Irwin DeShetler, Los Angeles regional director for the AFL–CIO, notified union locals to halt Perelli-Minetti shipments "even if you have to threaten them with a picket line, and etc."[49] Cases of Tribuno vermouth were mysteriously lost in the back rows of stockrooms, and shipments were misrouted. Union representatives notified shipping firms that shipments of scab products would endanger labor relations. Perelli-Minetti dumped its prize vermouth on the bulk market, so the UFWOC expanded the boycott to the bulk labels. In New York, union sympathizers organized picketing against Macy's, the giant department store, that had a sideline liquor business. The offending stock came off the shelves. Perelli-Minetti also produced a special kosher wine, so the pickets asked the rabbis who consecrated the wine to declare the wines unclean because they were produced with scab labor.

In February, 1967, the Perellis finally sued for peace, notifying UFWOC that the only barrier to a contract was the Teamster agreement. The UFWOC then asked Bishop Donohoe to intervene. After visiting Einar Mohn, the West coast Teamster regional director, Donohoe formed a committee of concerned bishops to oversee negotiations. After four months negotiations, they announced a jurisdictional settlement. The vineyard contract would go to the UFWOC, and the Teamsters jurisdiction would be limited to the truckers, canneries, packinghouses, and freezers. The UFWOC would hold exclusive claims to the field workers.[50]

The Perelli-Minetti boycott shook loose six more winery contracts. Card checks certified worker support for the UFWOC in the giant Gallo vineyards and the Almaden, Beringer, Franzia, Paul Masson, and Goldberg wineries, and the Novitiate of Los Gatos, another Catholic winery. The union had a toehold, eleven contracts covering around 5,000 workers, or about 2 percent of the state's farm labor force (R. Taylor 1975:204–206; *San Francisco Chronicle*, August 2, 1967; *California's AFLCIO News* August 11, 1967). Although the strikes had begun with support, they had eventually collapsed. The key leverage had come from boycotts. Sponsors had not only sustained the cadre and helped initiate negotiations, they also contributed decisively to the major disruptions.

The Great Grape Boycott

The UFWOC had not even signed the new wine grape contracts before it embarked on a new project: organizing strikes against the Delano table grape growers. The move signalled a return to the original base of supporters. The union still had a significant membership in the table grape industry. Although Kircher advised keeping up the wine boycotts until the rest had been signed up, Chavez and his lieutenants felt that the new contracts would make their organizing more effective. The contracts demonstrated what could be won and provided new organizing contacts. The move also signalled a commitment to use strikes as the major attack. This time, though, the target would be restricted to a single large ranch. This way the organizers could focus their energies and use neighboring ranches to recycle pickets.[51]

The logical target was the Giumarra vineyards, the largest of the Delano table grape growers, with 12,000 acres and a permanent crew of 200 ranging to a harvest force of 2,000. "If we can crack Guimarra," declared Dolores Huerta, "we can crack them all" (Meister and Loftis 1977:151). The union also had a base in the Giumarra vineyards, having used it to recycle pickets during the original grape strike. By late July the UFWOC was holding rallies and proselytizing. With a majority of the Giumarra workers signed up, Chavez asked for negotiations. When the predictable refusal came, the union called a strike meeting and, on August 3, pulled out around two-thirds of the 1,200 workers.[52] Giumarra enticed local workers with a wage premium and brought in truckloads of day-haul workers from Los Angeles. Shortly thereafter, several contractors returned with migrants from south Texas and green carders and illegals from Mexico. Giumarra also got crippling injunctions that barred bullhorns, limited picket teams to five, and required that they remain fifty feet apart. Even with the new wine contracts, the UFWOC still could not halt the strikebreaking.[53]

The union had little choice but to rekindle the boycott. The Migrant Ministry's student volunteer project was in its second year. Fred Ross, who had been lured out of retirement to become Director of Organizations for the union, gave the students a week's hasty training before assigning them to the cities where the wine boycott had been the most effective. Unlike the earlier teams of SNCC and CORE organizers, these volunteers were less experienced, and throughout the fall of 1967, the boycott had little effect. In October, Ross moved to New York to reorganize the eastern boycott effort. Although committed, the students had little experience, and many resigned. The average volunteer lasted less than six months (R. Taylor 1975:218; Meister and Loftis 1977:151–152). Ross decided that he needed loyal farm workers. Chavez selected fifteen of the most ardent picket leaders and sent them and their families to New York. Within a month, Ross had the boycott houses in New York, Boston, and Philadelphia reorganized, putting the farm workers in charge. The farm workers lent the boycott greater credibility and determination. Still the boycott had major problems. Table grapes were labeled only on their shipping boxes, making it difficult to identify scab shipments. Giumarra also began shipping under other labels, borrowing over 150 labels from other grape growers. Most important, the boycott relied on consumers rather than hot cargo actions by labor sympathizers.[54]

Over the winter of 1968, the cadre debated a new strategy. Previously, they had treated boycotts as a backup measure for strikes. But the failure of the Giumarra strike suggested that even with extensive preparations, strong initial support, and a vulnerable target, the workers were too disorganized and impoverished to support a prolonged strike. If worker support was insufficient, then they would have to organize boycotts. This would require a major change in strategies. Although the union would still use house meetings, service programs, and solidarity events to organize workers, the major mobilizing focus would now be the political allies. Dramatic protests designed to secure third party support would become central. Although the union would still conduct strikes, the major disruptive force would now come from enlisting these third party supporters behind boycotts.

The decision was not reached easily. Saul Alinsky counselled that a boycott of table grapes would have to be nationwide, and Kircher argued that unlike the wines, table grapes were poorly marked and the distribution network too diffuse (R. Taylor 1975:221–223). Although symbolic actions like the March on Sacramento and the Boston Grape Party had threatened the liquor industry with its sensitivity to negative publicity and small investments in the vineyards, the table grape growers were less vulnerable and also more resistant. The grapes were difficult to target, and the growers were heavily dependent on cheap labor. Moreover, unlike the liquor industry, they had no past experience with unions. A boycott would have to close them out of the markets. This would also be more difficult than in the Perelli-Minetti boycott, where the liquor store owners simply filled in shelf space with a substitute. The grocers would have to pull the product entirely. Eventually this would require a secondary boycott against the grocery chains. The major positive factor was the luxury status of table grapes. Grape consumers were in a higher income bracket and more willing to forego a luxury for a moral cause. The price structure was also inelastic, meaning that price cutting would not elicit increased sales. Giumarra also simplified the problem of a target by using multiple shipping labels. The UFWOC claimed that all of the table grape growers were now implicated and promptly called strikes throughout the rest of the industry, even though work was at a seasonal lull and many of the ranches had not actually been organized. When the growers refused to negotiate, the boycott was extended to all California table grapes.[55]

The union faced three major problems. After seven months of unsuccessful strikes and boycotts, morale had collapsed among the cadre and loyal supporters. There was talk of defying Chavez's leadership, especially on the issue of nonviolence. Chavez had early adopted the position that nonviolence was a moral and strategic imperative. Borrowing from Ghandi and the early civil rights leaders, he argued that nonviolence was morally superior. It was also strategically imperative. The growers and local police could crush the movement at any moment. Violence would also alienate many of the sponsors, whose support was essential. Although the nonviolent philosophy had its limits, barring attacks on persons while allowing property violence, it was a significant restriction. The emergence of the brown power movement encouraged several militants to challenge this approach. The union was also organizing a new group of workers who were less reluctant to use force. The table grape workers were more likely to be younger migrants. Third, the boycott needed an event comparable to the March on Washington and the Selma marches of the civil rights movement that would galvanize attention and thrust the movement into the national limelight.

Chavez addressed all three problems by going on a twenty-five-day fast. On February 15, he quietly retreated to a shed on the union's new headquarters at the Forty Acres east of Delano and began to fast, explaining that it was penitence for the dissension and talk of violence in the union. The fast created a powerful image of a dedicated, saintly martyr sacrificing for the workers. Although some opposed the fast, especially the student radicals and members who took offense at the religious imagery, the priest volunteers quickly organized nightly masses around the fast, using it to build a new base of worker support. The older workers and their families, who were more likely to be practicing Catholics, were the most responsive, and gradually its effectiveness won over initial opponents (R. Taylor 1975:223–225; Levy 1975:272–293).

The fast also became a mass media event, capturing national political attention. Eleven days into the fast, Giumarra inadvertently gave the event publicity by asking a local judge to haul Chavez into court to face contempt charges for defying an injunction on picket activity the previous fall. When Chavez arrived at the courthouse weak and disheveled by fasting, the 200-yard walkway to the courthouse was lined with row after row of silent kneeling farm workers. News reporters and cameramen thronged the courthouse steps. Chavez was too weak for a protracted court appearance, and as sooon as the story hit the national news wires, the Giumarra attorneys quietly urged the judge to dismiss the charges because of the adverse publicity.[56]

Meanwhile Chavez's aides petitioned Robert Kennedy to attend the mass at which Chavez would end the fast. Kennedy was about to announce his entry into the Democratic primaries against President Johnson and needed the support of Mexican-Americans and middle class liberal voters. Finally he agreed. On March 11, 1968, flanked by the news media and over 4,000 workers gathered in Delano's public park, Chavez broke his fast by joining Kennedy in a mass administered by Chris Hartmire. James Drake read the note of thanks that Chavez had written earlier but was too weak to deliver personally:

Our struggle is not easy. Those who oppose us are rich and powerful, and they have many allies in high places. We are poor. Our allies are few. But we have something the rich do not own. We have our own bodies and spirits and the justice of our case as our weapons. When we are really honest with ourselves, we must admit that our lives are all that really belong to us. So it is how we use our lives that determines what kind of men we are. It is my deepest belief that only by giving our lives do we find life. I am convinced that the truest act of courage, the strongest act of manliness is to sacrifice for others in a totally nonviolent struggle for justice. To be a man is to suffer for others. God help us to be men! (Cited in Levy 1975:286; R. Taylor 1975:223–225)

While Chavez was being loaded into a station wagon, the workers crowded around shaking hands with the famous visitor.

The events consolidated an important political alliance. Kennedy was attempting to unseat Johnson by appealing to minorities, the poor, and middle class liberals disaffected by the Vietnam war. A critical electoral base was the growing Mexican-American vote in the southwest. Chavez was also willing to reciprocate, serving as a Kennedy delegate to the Democratic National Convention and hitting the campaign trail over the spring in a "Viva Kennedy" effort in the Los Angeles and San Diego barrios that provided the electoral margin for Kennedy's critical victory in the California primary (Chester et al. 1969:112–115). Until an assassin's bullet cut down the hope, la causa had the promise of a presidential ally.

From late spring through early summer, the union rebuilt the boycott. Because a simple extension of existing labor legislation would prohibit the secondary boycotts, Chavez announced that the union wanted separate legislation for farm workers. The leadership of the AFL–CIO and the Campaign for Agricultural Democracy, a committee of prominent liberals and labor leaders set up to support labor legislation, were caught by surprise.[57] Assisted by Fred Ross, Chavez took personal charge of the boycott, training hundreds of loyal farm workers to restaff the boycott centers. Twenty major cities representing two-thirds of the national table grape market were targeted. Each team received a list of local contacts assembled from past boycotts and suggestions by the national AFL–CIO and the Migrant Ministry. Chavez contacted the national offices of minority organizations like MAPA, the GI Forum, and the NAACP and liberal civic associations like the Consumers League and the Urban League, asking for endorsements. The teams then used these contacts to solicit local boycott committees, using house meetings to organize endorsements, donations for the boycott house, and volunteer pickets. The support coalition was a familiar cast: labor leaders, ministers, civil rights activists, and radical students. The support was overwhelming. Union locals as well as international offices assessed their members for contributions and picket duty. Sympathetic ministers, priests, and nuns donated office space and joined the boycott teams. Chapters of student organizations adopted the boycott as a special project. As Chavez outlined the division of sponsorship: "I go to unions for publicity and money; to the Church for respectability; to students for bodies."[58]

The boycott enlisted three kinds of outside supporters: full-time cadres who lived in the boycott houses and worked 80–100 hours a week for the standard subsistence plus $5 per week; transitory teams of part-time volunteers who donated a few hours a week; and institutional supporters who diverted resources at their disposal to the effort. Cadres were predominantly radical students plus an occasional minister, priest, or nun. The part-time volunteers were the most numerous and diverse. Any sympathizer with discretionary time became a potential volunteer. In many ways, the brilliance of the boycott was its integration of thousands of part-time volunteers who no longer had to take a vow of poverty and leave school, their jobs, and families to support la causa. All they had to do was spend an evening a week checking grocery stores, phoning donors, or joining a weekend picket parade. The institutional supporters acted in their roles as church executives, union officials, and leaders of established political associations by endorsing the boycott, allocating spare buildings as office space, offering political advice, and soliciting their members and political allies for donations.

At first, the boycott teams tried a primary boycott against grapes and hot cargo actions by sympathetic unionists. Informants inside the transport industry kept the union posted on grape shipments. Nervous brokers refused shipments, afraid to jeopardize their relations with local unions. Whole shipments were mysteriously damaged by accident. Sympathetic Teamsters lost the loading orders. Warehousemen misplaced fruit, burying it deep in the back rows, where it sat for days before suddenly being discovered. If shipments made it to the grocery stores, the pickets contacted the manager, asking that he pull the scab grapes and substitute another fruit. Sympathetic members of the Butcher Workmens Union or the Retail Clerks walked out on sympathy strike. Then the serious picketing began, anywhere from three to forty pickets marching across the store entrance asking consumers to shun table grapes.

Soon the boycott turned into a secondary boycott against the grocery chains. Few of the chains pulled the grapes, and the most effective leverage was simply to cut off their trade. The lost grape sales paled against the loss of customers. Mass picket lines were organized to meet the prime Saturday morning traffic. A group of students with a cleric wearing a collar would mass around a store entrance, waving placards and chanting, cutting off access. One could see the customers approach the picket line, ducking their heads or simply pausing, uncertain whether to brave the picket line or return to their cars. Some would simply stand in amazement, watching the procession of priests, housewives, and students parading across the store entrance. The store manager would emerge, red-faced and shouting at the pickets. Soon the police would arrive and order the pickets out on the sidewalks or arrest them. Many of the grocery chains secured court injunctions against mass picketing, claiming their parking lots as private property. John Birch Society chapters organized counterdemonstrations.

Another tactic was the "shop-in," which had two variants. A respectable-looking housewife entered the store, filled her basket, and then suddenly discovered that these were scab grapes. She demanded to see the manager. How could he put scab grapes on the shelves when some farm worker's children were starving? The drama soon became the center of attention. With the eyes of checkers and customers riveted on the front of the store, the housewife lectured the grocer and then triumphantly marched from the store with children in tow. Meanwhile mounds of ice cream and frozen pics were melting on the counter. Other customers decided that they too should go elsewhere. A rougher version entailed boycott teams filling baskets with expensive frozen foods, mashing grapes and peaches underneath cans, and then abandoning the baskets in the back corner of the store. Several hours later the manager received an anonymous phone call, alerting him to the dripping baskets and recommending that he get nonunion grapes off the shelves.[59] Once the grapes were off in a particular store, the agreement had to be policed. No grocer could be counted on to honor the agreement. So store checkers had to spend several hours a day driving around, checking the shelves. Any infractions had to be followed up, if necessary, with another round of picketing, demonstrations, and shop-ins.

The boycott was more effective in cities where the grocery industry was more concentrated and labor unions were strong supporters. Initially the boycotters focused on the small chains and independents, thinking that they would be more vulnerable. But the smaller stores had greater consumer loyalty and, more important, did not sell many grapes. The larger national chains in the major metropolitan areas provided a more centralized and vulnerable target. As a rule of thumb, it took three months of picketing to force a chain to pull grapes. It was obviously more effective to picket a large chain which handled, say, a quarter of local grape sales than a small store that represented less than one percent. The concentration of over half of total grape sales in ten metropolitan areas and two-thirds of grocery sales in a handful of large chains made the task easier (Brown 1972:165–175).

The boycott was also strengthened by the support of local unions, especially those in the transport and grocery industries who provided information on shipments and hot cargo actions. The comparison between New York and Los Angeles highlights the difference. In New York, Dolores Huerta took charge in April 1968 and persuaded the New York Labor Council to endorse the boycott. From early June through mid-July, the Seafarers Union cut off all shipments through the New York port. Over 418 carlots of grapes, or roughly $500,000 worth, were lost. Although the Coachella Growers Association secured an injunction in late July, Teamster warehousemen and porters quietly diverted tons of grape shipments. Meanwhile the pickets attacked A & P, the largest chain and one reputed to be in financial straits. Teamsters, Butchers, and Retail

Clerks went on sympathy strikes, and within a month A & P sued for peace. Institutional buyers such as universities, churches, and government cafeterias boycotted grocery wholesalers who handled scab grapes. By January 1969, the New York market was largely cleared, grape sales cut by over thirty percent. Los Angeles, in contrast, was an "open shop" and politically conservative city. The Butchers and Retail Clerks Unions were too weak for "hot cargo" actions, and the major target, the Safeway chain, depended on California fruits and vegetables. Safeway obtained an injunction against mass picketing at the store entrance, forcing the pickets to resort to a simple consumer boycott, passing out leaflets and marching on the sidewalks. Grocery sales were highly concentrated, but the boycott only cut grape sales by around sixteen percent.[60]

By the end of the 1968 season, the boycott was showing its teth. Retail grape sales were down by twelve percent nationally and by over half in major cities like New York, Boston, and Baltimore. An estimated $3–4 million of grapes rotted on the vines for want of a market outlet, and prices plummeted as wholesalers had to dump shipments in new markets.[61] The growers organized a countercampaign. The California Farm Bureau and Safeway hired Whitaker and Baxter, a Los Angeles public relations firm with conservative ties, to promote grape sales with "Eat California Grapes, the Forbidden Fruit!" bumper stickers and newspaper ads trumpeting the health benefits of grape consumption. The Delano growers created an Agricultural Workers Freedom to Work Association, which sent Jose Mendoza, a former shoe salesman, on a speaking tour, claiming that: "What Chavez espouses is as Un-American as Karl Marx. . . . The Chavez movement is a fraud!" (Meister and Loftis 1977:160). Under instructions from the newly installed Nixon administration, the Department of Defense multiplied its grape purchases by five, and conservative politicians such as California's Senator George Murphy and Governor Ronald Reagan endorsed grape consumption and called for legislation to block the boycott (Meister and Loftis 1977:160–161).

In preparation for the 1969 season, the UFWOC renewed the strikes, extending them into Arizona and the Imperial Valley. In June, Chavez led a mass march on the Coachella and Imperial Valleys, marching to Calexico to turn back illegal and green card immigrants and dramatize the role that they played in breaking strikes. Jerry Cohen, the Union's head attorney and a former lawyer for the California Rural Legal Assistance Project, filed suits against the Delano growers, the Immigration and Naturalization Service, and the Farm Labor Service for promoting illegal immigration. The union also linked the boycott to increasing public concerns about the environment and the use of pesticides by filing suits against the growers for using DDT and Aldrin, claiming that these endangered the workers and were a public health threat (Meister and Loftis 1977:158).

The growers were under serious pressure. Ten percent of the 1968 crop was still in cold storage, and eastern wholesalers refused to handle shipments. On June 12, 1969, halfway through the Coachella harvest, ten growers announced they would open negotiations with the union. The Nixon administration ordered the Federal Mediation and Conciliation Service to oversee the talks, but after three weeks of tense negotiations, the talks collapsed, in large part because the union demanded controls over pesticides as well as a union-controlled hiring hall and significant wage hikes and benefits. The union leaders feared a partial settlement would weaken the boycott pressure against the rest of the growers and decided to bargain tough (R. Taylor 1975:240–244; Meister and Loftis 1977:160–161).

Over the summer and fall, the boycott teams intensified the pressure and, by the end of the 1969 season, shipments were down by over a third. Wholesale prices dropped below production costs, and fruit dealers refused to cite prices in advance, accepting grapes only on consignment.[62] In February 1970, forty Coachella growers finally asked for negotiations. After two months of negotiation overseen by the National Catholic Conference, the negotiators announced an agreement. One grower, Keene Larson, demanded an election to prove worker support, which the UFWOC handily won 152–2, and the rest signed contracts providing for a 25-cent raise, a union hiring hall, grievance procedures through a local ranch committee elected by the workers, limits on pesticide use, rehiring of strikers, contributions to the union's health fund, and a successor clause (Meister and Loftis 1977:162).

The Coachella grapes protected by the union's "black bug" sold off immediately, putting pressure on the Delano growers. Safeway and Bank of America, both with major ties to the industry, quietly advised the growers to settle, and three smaller Delano growers signed. The union tightened the boycott. Finally, on July 15, 1970, the twenty-six Delano growers representing half of the state's table grape crop and over 8,000 jobs agreed to sit down at the bargaining table. At the last minute, they

171

announced they would negotiate only if the boycott was called off, Governor Reagan suddenly offered to hold state-supervised elections. But the UFWOC had no need for half offers. Within a week the growers were back at the table, accepting the same terms as the Coachella growers. As one of the hold-outs explained: "I gotta have that black bug." Dolores Huerta, negotiating for the union, toughened the negotiation stance by bringing workers into the negotiating room to approve or reject terms and back up her demands for concessions. Several growers walked out in protest but soon returned. The final demand was the toughest. The contracts would be signed in the union headquarters on the Forty Acres on the east edge of town. The growers swallowed and finally conceded (Taylor 1975:248).

At 11 A.M. on July 29, 1970, the twenty-six Delano growers quietly filed into the union's new hiring hall. The workers surrounded the building, singing "Nostros venceremos, nostros venceremos . . . we shall overcome, we shall overcome" broken by "Viva la huelga! Viva la Virgien de Guadalupe! Viva Cesar Chavez!" Chavez, wearing a Mexican wedding shirt, emerged into the morning sunlight, smiled, help up his hand with a V-sign and offered one word: "Victory." Johnny Giumarra, the key negotiator for the growers, put his signature on the contract, looked up into the news cameras, and proclaimed it a "new era" and "an experiment in social justice." Chavez merely grinned, "From now on, all grapes will be sweet" (R. Taylor 1975:242–249; Matthiessen 1969:331). Delano had fallen. The union now held a base from which to mobilize further insurgency. With over 150 grape contracts, 10,000 members, and control over nearly 20,000 jobs, the union finally appeared on the edge of a sustained insurgency.

A Sustained Challenge

The UFWOC held the promise of a sustained challenge. With over 10,000 members and 150 contracts, the union had sufficient support to weather most obstacles. At the minimum, the growers could no longer ignore the forces for change. What had led to this turn of events?

The UFWOC enjoyed a more favorable organizing environment as well as using a more effective mobilization strategy. As we saw in chapter 4, the changes in the labor market—less migrancy, greater specialized work, fewer permanent hands, and less ethnic diversity as well as the end of the bracero program—made it easier to mobilize farm workers. The cadre also adopted an effective mobilization strategy using solidarity events like festivals and religious symbolism and benefit programs to sustain support. Professional organizers made long-term commitments, used bloc recruitment, and trained indigenous leaders, thereby insuring a more rapid and durable mobilization. Although Chavez's original plan had been to invest a decade in preparatory organizing, the AWOC strikes pushed up the time schedule considerably. It is impossible to be certain, but it seems plausible that had the original schedule been adhered to, the association would have been able to organize more effective and perhaps successful strikes. In any case, the UFW clearly had a better base of farm worker support. The UFW was also extremely adept at mobilizing external support, using protest tactics, and building political alliances with liberal politicians and reform organizations. Yet despite these advantages, the union still could not conduct effective strikes. Because of the fluidity in the labor market, there were potentially 100,000 to 150,000 workers available for any particular firm. The union either had to organize mass strikes or, like the strikers in the 1930s, use coercion. Violence, of course, would have alienated its sponsors, provoked official repression, and probably destroyed the challenge. The boycott allowed the union to sidestep this problem, organizing disruptions in the metropolitan fruit markets. Significantly, the boycott also reduced the costs to the workers, making support easier.

Without sustained sponsorship, the challenge could not have developed beyond the initial association of 1,000 farm workers. The early support of the Migrant Ministry, AFL–CIO, UAW, student radicals, and civil rights activists provided subsistence support for the cadre, basic organizing resources like loudspeakers, cars, and mimeograph machines, invaluable tactical advice, and political contacts that kept the insurgency alive. These developments, in turn, were linked to the economic affluence and favorable political alignments of the 1960s.[63] Economic prosperity increased the discretionary resources and staff autonomy of social service organizations like the National Council of Churches and the Catholic Campaign for Human Development. Staff who were committed to experimental projects in solving social problems eventually brought their organizations behind the challenge. The Democratic reign of the mid-1960s also strengthened the political influence of these sponsors and their potential gains from sponsoring a new challenger. The Democrats eliminated the bracero program and created expanding budgets for social programs like poverty law and citizenship training on which the insurgents could draw. The Democratic reign also meant that the challenge would not dissolve under another wave of official repression. Political contenders like Robert Kennedy and George McGovern, pursuing the votes of minorities and middle class liberals, endorsed the boycott and publicly attacked police violence and harassment. Successful challengers like those in the civil rights movement furnished models of effective tactics and created a fall-out of trained cadres on which the new challenge could draw.

Yet, as we will see, even this combination of favorable conditions could not guarantee that the UFWOC itself would be the agency that would institutionalize gains for farm workers.

7

La Causa on Trial: Counterattack and Renewal (1970–1980)

A UNION OF OUR OWN

use this quote in the beginning

There's so much power in this land
Resting in the growers' hands.
Why should woman, child, or man,
Bend their back to work the land,
To fill your table everyday
And go home hungry anyway?

We've lived our lives as rented slaves,
Worked us into early graves,
But that's over now.
We've built a union of our own!

Built it with our blood and bone.
We've nurtured it and watched it grow.
And we don't need no Einar Mohn
To tear it down and tell us "no."

The UFWOC was on the brink of a sustained challenge when
it was suddenly rocked by a threat to its very existence. On the day
before the historic meeting in Delano, 170 lettuce and vegetable growers in the Salinas and Santa Maria Valleys signed sweetheart contracts
with the Teamsters union. Although the lettuce growers were ready to
concede the inevitability of unionization, there was a vast difference between the UFWOC and Teamster contracts. The Teamsters provided only
wage gains and medical benefits that, as soon as the UFWOC threat was

175

defeated, would be rescinded, leaving the workers covered by a paper union. In contrast, the UFWOC contracts made for lasting gains and expanding insurgency. The key was the ranch committees elected by the workers to negotiate contracts and grievances. The committees provided a grass-roots base that could mobilize continued pressure. They also served as training schools, recruiting new organizers and generating an insurgent consciousness among the rank-and-file. The UFWOC also used seniority and "good standing" rules to mobilize pickets and collected contributions to the Robert F. Kennedy Educational Fund for further organizing.

The UFWOC was quite vulnerable to a union substitution attack. The boycotts depended on external support which the Teamster contracts would weaken. Moreover, the union's support among the workers was uncertain. Many were new to the union, having been strikebreakers before the contracts. Nor was it clear that the new contracts would suddenly make strikes effective. The problem of farm worker powerlessness still existed and the growers still had solid support from local police and courts. Although the UFWOC still enjoyed strong sponsorship, this support would wane in the early 1970s, especially among organized labor. National political alignments also shifted steadily in a conservative direction, forcing the union to rely increasingly on political allies within California. In this context, organizing farm workers for effective strikes became decisive in the bid to renew the challenge.

Los Teamsters and the Grower Counterattack

The grower move forced the UFWOC to shift immediately to the Salinas and Santa Maria Valleys, organizing mass strikes in a bid to break the Teamster contracts. The Salinas Valley, known as "America's Salad Bowl," was a hundred square mile area containing 70 percent of the nation's iceberg lettuce and most of the strawberries, broccoli, tomatoes, cauliflower, carrots, artichokes, and celery grown in California. Over 50,000 workers were involved in these crops, generally in large crews of 100 or more. Ecological concentration facilitated organizing, yet most of the workers were migrants and would be less attracted to benefit programs and community events. Although the lettuce workers were specialized, organized in cohesive crews and highly committed to their jobs, the other vegetable workers were mostly unspecialized migrants, frequently illegal immigrants from Mexico. Like the Filipino grape workers, the lettuce workers would support militant strikes, especially if abused by the growers, but without strong community ties they would not support sustained strikes. They were also less receptive to the benefit programs and ethnic appeals, the UFWOC's distinctive organizing incentives. As for the vegetable workers, they often lacked community and job commitments, and many were vulnerable to deportation.

The Santa Maria Valley was largely devoted to vegetable farming and was worked by about 4,000 to 5,000 unspecialized Mexican-Americans who lived in the small towns and barrios along the coast. Although they had strong ethnic and community ties, few were specialized or worked more than sporadically in the fields. Their weak job commitments and ecological dispersion would make them difficult to organize.

Although Chavez had originally planned to move into the citrus groves, the UFWOC had made preliminary organizing forays among the lettuce and vegetable workers. In 1967, Manuel Chavez began working out of the new farm worker service center in Mexicali, organizing wage strikes among the lettuce and cantaloupe workers who migrated from the Imperial Valley to Arizona, and then to Salinas in the spring. The next spring, Gil Padilla began organizing the local workers in the coastal valley region by holding house meetings to create a base similar to the original NFWA. The lettuce workers were the most receptive, and as early as the winter of 1968, they sent a delegation to Delano, asking support for a strike. Because of the grape boycott, Chavez asked them to hold off until the grape workers had been organized, promising to return as soon as the grape contracts were signed. In the spring of 1970, the lettuce workers again sent delegations to Delano, arguing that their turn was next now that the grape contracts were coming in. After a Cinco de Mayo rally in Delano, Chavez forwarded a letter to the Western Growers Association in Salinas, demanding they open negotiations (R. Taylor 1975:252–254).

The growers responded immediately by meeting secretly with the Teamsters union to negotiate sweetheart contracts. They were determined to block the union, and since Bud Antle had demonstrated the advantages of a Teamster contract, they decided Teamster contracts were better than battling the Chavistas. The Teamster's stake remained the same. They wanted to protect their contracts on the truckers and packingshed workers as well as the field contract on the Bud Antle ranch.

The emerging leadership battle inside the Teamsters Union also contributed. Frank Fitzsimmons, hand-picked by Jimmy Hoffa as his successor, and Hoffa, newly released from prison on a Presidential pardon, were battling for the Presidency. Einar Mohn, Director of the Western Conference, was a Fitzsimmons ally, vying with William Grami, the ambitious Director of Organizations for the Conference and a Hoffa ally who saw the move into farm worker contracts as an opportunity to seize the directorship (Levy 1975:355; Walsh 1981). In early July, the Teamsters called a truckers strike, partially to cover their new actions, declaring that the truckers refused to return to work unless the contracts were extended to the field workers. On July 26, the growers hastily signed contracts, leaving all terms "to be filled in later" (*San Francisco Chronicle*, July 30, 1970).

Chavez immediately criticized the "Pearl Harbor type of sneak attack . . . an act of treason against the legitimate aspirations of farm workers" and declared "all-out war between the Chicanos and Filipinos together against the Teamsters and the bosses" (cited Meister and Loftis 1977:168). The UFWOC immediately moved the union headquarters to Salinas, and by August 1, Chavez was leading marches through Watsonville, holding rallies in Salinas and Hollister, and organizing strikes against the Teamster-grower alliance. Boycott teams were ordered to return immediately to Salinas. Meanwhile, the Teamsters sent organizing teams out into the field to sign up workers and began collecting the $1.50 dues from weekly paychecks. Although the Teamster contracts provided wage gains of 10 to 50 cents an hour, they provided no grievance procedures, restrictions on hiring policies or the use of labor contractors and pesticides (R. Taylor 1975:254–259; Meister and Loftis 1977:167). The workers were outraged, especially by the forced dues collection and the lack of consultation, and rallied around the UFWOC strike call. Over 1,000 workers at the giant Freshpict farm refused to sign the Teamster authorization cards and marched out on strike. The next day the UFWOC filed suit against the two largest lettuce growers—Interharvest and Bruce Church—charging conspiracy and threatening to boycott the most vulnerable lettuce firms—Interharvest, which was a subsidiary of United Brands, owner of Chiquita bananas; Freshpict, a subsidiary of Purex Corporation; and Pic N Pak, a strawberry subsidiary of Dole.[1] The Western Growers Association, supported by Freshpict, secured an injunction against the picketing and threatened boycott, charging that the dispute was simply a jurisdictional dispute. Certain of worker support, Chavez decided to defy the injunction, calling new strikes and planning to use the arrests to publicize the Teamster raid (R. Taylor 1975:260).

Meanwhile the Teamsters were under pressure to rescind the contracts. They had just formed a national Alliance for Labor Action with the United Auto Workers, who pressed the Teamster leaders to withdraw. At the same time, the AFL–CIO intervened, asking for negotiations. After two weeks of negotiations supervised by the Catholic Bishops Committee, the Teamsters and UFWOC announced a truce, reiterating the 1967 jurisdictional agreement (Meister and Loftis 1977:168). But then the growers refused to give up the Teamster contracts, threatening to sue if they backed out. "If we could get the Teamster contract from Chavez," announced Herbert Fleming, President of the Western Growers Association, "then maybe in the long run Chavez would have to shape up and act like a businessman and it would work out. But as of now, we growers here are ready to fight to protect our workers from intimidation and our rights as farmers. We have the proper and legal contracts with the Teamsters Union; the Teamsters have assured us they will honor these contracts and we intend to do the same (*Salinas Californian*, August 9, 1970).

On August 14, Interharvest, worried that the threatened boycott of Chiquita bananas would destroy their lucrative trade label, asked for a recission. At first, William Grami refused, stating that he could not sign the recission, but finally Einar Mohn stepped in. The UFWOC promptly called off the boycott and, following a card check, signed a new contract covering 2,000 workers with a base pay of $2 an hour, paid vacations, health and welfare benefits, and a hiring hall that included the ranch foremen.[2] The growers retaliated, organizing a counterpicket that carried American flags and signs proclaiming themselves to be "Citizens Against United" and "Citizens Committee for Agriculture" and closed off the Interharvest packingsheds until a week later, when a local judge issued an injunction. Shortly afterwards, Freshpict sued Interharvest for violating an agreement that the growers would honor the contracts unless they unanimously agreed to rescind them (*Salinas Californian*, August 13 and 15, 1970).

The UFWOC called strikes against Freshpict and Pic N Pak, and the workers responded enthusiastically, over 5,000 marching out on 150 farms. Over the next two weeks the strike continued to build, and by the end of August, the Salinas and Santa Maria Valleys were in turmoil, with over 10,000 workers on strike. Grami imported Teamster guards, large burly men weighing over 200 pounds armed with shotguns, billy sticks, and chains, who attacked the pickets. Later, "Speedy" Gonsalvez, the business agent for a nearby Teamster local who directed the guards and toured the strike zone in an armored black limousine wearing a black suit with white tie and carrying a violin case rumored to contain a machine gun, was removed from office for stealing $25,000 in union funds to hire the guards.[3] Several guards were also jailed for extorting $12,000 in "expenses" from several growers for their services.[4] The UFWOC replied in kind, intensifying the picketing, manhandling several of the Teamster organizers, and calling a strike on the Antle ranch. William Kircher, a veteran of Teamster raids on the east coast, called on the Seafarers Union, who sent fifty seamen to serve as guards for the UFWOC and, in one case, narrowly escaped a beating by Gonsalvez's crew at an ambush set up by a grower claiming that he wanted secret negotiations.[5] The valleys seethed in turmoil as roving pickets toured the backroads, attacking teamster organizers and blocking growers from bringing in strikebreakers. Lawmen and Teamster guards battled the pickets, putting several in the hospital and shooting three. The UFWOC office in Watsonville was bombed. On August 24, Jerry Cohen, the UFWOC's head lawyer, was attacked by Teamster guards and beaten unconscious when he tried to enter a struck ranch to help workers remove their personal possessions from a bunkhouse.[6]

Despite the violence and over thirty injunctions against the picketing, the strike was remarkably effective. Unable to delay the harvest of their highly perishable vegetables, the growers lost an estimated $500,000 per day. Produce shipments were cut from 200 railway carloads per day to fewer than 75.[7] The growers secured more injunctions against picketing and the boycott, but the UFWOC kept up the pressure. Freshpict, threatened by the Purex boycott, sued for peace, accepting the Interharvest contract terms and shortly afterwards was joined by Pic N Pak and three locally owned vegetable growers crippled by the strike (R. Taylor 1975:259–260). For the first time, the union was making gains on the basis of strikes. But it was also running out of money despite union contributions and a $150,000 loan from the Franciscan Brotherhood, using over $100,000 per week to pay $25 per week strike benefits to each picket. The growers again went to court, after the California Supreme Court lifted the original injunctions on the ground that Judge Brazil had listened only to the testimony of the growers, and on October 15, secured a new injunction, cutting the picket lines to one informational picket at only twenty-two of the Salinas farms and barring all boycott actions (*Salinas Californian*, October 16, 1970). With strike funds exhausted and the workers beginning to sneak back into the fields, the UFWOC decided to comply with this injunction and called off the pickets, after nailing down another contract with Mann and Hill Packing Company.

The UFWOC immediately announced a boycott against Antle, using Antle's financial ties to Dow Chemical, then a target of antiwar organizers, to publicize the boycott. Antle sought another injunction, claiming that the UFWOC was violating the California Jurisdictional Act because of the standing Teamster contract. The UFWOC reinstated the picket lines, and on December 4, Judge Campbell ordered Chavez to appear to show cause why he and the union should not be held in contempt. The Antle lawyers realized the trap too late. On December 4, over 3,000 farm workers marched with Chavez to the Monterey County courthouse, ringing the courthouse and kneeling in the hallways. After three hours of hearings, the Antle lawyers suggested the judge merely fine the union. But Chavez's refusal to call off the boycott infuriated the judge, and he ordered Chavez jailed. As he was being hauled away, Chavez shouted triumphantly: "Boycott the hell out of them" (Levy 1975:425–429; R. Taylor 1975:260). The UFWOC then organized round the clock prayer vigils and highly publicized demonstrations outside the jail. Ethel Kennedy and Coretta King made special visits, bringing additional notoriety to the boycott. On December 23, Judge Campbell finally decided to release Chavez pending the outcome of the UFWOC appeal (*New York Times*, December 24, 1970).

Meanwhile the union trained new boycott teams to be sent to sixty-four cities. The grape boycotters had been called home in early August, and in recognition of their sacrifices, the 150 grape workers were allowed to go back to work. New teams drawn from the lettuce workers had to be trained, and because the lettuce workers were not as committed, the boycott did not really get underway until the winter of 1971. Then came a series of Teamster negotiations that cut into the boycott's effectiveness. On March 26, 1971, the Teamsters and the UFWOC signed another jurisdictional agreement, countersigned by George Meany and Frank Fitzsimmons, in which the Teamsters pledged to withdraw from their contracts, placing dues in escrow and pressing the growers to accept the UFWOC contracts. In exchange, the UFWOC promised to call a moratorium on the boycott that was hurting the Teamster truck drivers and warehousemen as well as the growers (Meister and Loftis 1977:172). But only one grower switched and the Western Growers Association announced that its members would honor the Teamster contracts. The head of the Salinas Teamster local challenged anyone to "arbitrate away our contracts." Although the growers reopened negotiations on May 7, it soon became clear that they were only attempting to defuse the boycott. Despite UFWOC offers to drop pesticide clauses and accept lower wage demands, the growers would not agree to terms. In November, the growers finished the harvest and withdrew, and the UFW resumed the lettuce boycott (R. Taylor 1975:262–263; Meister and Loftis 1977:172).

Although the union finally rebuilt the boycott organization, the lettuce action was never as effective as the great grape boycott. The most important factor was the loss of labor support. Because of the Teamsters' control over transportation, they had significant influence over other unions, making or breaking their strikes by hot cargo actions (Romer 1961:223–230). The Teamster truckers and warehousemen refused to support the UFWOC boycott pickets and pressured other unions to do likewise. Key labor sympathizers were also alienated by the persistent boycotts. The Retail Clerks and Butchers Unions decided that they could no longer support boycotts because they cut into their own jobs, and when the UFWOC announced a secondary boycott against Safeway and A & P in 1973, they successfully lobbied the AFL–CIO Executive Council into refusing to endorse the boycott. The problem was illustrated by the Heublein boycott. Shortly after the lettuce strike, the UFWOC called a boycott against Heublein Corporation, a conglomerate with a winery as well as vineyards. The move threatened Distillery Workers and Glassblowers Union jobs. The UFWOC had to resort to a primary or consumer boycott and secondary actions against the grocery chains. Lettuce was also less vulnerable to a primary boycott because it was viewed as a necessity and consumed in many ways, in salads and sandwiches as well as households. The Teamster contracts also allowed the growers to confuse the issue by pointing to the Teamster label, claiming that their lettuce was already harvested by union labor. The UFWOC, aware of its weak position, allowed itself to be drawn into off-and-on negotiations that required boycott moratoria and thoroughly confused the boycott teams as well as consumers.[8]

The growers, reinvigorated by the installation of the newly elected Nixon administration, also mounted an effective political attack. On September 24, 1971, the UFWOC was notified by a Treasury Department agent in Bakersfield that there was an assassination plot against Chavez's life. While investigating illegal drug traffic, the agent had learned of a $25,000 pay-off made by an unidentified group of growers, presumably in the Delano area since the contract was let in Bakersfield, to have Chavez murdered. Chavez immediately went into hiding, traveling incognito for three months, losing contact with the workers and denying the boycott a critical public figure. Although the sources of the plot were never identified, the hired gunman was later imprisoned for another contract killing and the threat demoralized the cadre (Levy 1975:443–446). In December, Peter Nash, newly appointed general counsel to the National Labor Relations Board, filed for an injunction against the UFWOC wine boycott against the Heublein Corporation, claiming that the aim was to organize the shed and winery as well as field workers of the Allied Grape Growers, which owned a commercial shed covered by the National Labor Relations Act. The court agreed. The Heublein boycott also alienated labor and Catholic supporters, in part because the UFWOC had not actually organized the Allied Grape field workers. The Distillery Workers also protested to the AFL–CIO, which ordered all affiliates to ignore the boycott. Finally the UFWOC backed down, negotiating a single contract with Heublein and dropping the boycott in exchange for a withdrawal of the suit.[9]

Senator Murphy (R.-Calif.) reintroduced labor legislation, this time providing for recognition elections limited to year-round workers and bars on boycotts and harvest strikes. The Farm Bureau Federation asked the lettuce growers to hold out, promising national legislation that would halt the boycotts, but they could not get the bills through the Democratic-controlled Congress. The Farm Bureau then shifted to state legislatures, securing restrictive labor bills in Kansas, Idaho, Oregon, and, most critically, Arizona (Meister and Loftis 1977:179).

The UFWOC ordered the boycott offices to organize protests, holding demonstrations at Farm Bureau offices in thirty-four states and successfully pressuring the governor of Oregon, Tom McCall, to veto the Oregon bill. Because most of the lettuce workers also worked in Arizona, the union decided to fight the Arizona bill. Strikes were organized in the cantaloupe and lettuce fields, most of which were owned by the Salinas-based growers. Then the union mounted a recall campaign against Governor Jack Williams, who had just signed the Farm Bureau bill. After mass rallies, a 24-day fast, and a registration campaign that signed up 100,000 new Mexican-American voters, the union submitted 175,000 signatures on the recall petition. Although only 108,000 were required for a recall election, the Attorney General ruled out most of the signatures, claiming that though the signers were registered to vote, they had not been registered at the time they signed the petitions and that many signers had been intimidated. Although the campaign was defeated, it did strengthen support among the lettuce and melon workers and created a new voting block (Meister and Loftis 1977:179–180).

The California growers then filed a 7,000-word initiative known as Proposition 22 modelled on the Farm Bureau's labor bill. The bill limited elections to permanent workers, imposed a mandatory sixty-day cooling off period that would have effectively barred harvest strikes, prohibited negotiations on work rules, and subjected union adherents to potential $5,000 fines for violations while leaving grower violations unpunished (*Los Angeles Times,* September 21, 1972). The growers put up $224,000 to qualify the proposal, hiring professional petition circulators, who gathered 388,000 signatures. At first, the UFWOC reeled under the attack. Borrowing from the Boston boycott, human billboards—workers with "Vote No on 22" signs on their backs—were stationed at expressway exit ramps and outside sports events, but it was difficult to counter the apparent neutrality of legislation that promised recognition elections (*Los Angeles Times,* October 25, 1972). The growers invested another $500,000, complete with television commercials displaying violence said to have been instigated by the UFWOC in the Salinas strikes.

Then a break came when several signers of the petition phoned the boycott office in Los Angeles, claiming they had been told by the petition circulators that it was a UFWOC-supported bill. Bonnie Chatfield, the wife of Leroy Chatfield, who was in charge of the anti-Proposition 22 campaign, began checking the signatures and quickly uncovered wholesale fraud, whole petition sheets signed in one hand and many signers retelling the same story of the bill being promoted as a UFWOC measure. Chavez appealed to Secretary of State Jerry Brown, son of the former governor and a former activist in the grape boycott, who promptly filed suit to remove the measure from the November ballot (*Los Angeles Times,* November 4, 1972). Although Brown's suit was rejected, the fraud provided the UFWOC with an issue. News headlines trumpeted the charges, and while the UFWOC hastily registered voters in the barrios, support for the grower measure unraveled. On November 3, 1972, the voters resoundingly rejected the measure—58 percent to 42 percent— despite Richard Nixon's landslide victory over George McGovern.[10] The union had won despite a generally conservative election.

The growers returned to their main line of attack—"union substitution" and, if possible, outright destruction of the union. The initial testing grounds were the Tenneco asparagus ranch near Schafter and the White River Farms, the renamed Schenley vineyards that had been purchased by Buttes Land and Oil in 1971. In the fall of 1971, the UFW lost its first representation election among the asparagus workers on the Heggblade-Marguleas asparagus farm near Schafter, the farming subsidiary of Tenneco. The union had done little organizing, instead threatening a boycott against Tenneco, and was opposed by crews of Filipino migrants who saw the UFWOC as the "Mexican union."

The White River Farms conflict was even more threatening. Under a successor clause, the UFWOC held onto the original Schenley contract and entered negotiations for a renewal in early June. The Buttes management claimed that the UFWOC demanded the contract be extended to another grape ranch 150 miles northward which had not organized, while the union denied the claim. Regardless, the union leaders were preoccupied with the Proposition 22 campaign and, since relations had previously been smooth, decided to hold back from a strike when the harvest began on August 10, despite the expiration of the contract. On August 14, the union negotiating committee offered a final compromise, wages 20 cents below the standard contract. The management dawdled and then refused. Two weeks later the ranch committee finally called a strike, pulling over 1,000 workers out. The White River Farms management immediately began hauling in strikebreakers, mostly local workers eager to get the better jobs. When the huelgistas attacked the strikebreakers, injuring several, the management asked for help from the neighboring Niesi Growers League. The League was composed of smaller Japanese growers, who ferociously resented the union. They quickly organized work crews to save the crop, and, supplemented by busloads of

Mexican illegals, finished the harvest. Although Buttes lost a significant portion of the crop, the manager replied to a news interviewer: "Money is no object. We'll spend a fortune to get this crop harvested and after we're through we'll plan out how to run this farm permanently without a union." (R. Taylor 1975:284–286; Sosnick 1978:334). The determination to rid itself of the union stemmed in part from the fact that the farm was a tax write-off for a conglomerate corporation.[11] It also signified the new militancy of the growers. Symbolically, it was the UFWOC's first contract, and now the growers knew that the UFWOC could be broken even on organized ranches (Los Angeles Times, December 13, 1972).

The grape growers immediately opened secret negotiations with the Teamsters. On December 12, Frank Fitzsimmons spoke at the annual convention of the American Farm Bureau Federation, offering an "alliance between organized labor and the farmers" and urging support for extension of the NLRA. Two days later, the Western Conference announced the new Agriculture Workers Organizing Committee, headed by Ralph Cotner, a tough Teamster organizer who began working the Coachella vineyards. The national Teamster leadership continued to claim they did not want the lettuce contracts and, largely because of worker resistance, left them unenforced. Suddenly, on January 17, Bill Grami met with the Salinas lettuce growers to announce the renegotiation of the still unexpired 1970 contracts and a campaign to sign up the workers (San Francisco Chronicle, December 30, 1972 and January 17, 1973). In secret negotiations with twenty-five Coachella growers, Cotner offered the Salinas union substitution solution, the elimination of the hiring hall and ranch committee in exchange for higher wages and small health benefits. Because work was at the winter ebb, Ray Huerta, the director of the UFWOC's Indio hiring hall, ignored the rumors that the Teamsters were passing out petitions, assuming they were after the packingsheds. Then, on March 16, the UFWOC received a shock that confirmed their worst fears. A Riverside journalist decided to check out a claim by one of the Teamster organizers that the Teamsters were taking over the Coachella grapes and had already signed over 4,100 workers. The journalist checked with the local farm labor placement office, confirming that there were only 1,200 to 1,500 workers then in the Valley, and phoned the UFWOC office (Riverside Press Enterprise, March 17, 1973).

The Teamster raid caught everyone by surprise. Significantly, the initiative had originated in the Nixon White House. Working through Charles Colson, President Nixon's chief counsel, Fitzsimmons reached a secret agreement to support Nixon's reelection, carry out the anti-UFWOC raid, and provide evidence against former Teamster officials under investigation for income tax evasion in exchange for the release of former Teamster President James Hoffa—released on condition that he not run for the Teamster Presidency—dropping legal charges against Fitzsimmons' son and tax evasion suits against other Teamster officials.[12] President Meany, informed of the threatened raid, sent word back through his press secretary: "No comment." The UFWOC had been granted a union charter in February 1972, renamed the United Farm Workers of America, and was now officially on its own. Even when the Teamster move became more clear in March, Meany refused to intervene, citing the Antle strike in 1970 as a threat to the Teamster jurisdiction and attacking the secondary boycotts (R. Taylor 1975:294–295).

Nor was the UFW prepared. During January and February, Chavez had organized industrywide negotiations, supervising the selection of a ten-member negotiating committee elected by the ranch committees that met regularly with the Coachella and Delano grape growers beginning in late February. Negotiations continued to stall around the hiring hall issue, and on April 9, one week before the contracts were to expire, a grower attorney finally challenged the UFW's support from the workers, claiming that until the jurisdictional issue was settled he could not negotiate. The other growers quickly withdrew, and on April 15, the Teamster and grower representatives announced that they had negotiated new contracts. The Teamsters not only would do away with the hiring halls, but they would also allow labor contractors (R. Taylor 1975:296; Meister and Loftis 1977:185).

The hiring hall was the major point of contention. The growers complained that the UFW maladministered the hall, failing to dispatch sufficient workers on time.[13] Although the charges were not entirely unfounded, the growers' major objection was actually that the hiring halls allowed the union to thoroughly mobilize the workers. The union used the hiring halls to collect dues, recruit pickets, organize solidary events, and deliver services as well as make certain that priority jobs went to loyal supporters. The growers, of course, preferred their own hiring and supervisory controls and the continued use of labor contractors. The UFW had also alienated some of the workers, insisting on union rather than

187

ranch seniority to protect loyal supporters and demanding volunteer picket duty on the boycott and other ranches. Many Filipino migrants also saw the union as Mexican dominated and resented the bars on contractors. The migrants also complained that there were long waits in the hiring halls and that loyal Chavistas got first crack at the better jobs.[14]

These disputes made the UFW contracts vulnerable to the Teamster raids. The UFW began organizing rallies and on April 16 called strikes, pulling over 1,000 of the 1,300 workers then working in the grape vineyards. The growers filed for injunctions, which the UFW decided to defy, and recruited strikebreakers. The UFW put up $1 million for strike relief and petitioned the AFL–CIO for an emergency meeting of the Executive Council. Within two days, over 500 pickets were in jail and the AFL–CIO announced a special levy against all affiliates, raising over $1.6 million to defend the contracts. As Meany announced: "[The Teamsters] are clearly union busting in a concerted campaign to wipe out the United Farm Workers. This is the most despicable strikebreaking, union-busting activity I have ever seen in my lifetime in the trade union movement."[15] For the first time, the UFWOC was able to pay significant strike relief, $35 to $90 a week for picket line duty, and it hired a large legal staff to battle the court injunctions.

The funds reinvigorated the picket lines, and on April 20, the union scored a major legal victory when Judge Metheny rescinded the original injunction against all picketing, substituting an order that pickets stay sixty feet from the vineyards (Levy 1975:483). The Teamsters again called in guards, this time 500 strong, several of whom were identified as muscle men for Las Vegas casinos reputed to have gangster connections. The guards—large, muscular men who "acted like extras from a Hell's Angels movie"—set up counterpickets, traveling up and down the backroads on an open-bed truck the Chavistas called "the garbage truck" and armed with clubs, chains, and tire irons. Whenever they spotted a UFW picket line, the "animals," as one Teamster official called them, leaped off the truck and charged the picket lines. "They would grunt and snort and paw the ground: they dragged effigies of Chavez aroung to stomp on. The strikers were intimidated but they did not give up (R. Taylor 1975:299-300).

The sheriff's deputies made dozens of arrests, seizing both Teamsters and UFW pickets, but could not police the huge vineyard area where the guards and pickets clashed. Paul Hall, President of the Seafarers

Union, was sent in by George Meany as an observer and, shielded by fifty burly seamen, provided protection for the UFW leadership and offered to remove the Teamsters. "You gotta break those bastards' legs," claimed Hall, "that's the only thing they understand."[16] Chavez refused the offer but accepted the protection.

The strike area was a battle zone, with daily bulletins of violent skirmishes and mass arrests.

May 30, 1973—*Wall Street Journal:* "*Wall Street Journal* reporter William Wong and Father John Bank, a 33-year-old Ohio priest doing public relations work for the UFW were seated in the Trukadero Restaurant today after several hours on the UFW picket lines. A Teamster member, Mike Falco, challenged Bank and, without warning, smashed Father Bank in the face, breaking seven bones."

June 20, 1973—*Riverside Enterprise:* "A Las Vegas public relations man, Murray Westgate, dispatched to this area as part of a multi-million dollar effort to improve the image of the Teamster Union, has filed a complaint against a Teamster who he says hit him in the face Monday night and told him to 'get out of town.'"

June 21, 1973—*Riverside Enterprise:* "Two Teamsters were arrested yesterday morning by Riverside County Sheriff's deputies on charges of attempting to commit murder and kidnapping. The victim, Israel Guajardo, 28, of Mecca, was mistaken for a UFW Member by the Teamsters, sheriff's deputies said. Guajardo was taken to Indio Community Hospital with six ice pick wounds to the back of his shoulder and neck."

June 23, 1973—*Riverside Enterprise:* "Francisco Campos, his wife Patricia, and their two-and-a-half year-old daughter Elisa, all of Brownsville, Texas, nearly died this morning when their small trailer was destroyed by flames in an open field. A neighbor saw two cars drive into the field where the trailer was located and heard someone yell, 'We're going to burn down your house, Cisco!' Campos joined the UFW in February and has been a picket leader at the Richard Glass vineyards."

June 28, 1973—*Riverside Enterprise:* "Factfinders sent into Coachella Valley by Teamster President Frank Fitzsimmons have been attacked and beaten by agents for Ralph Cotner, head of the Teamster Agricultural Workers Organizing Committee. Spokesmen for the Riverside County Sheriff's Department say the Teamsters have instigated all of the violence that has occurred in the past week. A melee that occurred in an asparagus field east of Thermal on Saturday June 24 was, according to Lieutenant Paul Yoxsimer, field commander for the sheriff's department strike task force, 'the most violent eruption of the entire strike.' Fifty-six persons were hospitalized and five arrested after the melee involving over five hundred people."

July 5, 1973—*Riverside Enterprise:* "William Grami, Director of Organizations for the Western Conference of Teamsters, announced yesterday that his union 'will immediately withdraw all guards from agricultural areas being picketed by the United Farm Workers Union. We believe that local law enforcement agencies have realized the need for increasing their forces to the point where their protection appears adequate.' "

July 7, 1973—*Riverside Enterprise:* "More than 2,000 UFW pickets demonstrated at orchards and vineyards in five California counties yesterday, but for the second straight day, no incidents were reported. Law enforcement authorities in Riverside, Kern, Fresno, Tulare and Monterey counties cited the absence of Teamster union guards as the major reason for the lack of confrontation between opposing labor unions."

In spite of the mass picketing, the Coachella growers managed to harvest most of their crop by bringing in migrants from the Mexican border towns who were inexperienced, destroyed grapes in packing, and left many rotting on the vines (*Los Angeles Times,* June 5 and 13 and July 5, 1973). The loss was worth it, however, if it meant ridding themselves of the UFW. Only two growers—Lionel Steinberg and Keith Larson, the first two to sign contracts in 1970—held onto their UFW contracts. The next year, Larson followed suit, signing Teamster after a rigged election conducted by an anti-Chavez priest.[17]

The strike then moved northward to the wine vineyards around Modesto and Delano. On June 27, Gallo announced a contract with the Teamsters. The UFW had held the contract for over six years and, despite the expiration of the contract on April 15, had not struck because their major supporters, the Mexican migrants, were not at work. The Gallo vineyards, which provided less than 10 percent of the winery's grapes, employed 150 permanent workers, mostly Anglos and Portuguese immigrants who had formerly been goat herders in the nearby hills, and around 600 Mexican migrants. Suddenly, in the midst of negotiations, Gallo demanded the UFW give up the hiring hall and the right to determine union seniority and good standing, claiming that the UFW was abusing its disciplinary powers. The UFW refused and, when Gallo rejected another election to demonstrate worker support, withdrew from the talks and called a strike meeting. Meanwhile, Teamster organizers entered the fields, forcing workers to sign authorization cards. Those who refused were fired. The UFW called a strike and over half of the workers walked out. Gallo promptly brought in more Portuguese workers and finalized the Teamster contract. The migrants conducted a sit-in in the camp housing until sheriff's deputies, armed with eviction notices, forcibly removed them. As soon as the strikers had been evicted, Gallo held a new recognition election to ratify the new contract—158, Teamster; 1, no union (*Los Angeles Times*, June 27 and 28, and July 11, 1973). The next week, the nearby Franzia vineyards followed suit (*San Francisco Chronicle*, July 17, 1973).

At the same time, the UFW began organizing the Delano workers for a strike. On July 21, the UFW called a strike meeting attended by over 2,000 workers, voting to strike if the contracts were not renewed before they expired on July 29. Bill Kircher, speaking to the strike meeting, pledged full AFL–CIO support: "This is Delano. This is the heart of the union, the core of the farm workers movement, and there isn't a power on earth that can destroy it (Cited in Levy 1975:498). A week later, the workers committee defiantly marched out of the negotiations chanting "Huelga." Giumarra, the head negotiator for the growers, had made the final offer, demanding the elimination of the hiring hall. That night at the Forty Acres, an old NFWA sign was on the back of a flatbed truck used as a speaking platform. "That's our sign of victory," Chavez told the 2,000 workers.

"Eight years ago in Delano, the idea that workers should have a union came forth out of some of us here. There were few of us. Eight years ago we were being paid ninety-five cents an hour. What the growers are trying to do with the Teamsters is a fraud. We shall take out our huelga flag all across the country, and we shall go to the picket lines. We'll make sure the growers pay double for the price of picketing. We'll make sure the quality is disastrous, and that wherever possible the grapes turn to raisins on the vine. Now we're in heaven compared to eight years ago. In those days we were inspected by every department in one week. We had no place to meet, no money, no cars. Now we have a trained staff, a hall. We'll have it thirty times easier this time!" (Cited in Levy 1975:499)

The next morning the UFW organized mass picket lines around the vineyards, pulling virtually all the workers out of the fields. This time, however, the sheriff's deputies mounted the violence. The Tulare County Sheriff put over 100 deputies in the field, outfitted in green flight suits, heavy boots, and visored riot helmets, armed with pistols, yard-long clubs, and tear gas canisters. Behind the deputies stood the grower's private patrolmen armed with shotguns and Teamster guards. When the pickets massed outside the fields, rather than arresting them for violating the injunctions, the deputies attacked, clubbing the pickets and spraying them with mace: "Tulare County—a bunch of dogs. They had a legal goon squad of twenty-four deputies in riot gear that went around threatening people, macing them, and beating people up. Tulare just didn't give a damn. They were going to break the strike."[18] The UFW vowed to build a "perpetual strike" and defy the court injunctions, filling the jails and using the police violence to publicize the boycott. Church allies were called to the strike zone and asked to be arrested on the picket line. Dorothy Day, the celebrated 76-year-old leader of the pacifist Catholic Worker Movement, came from New York to be arrested along with seventy priests and nuns. In four months' time, there were fifty-eight injunctions and 3,589 arrests, the largest number in Fresno.[19] Soon the jails were overcrowded, forcing the courts to release the pickets uncharged. Court calendars were so clogged with strikers demanding jury trials that the deputies stopped arresting pickets.

The police violence also mobilized outside support. On August 1, Meany called an emergency meeting of the AFL–CIO Executive Council and sent three vice presidents and the AFL–CIO's chief legal counsel to negotiate with the Teamsters. The UFW intensified the picketing, and the growers made another offer to renew the contracts if the UFW would drop the hiring hall. The UFW suggested a joint operated hiring hall, and Meany offered the AFL–CIO's guarantee that the UFW would live up to its contracts.[20] Meanwhile the Teamsters offered to return the grape contracts in exchange for the UFW's endorsement of an extension of the National Labor Relations Act, guarantees by the AFL–CIO that the UFW would honor Teamster contracts outside the fields, and arbitration of any disputes by Fitzsimmons and Meany (*San Francisco Chronicle*, August 4, 1973). Suddenly, Einar Mohn announced that Jimmy Smith, the organizer in the Delano office, had mistakenly signed twenty-nine contracts with the Delano grape growers. Chavez immediately stormed out of the session, past the reporters waiting outside to hear word of the new peace treaty. "Stabbed in the back!" shouted Chavez as he slid into the front seat of the waiting car. "Just like Pearl Harbor!" added Jerry Cohen, the UFW attorney (cited in Meister and Loftis 1977:189).

The UFW decided that the negotiations were merely a cover and renewed the picketing, focusing on the Giumarra ranch. Both Mohn and Fitzsimmons disclaimed the contracts, but the growers acted as if they were in force. Two UFW pickets were wounded by gunshots from passing trucks, but the deputies failed to identify suspects (*Los Angeles Times*, July 31, and August 2, 11, and 22, 1973). The picketing was intense, but the Filipino labor contractors brought in illegal immigrants and Arab workers. Meanwhile the growers paraded their Teamster contracts. Asked about the conflicting claims, Johnny Giumarra, Jr. replied: "My response would be ha, ha! The UFW? I think they're out of business now!" (*Los Angeles Times*, August 22, 1975). Three days later, one of the UFW's Arab members—Nagi Daifullah—was struck by a sheriff's deputy with a flashlight during a scuffle outside a Delano bar and died of a concussion two days later. The UFW immediately organized a funeral procession, appealing to the Arab strikebreakers to come out of the fields. The next day, a sixty-year-old striker, Juan de la Cruz, whose involvement dated to the 1966 DiGiorgio strike, was shot to death on the picket line by a labor contractor in a passing truck driven by one of the growers. The UFW organized a second funeral procession, this time 5,000 workers marching five miles from the Arvin city park to the cemetery, and called a moratorium on the picketing (*Los Angeles Times*, August 17, 1973). Chavez immediately called an emergency meeting of the Executive Board, and after extensive debate, the board voted to call off the strike. Mass picketing had failed to halt the Teamster raid, and amid escalating violence, Chavez feared the loss of more lives.[21]

This time Chavez took charge of organizing the boycott, selecting 500 loyal huelgistas. The major target was the Safeway grocery chain, concentrated in the southwest, the largest retailer of California fruits and vegetables and, having recently advocated a simple extension of the NLRA, seemingly the softest opposition. Although hampered by weak labor support and consumer confusion, the boycotters turned away an estimated 30,000 customers per week, leading Safeway to file for injunctions and a $150 million damages suit.

The board also decided to proceed with plans for the union's constituting convention to be held September 21—23 in Fresno. President Meany had recently echoed the grower complaint that the union had misadministered the grape contracts, and other sponsors wondered about the union's survival. Although the UFW had lost over 90 percent of its contracts and membership had shrunk from over 40,000 to 6,500, the convention would project an image of stability. Over 400 delegates attended, the majority elected by ranch committees now under Teamster contracts; they elected a slate of officers hand-picked by Chavez and ratified a 111-page constitution.[22] As soon as the convention closed, Chavez flew off to Washington, where Meany and Fitzsimmons were negotiating still another jurisdictional agreement. The Teamsters promised to give up the grape contracts immediately and transfer the lettuce contracts as they expired over the next two years. In exchange, the UFW would support a simple extension of the NLRA and drop the lettuce, grape, and Safeway boycotts (*San Francisco Chronicle* September 28, 1973).

But this agreement dissolved as quickly as the others. The Delano growers threatened to sue, and behind the scenes the Nixon White House urged another attack. While Fitzsimmons was consulting his lawyers, Jimmy Hoffa announced that he would run against Fitzsimmons for the Teamster presidency and promised to "fight Chavez, just like the growers."[23] Fitzsimmons then announced a new organizing drive under the leadership of David Castro, a Mexican-American Teamster cannery official, and promised a $100,000 a month budget and staff of 100 (*Los Angeles Times*, March 29, 1974). Over the summer of 1974, the Teamsters actually made their first and only serious effort to organize the workers, establishing offices throughout the state and providing the benefits promised in the contracts. Then the leadership battle came to an end. Andy Anderson, the new Director of the Western Conference and a Fitzsimmons ally, fired Castro, dissolved Local 1973, and transferred Grami out of the organizing position (*Fresno Bee*, November 4, 1974). Shortly afterwards, Hoffa disappeared, presumably assassinated by his enemies. The Teamster leadership was no longer interested in the contracts.

Still the UFWOC was on the defensive. Responding to pressure from union opponents of the boycott, the AFL–CIO refused to endorse the boycott or provide financial support. Meany forced Bill Kircher into retirement and charged that the UFW had simply failed to organize the workers: "It was Chavez's own people who went to work behind the picket lines in Coachella last year and that didn't indicate much support from the workers there for Chavez" (*Los Angeles Times*, February 23, 1974). The decline in student radicalism also cut the supply of student volunteers, prompting one boycott organizer to comment: "It is not the nineteen-sixties anymore" (*New York Times*, November 25, 1975). Yet the Catholic Church increased its support, the bishops endorsing the boycott and instituting a new leave policy that facilitated the move of priests and nuns into UFW staff positions. By the summer of 1974, the UFW staff was transformed as over 700 priests and nuns took leaves, boosting the full-time staff to a peak of almost 1,500.[24] Although they were not as politically experienced as the student radicals, the priests and nuns lent credibility to the boycotts and were less likely to challenge union policies.

Meanwhile, the boycott sputtered along, producing no contracts despite a slight increase in consumer support. Twelve percent of the population replied to a Harris poll that they had stopped buying table grapes, 11 percent lettuce, and 8 percent Gallo wines (*Los Angeles Times*, October 30, 1975). But without strong labor support, the campaign had been largely reduced to a consumer boycott. In March 1974, Chavez and Meany finally reached a truce. The UFW would drop the secondary boycott against Safeway and A & P, and the AFL–CIO would urge all affiliates to support the lettuce and grape boycott.[25] The endorsement, however, had little effect. Meanwhile, the UFW organized another series of strikes and held marches along the border to highlight strikebreaking by illegal immigrants. Still the growers would not budge. Then the UFW hit on another tactic, shifting the boycott target to Gallo wines. Although Gallo had been on the list before, it had not been a priority target. Since the boycott had now effectively been reduced to a consumer boycott, the best strategy was to pick a highly visible trade label like Gallo which represented a third of the domestic wine market. Increasing competition from imports and a campaign by the National Student Association among Gallo's major clientele—college students—cut Gallo sales by 7 percent (Meister and Loftis 1977:197–208). Still the loss was not enough to bring negotiations.

The UFW leadership decided that it was time for a political settlement. The union had immensely more worker support than the Teamsters, but it could not demonstrate this through elections or convert it into effective strikes. The boycott still enjoyed significant consumer support, but with the decline of the student and civil rights movements and the withdrawal of organized labor, it could not force contracts. The 1974 elections also created new political opportunities. Buoyed by the Watergate revelations and restrictions preventing Ronald Reagan from running for a third term, the Democrats seized control of both the state legislature and the governorship. Jerry Brown, a former priest who had marched in the grape and lettuce boycotts, became governor. As the 1974 legislative session drew to a close, the UFW tested the political waters by pushing for a labor law that would provide secret ballot elections while allowing boycotts and harvest strikes. The Assembly passed the bill, only for it to be killed in the Senate (Meister and Loftis 1977:215–216).

The union immediately launched a series of marches to simultaneously galvanize worker support, renew the Gallo boycott, and reinvigorate the outside supporters to pressure the governor and legislature to support the new labor legislation. On February 22, 1975, a crowd of 3,000 gathered in Union Park in downtown San Francisco to begin a 110-mile march to Modesto, the Gallo headquarters. While the marchers gathered around, the speakers stood chanting "Cesar si, Teamsters no, Gallo Wine has got to go!" Gallo employees overhead unfurled a massive poster from the upper floor of the stately St. Francis Hotel reading: "Gallo's Farm Workers Best Paid in U.S. Marching Wrong Way, Cesar?" A week later, over 15,000 marched past the Gallo headquarters into Modesto's Graceda Park, where Chavez promised that "we will win our contracts back!" The audience of farm workers, students, priests, nuns, ministers, and an assortment of Old Left representatives thundered applause. The Modesto Labor Council sent a message protesting the rally, and the AFL–CIO did not send representatives. But the message was clear. Although it had lost most of the contracts, the UFW still enjoyed the support of the workers and a broad political coalition (*San Francisco Chronicle*, February 23 and September 30, 1975).

Meanwhile, Governor Brown put his staff to work on a new farm labor bill. The growers were ready to sue for peace, finally convinced that the Teamster contracts had not really protected them from farm worker insurgency. Now that the contracts were no longer a basis for leadership rivalries, the Teamster leaders were also ready to negotiate. The growers and Teamsters asked for a bill outlawing harvest strikes and boycotts and restricting ballots to the more conservative permanent workers. The UFW advanced a bill allowing unrestricted strikes and boycotts and elections timed for the harvest peak when its migrant and local supporters would control the vote. Governor Brown took personal charge of negotiating a compromise bill, meeting separately with each of the parties (*Sacramento Bee*, April 23, 1975). Once he had hammered out a compromise bill, he submitted it simultaneously to the Assembly, where the UFW was influential, and the Senate, where Teamsters and growers prevailed. Everyone attacked the bill, the Teamsters calling for protections on their existing contracts, the growers for bars on secondary boycotts, the UFW for rights to recognition strikes and unlimited boycotts, and the AFL–CIO Building and Construction Trades Council and the Packinghouse Workers for removal of a UFW proposal to include packingshed workers and carpenters under field worker jurisdictions. In another round of bargaining sessions, Brown finally hammered out the final compromises, giving the growers protections against boycotts and strikes until after recognition elections; the Teamsters guarantees on their contracts until contested by elections or in court; the UFW elections timed for the harvest peak, the right to strike and boycott after recognition, and the right to challenge the Teamster contracts in court; and the AFL–CIO separate jurisdictions. Brown then called a special session of the legislature, and the bill sailed through.

It was an historic breakthrough, providing the first protections on collective bargaining by farm workers outside of Hawaii. Secret-ballot recognition elections had to be held within seven days after the receipt of a valid petition from half of the workers with at least half of the maximum work force participating. Strikers who had been on the payroll during the previous year could vote, and growers were barred from coercing or intimidating workers. After a recognition election, a certified union could call strikes or boycotts, and a struck employer could hire non-union replacements.[26] Brown used the victory to press for further reforms, getting an extension of unemployment insurance that would also discourage short-term hiring and bars on the short-hoe that kept farm workers bent over double in the fields (*Los Angeles Times*, September 23 and October 6, 1975).

The growers demanded that the boycott be called off, but the UFW, hoping for quicker elections, intensified the pressure. In June, the UFW launched an organizing campaign, Chavez heading up a 59-day, 1,000-mile march winding from the Mexican border throughout the state. Since they could not get onto the farms, Chavez spoke at public rallies along the way about their victories and the advantages of the service centers and hiring halls. The Teamsters held the first meeting of their farm worker union, which was broken up by 1,000 chanting Chavistas, signed 165 new lettuce contracts, and pointed to their higher wages and the freedom to work anywhere the worker pleased. The growers, hoping to get rid of the UFW, allowed a whopping 16 percent raise in the new Teamster contracts, raising base hourly wages to $2.96, as opposed to the $2.45 in the UFW's lettuce contracts.[27]

Meanwhile the battle began over the composition and rules of the Agricultural Labor Relations Board. Brown nominated a pro-UFW majority to the board, including LeRoy Chatfield, Brown's staff director and a former aid for Chavez for over eight years; Bishop Roger Mahoney, who had arbitrated the DiGiorgio negotiations and engineered the Church's boycott endorsement; and a sympathetic Mexican-American lawyer. The growers and Teamsters failed to block the appointments, so they focused on the Board's rulings. The UFW convinced the board to use its black eagle "bug" on the ballots for the benefit of the thousands of illiterate farm workers, while the Teamsters got the right to call elections by presenting a simple majority of authorization cards on ranches where they already held contracts.

The major controversy, however, was over the ranch access rule. Because many of the workers resided on ranch property, the UFW demanded unrestricted access, while the growers demanded protections on their property rights. The board finally compromised, ordering limited access during lunch and for one hour before and after working hours. The growers, however, decided to resist the ruling and, encouraged by the rural judges and sheriff's departments, organized vigilante committees armed with shotguns to deter the UFW organizers while giving Teamster organizers free access (*Los Angeles Times*, September 19, 1975). Although the Labor Board secured an injunction from the State Supreme Court, overruling lower court orders against the access rule, the rural sheriffs ignored the ruling, arrested hundreds of UFW organizers for trespassing, and allowed the growers to post armed guards at their ranch entrances. In one incident near Stockton, UFW organizers were confronted by forty armed members of the Posse Commitatus, a vigilante group led by a telephone installer who declared their right to enforce their own interpretation of the Constitution. The UFW backed off, but when the sheriff's deputies moved in, one of the posse fired over the head of the deputies, touching off a melee that led to the arrest of three people, including a 14-year-old toting an Army rifle.[28] The growers also threatened the workers. At Gallo, for example, the ranch manager took pictures of UFW organizers talking to Gallo workers, fired forty-one UFW supporters, hired pro-Teamster replacements, and openly displayed pro-Teamster literature, asking workers to vote Teamster. The UFW later lost the election, but the Farm Labor Board waived it, charging Gallo with sixty violations, and ordered the workers rehired (*Los Angeles Times*, October 7, 1976).

The elections began on August 28, 1975, in a tense atmosphere. Although the UFW assigned observers, the growers took every opportunity to sway the outcome. The voting was held on farm property, workers were transported to the polling place in company buses where the foremen could make their last minute bids for Teamster support, and on several ranches, armed guards surrounded the voting boxes. The UFW filed over 1,000 complaints, charging the growers with padding voting lists, threatening workers, firing over 1,800, and calling in the Immigration authorities to remove pro-UFW illegals (Meister and Leftis 1977:222). The Labor Board proceeded anyway, deciding to investigate complaints afterwards because of the short harvest season.

The first month showed the UFW and Teamsters neck and neck, the UFW with 74 wins to the Teamsters' 73 (*New York Times*, September 28, 1975). The UFW soon took the lead as the voting extended into the vegetable fields. In the 361 conclusive elections during the first year, the UFW won 198, covering 27,000 jobs, while the Teamsters won 115, covering 12,000 jobs. Significantly, however, the UFW failed to dislodge the Teamsters, picking up only 56 of the 156 ranches previously under Teamster contract. The Teamsters kept ninety-two, or about 60 percent, and picked up 51 percent of the elections on previously non-union ranches (Sosnick 1978:379-380). In other words, the UFW won a solid majority, but the Teamsters also held onto a significant base of support.

There were several reasons for the UFW losses, not the least being the growers' campaign of intimidation and violence. As a top official for the Labor Board conceded, grower intimidation probably cost the UFW 15 to 20 percent of the votes (*Los Angeles Times*, November 17, 1975). The Labor Board's staff was also poorly prepared and overwhelmed by the work load. There were 361 elections conducted in the first year (over five times the number held by the National Labor Relations board in its first year), and 80 percent were challenged. The elections also had to be held quickly, leaving little time for preliminaries or corrections of abuses. In September 1976, the board ran out of money, using up its original $1.3 million appropriation and $1.25 million in loans from other state funds. The growers then used their legislative influence to block refunding, demanding bars on access, their own right to call elections, a longer time (twenty-one days) between the petition and the election, a shorter validation for union authorization cards, multi-employer bargaining units, and restrictions on union good standing rules (Meister and Loftis 1977:222–223). The Teamsters also held the advantage, holding more contracts, using the benefits and access to enlist support, and enjoyed active grower support.

The UFW also had problems mobilizing the farm workers. The vestiges of farm worker powerlessness still persisted. Some workers were easily impressed by the Teamster wages and their image as a powerful union. Others perceived no advantage in the UFW program of workplace reform and stabilized employment. Still others resented the UFW's incessant demands for picket duty, hiring hall regulations, and the collection of back dues. The union also lacked a firm strategy for organizing the migrants, having originally been built around the problems of local workers. Ethnic rivalries also persisted, exacerbated by the UFW's use of ethnic symbolism in organizing drives. The Anglo, Filipino, and Arab workers rallied to the Teamsters, hoping to hold onto their privileged jobs and fearing the "Mexican union." Meanwhile, the UFW expanded its support among the Mexican workers, dropping its demand for immigration restrictions, attacking the Border Patrol, and openly organizing sindocumentos. The migrants were more difficult to organize than the locals, continually on the move and not approachable until a few days before an election. Where the ethnic labor contractors remained strong, as in the grape and broccoli fields, they pressed their workers to vote Teamster or no-union.

The UFW's problems also stemmed in part from its reliance on the boycott. With the most loyal supporters out on the boycott and the emphasis off organizing strikes, the union had abandoned Chavez's original community organizing strategy. Strikes trained indigenous organizers and developed strong commitments among the rank-and-file, while boycotts emphasized political alliances and dramatic protests by a small group of ardent supporters. Winning contracts by strikes prepared a base of indigenous support and leadership, while boycotts left these problematic. Suddenly the union found itself organizing workers with whom it had had little contact. The workers could not readily see the advantages of grievance procedures, pesticide controls, hiring hall regulations, and health benefits, but they could easily see the larger Teamster paychecks. The union had had the same problem with the grape contracts in the early 1970s. As Fred Ross had told a news reporter in 1973: "This was the first time we'd gotten so close to so many of these workers. They'd been imported as strikebreakers and now, overnight, they were blanketed by a union" (cited in R. Taylor 1975:265). It had been difficult to train indigenous leaders to operate the hiring halls and ranch committees. Since the benefits had come free, many saw no need to volunteer for picket duty or attend meetings. They had also missed the mobilizing experience of the picket line, where grower arrogance and police harassment created commitments to la causa. As one farm worker complained: "They (the UFW) were always making us go to meetings and rallies (Meister and Loftis 1977:223). In some cases, the cadre used coercion, revoking an uncooperative worker's good standing or refusing a dispatch from a hiring hall. The main problem, though, was the lack of preparatory organizing and solidary experiences that had welded the huelgistas together. Many workers wanted a union that provided benefits but asked little in return. As Meister and Loftis put it: "They did not necessarily want a union of their own; they wanted a union that would *serve them* without requiring them to do much in return" (1977:223).

There were also genuine grievances against UFW policies, especially among the migrants. The union had designed the hiring halls, service centers, and annual dues with the local workers in mind. But many of the migrants were sojourners with little interest in stabilized employment or year-round health benefits. They also resented infringements on their mobility and chafed at the hiring hall queue. Hiring hall managers refused to refer families or crews intact and dispatched workers according to union rather than ranch seniority. This rewarded loyal supporters, generally local workers, and stabilized employment, but it also interfered with the migrants' traditional work patterns. As one migrant grape picker commented: "With the Teamsters, it's like not having a union at all—you are free to work where you want" (Meister and Loftis 1977:223). The union also kept the annual dues policy, requiring workers to pay back dues before receiving a hiring hall dispatch. This made sense for the locals but alienated the migrants who could use the services only during part of the year.

The UFW also experienced continuing staff problems. The boycott strategy reduced the emphasis on training indigenous leaders who could take over the hiring halls and ranch committees. When the UFW took over the grape contracts in 1970, student volunteers had to be used. The volunteers often were unfamiliar with local conditions and were resented by some of the workers. Because of the highly moralistic basis of their commitment, they often needlessly antagonized the growers. They were inclined towards a simplistic Manichean outlook, seeing the UFW as absolutely good and the growers, Teamsters, and uncooperative workers as absolutely bad, which led to friction with workers as well as growers.

Will the UFW Survive?

The September 15, 1974 issue of the *New York Times Magazine* carried an article by the journalist Winthrop Griffith asking "Is Chavez Beaten?" "No one who sympathizes with him wants to admit that he is defeated. Some of his Anglo supporters still pace the sidewalks in front of city supermarkets, imploring customers to boycott the grapes and lettuce inside, but their posture now indicates to the skeptical outsider that they are engaged in a lonely vigil, not a dynamic national movement."[29] Written weeks before the Teamster Local 1973 was disbanded, Griffith's article argued that the Teamsters' superior organizational muscle, the conservative trend in national politics, and the psychological exhaustion of its supporters left the UFW struggling for its existence. Shortly afterwards, Peter Barnes wrote a much more informative assessment of "Chavez Against the Wall" for the *New Republic*, arguing that while the UFW was temporarily blocked by the Teamster-grower alliance, reports of the UFW's demise were "premature." Pointing to the UFW's solid base of farm worker support, Barnes suggested that the passage of an agricultural labor relations act giving the union a genuine opportunity to campaign for worker votes would restore the UFW's fortunes.[30]

Barnes proved a better diviner. The major factor behind the UFW's survival has in fact been its base of farm worker support. The mobilization strategy of bloc recruitment, indigenous organizers, preparatory efforts, and programs emphasizing ethnic solidarity, moral commitments to la causa, and selective incentives created a solid base of support that Teamster raids, grower harassment, unpopular union policies, and the vestiges of farm worker powerlessness could not destroy. Throughout the early 1970s, the UFW organized wildcat strikes against the Teamster contracts, and by the late 1970s, it had won over two-thirds of the elections, and its membership returned to over 100,000. In March 1977, the Teamsters announced that they would no longer contest elections and would allow their existing contracts to expire in the early 1980s.[31]

The UFW's largest problem has been converting electoral victories into union contracts. The Agricultural Labor Relations Act compelled growers to bargain in good faith but not to sign contracts. Although the UFW could still strike and boycott, the lettuce and wine boycotts had not proven effective. The political environment of the late 1970s was less favorable, and many sponsors mistakenly thought that the passage of the Labor Act removed the need for continued support. The question now was whether the UFW could organize effective strikes. Many of the Salinas vegetable growers were convinced it could, seventy signing contracts in the first two years after the elections. The UFW also altered controversial policies and adopted organizing strategies to maximize support among the migrants. Dues were changed to a proportion of salary and seniority to a ranch basis. Hiring hall managers were instructed to keep crews and families together. In several grape contracts, the union lost the hiring hall, in part because of worker opposition. The UFW downplayed the use of volunteers, relying exclusively on workers for picketing and, for the first time, began paying strike benefits for routine picket duty. The service centers along the border and coastal valleys were expanded, and the organizers emphasized bread-and-butter issues like wages and fringe benefits. The union also revised its action strategy, relaxing the restrictions on strike violence. Although nothing was ever said officially, personal attacks as well as property damage became more frequent while Chavez looked the other way. Since the boycott was no longer as central, external support was not as critical. The UFW had a more secure political position and could also afford to escalate its tactics.

The new approach paid off. In the spring of 1978, the union ran a mass strike in the Santa Maria Valley that brought out over three-fourths of the workers and forced the Coastal Growers Association to sign a master contract.[32] The next year, the UFW moved back to the Salinas Valley, seizing several Teamster lettuce contracts and winning 25 percent wage boosts, a cost of living escalator, and strong "good standing" provisions (*Los Angeles Times*, April 1, 1978; April 19 and 26, June 11, and August 13, 1979). Over the next two years, the strike wave spread to the Imperial Valley, the traditional graveyard for labor unions, and the Arizona lettuce fields. The UFW was now organizing powerful strikes; although the boycotts were still in effect, the victories now came from these mass strikes.

The union has survived several grower attacks on the Agricultural Labor Board. In the summer of 1976, the growers blocked the refunding of the board in the state legislature, bringing the elections to a halt for several months. The UFW mounted another initiative campaign, collecting 720,000 signatures for Proposition 14 that would have made the Labor Act part of the state constitution and expanded their ranch access. The growers relented, refunding the board, but attacked the Proposition with a $1.8 million advertising campaign that portrayed the access rules as a threat to private homeowners. In a television ad, an aging farmer pleaded: "Help me protect my personal property rights and yours. I've raised my family and *daughters* on this farm and *we* feel threatened." Although some voters were swayed by the ads, most doubted the need for a constitutional amendment once the board had been refunded, and the amendment was defeated 62 to 38 percent.[33] The UFW also survived a wave of legal challenges to the board's authority and more conservative board appointments. Yet the danger remained that Republican or conservative Democratic control of the state legislature and governorship might lead to restrictions on ranch access and delayed elections.

The union has also run up against barriers in expanding its base. The smaller, more dispersed farms have been more difficult to organize and the highly migratory sindocumentos and unspecialized workers less receptive to union appeals (Fuller and Mamer 1978; Thomas 1981a, 1981b). The UFW has also found it impossible to expand outside of California, indicating the importance of protective labor legislation. Despite a strong base of support in the Arizona lettuce fields, the growers have defeated several mass strikes. A merger with a union of Puerto Rican migrants in the east coast vegetable fields; several organizing drives in south Texas rivaled by the Texas Farm Workers Union, led by former UFW organizer Tony Orendain; and an alliance with the Farm Labor Organizing Committee centered in the Ohio Valley have not yet produced results. There is also the danger of a new bracero program which could be used to destroy the union. A bracero program has been included in legislation to restrict illegal immigration and, if administered like the earlier program, would blunt the UFW's new strike capacity.

The UFW also experienced factional disputes giving rise to charges that Chavez was inflexible and autocratic. In November 1971, Larry Itliong resigned, charging that Chavez had been "swayed by the grandiose thinking of a brain trust of intellectuals. . . . I couldn't get through to him" (*Los Angeles Times*, November 21, 1971). Three years later in the midst of a reorganization of the union's new offices in La Paz, an abandoned tuberculosis sanitarium in the remote Tehachipi Mountains, Jack

Quiggly, the union's business manager for over three years, resigned; he was protesting Chavez's interference in routine administrative matters with actions that included ripping out phones and holding heated disputes over the depth of staff commitments. Despite a constitution guaranteeing open elections, Chavez has closely controlled nominations to the Executive Board, filling positions with family members and close personal friends. In March 1979, Jerry Cohen, the UFW's long-term chief attorney, resigned after Chavez convinced the Executive Board to reject his proposal to pay staff salaries rather than in-kind subsistence. After the narrow victory, Chavez purged the board of dissenters at the next annual convention. Shortly afterwards Marshall Ganz, a key staff figure since the Delano grape strike and the major architect of the powerful 1979 vegetable strikes, resigned amid rumors that Chavez had forced him out over personal disagreements. About the same time Jim Drake resigned, becoming an organizer for a lumbermen's union in the south. Nor have union locals been allowed their autonomy, the most serious dispute being over Chavez's attempts to replace duly elected officials in the Salinas Valley local.[34]

As early as 1974, sympathetic observer Ronald Taylor concluded: "If *La Causa* is to make the transition from cause to stable union structure, its leadership must begin to accept the idea of a membership and union bureaucracy beyond the absolute control of any single individual. Chavez has been trying to delegate more and more authority, but in this effort he is clearly a man at odds with himself" (1975:331).

A long-standing thesis in social movement analysis has been that leadership styles change as social movements become institutionalized. The argument has illustrious ancestors, ranging from Max Weber's analysis of the "routinization of charisma" to Troeltsch's distinction between the church and the sect. In recent formulations, the argument has been posed in functional terms. As successful social movements grow and become institutionalized, they require a new type of leadership to handle new organizational tasks. Lang and Lang (1961:517–524), synthesizing the work of Dawson and Gettys (1935) and King (1956), have argued that there is a functional requirement to shift from the iconoclastic "agitator-prophet" who generates the movement to the more flexible "administrator-statesman" who negotiates alliances and implements changes. If the leadership fails to make this transition, the movement experiences internal strains and antagonizes potential allies.

Was the UFW experiencing a leadership crisis? There is no doubt about Chavez's determination to personally control the UFW's future. Yet it is also true that these clashes reflect long-standing decisions as well as personal proclivities. Chavez's reluctance to allow staff autonomy stemmed from the early community organizing approach, the treatment of student volunteers as servants of the movement and the early staff decision to give the boycott a focus by promoting Chavez's charisma. In the early organizing, Chavez built on the Mexican custom of compadrazgo (or fictive kinship), serving as a personal friend and protector for individual workers. The custom held on despite the union's growth, "every worker believ(ing) that his complaint about the union should be personally handled by Chavez" (*New York Times*, April 13, 1974). The first student volunteers had to accept vows of poverty, subsisting off union housing and meals plus $5 per week rather than salaries. They were also excluded from policy decisions, and Chavez upbraided and dismissed those who failed to exhibit sufficient dedication. The policy not only saved scarce resources, it also protected against a take-over by the student radicals who often had their own visions of the union's future. In the long run, it also strengthened the impetus for expansion since only those who were highly committed to social change stayed on. The key drawback, of course, was high rates of staff turnover. The focus on Chavez's personality was also a strategic decision, stemming from the staff conclusion that the boycott and protests would project in the mass media more effectively with a saintly martyr. On all three issues, the UFW has confronted an organizational dilemma. Compadrazgo cannot be transferred to a cadre of administrators. A staff committed to visions of social change is more likely to keep its missionary impulse and maintain pressure on the growers. The "saint" image is still politically useful, although it has been sullied by in-fighting and the conclusion that the UFW is just another union. The question is whether the benefits are outweighed by the costs of staff turnover and low morale. The union has lost virtually all the original cadre and new recruits from the farm worker ranks are discouraged by the poverty vow and demands for total dedication. The organizing pace has slowed in the early 1980s, leaving the prospects of union expansion ambiguous. At best, the UFW is experiencing leadership difficulties whose resolution or significance remains unclear.

There is, however, no doubt about the UFW's overall success. In chapter 1, the notion of insurgent success was measured by a hierarchy

of three dimensions: policy changes that produce tangible benefits; regime successes that alter the routines of institutional decision-making;
and distributional changes that redistribute societal resources. The UFW
has experienced successes along the first two dimensions. There have
been innumerable policy changes, the most significant being the increase in real wages. In 1964, farm wages in California averaged $1.10
to $1.35 per hour. By 1980, union lettuce workers were paid over $5 per
hour, representing a 70 percent increase in real wages. Work rules have
also been reformed. The short-hoe has been abolished. Dangerous pesticides are barred, and others cannot be used without notice. Growers
can no longer arbitrarily fire workers. Seniority rules facilitate stabilized
employment. Employers contribute to health care, disability, and insurance benefits.

There have also been significant changes in the authority structure of
the farm enterprises and the larger polity. Farm workers have for the
first time an institutionalized voice in key decisions. There are standard-
ized grievance procedures, hiring halls that control access to jobs, and
ranch committees that enter into contract negotiations and handle grievances. At the polity level, the Agricultural Labor Relations Act guarantees basic rights to organize and select union representatives, institu-
tionalizing these arrangements. The UFW has also forged strong political
alliances with Mexican-American political organizations and the Democratic party. By organizing voter registration campaigns and actively
campaigning for candidates in the urban barrios as well as among union
members, the UFW has made its endorsement and the farm worker vote
into a significant electoral force.

The challenge, however, has not brought major redistributions.
Unionization is still limited to less than a third of California's farm workers, leaving the general distribution of economic rewards roughly constant. In the decade and a half since the first contract, increases in farm
worker real income have kept pace with but not surpassed increases in
grower real profits.[35] Insurgency has also improved the workers' pride
and self-image, yet the general position of farm workers in the structure
of social prestige remains extremely low. The major distributional gains
have been in the political arena. The growers are still influential but they
no longer have an exclusive voice in public policies. Farm workers are
organized, have routine access to centers of decision-making, and as the
series of policy gains suggests, hold claim in an arena previously domi-

nated exclusively by the growers. Even if the UFW does not survive and prosper as an organization, it has clearly been the central agency in transforming farm workers' lives and rural California.

The Formula for Success

The UFW success stemmed from effective strategies and increased political opportunities. Although changes in the labor market did make for easier organizing, the farm workers were still structurally powerless. Braceros disappeared, local and specialized workers increased, ethnic diversity declined, and larger farms created more ecological concentration. Yet the UFW still could not organize effective strikes. Mexican immigrants, casual workers, and crews rounded up by contractors crossed picket lines. The initial victories came from boycotts and political campaigns.

Yet the UFW did build a sustained base of farm worker support which was decisive. Farm workers were the backbone of the boycott cadre, and their support allowed the union to survive the Teamster-grower attack and eventually organize effective mass strikes. The UFW mobilized the workers by emphasizing collective incentives and effective organizing tactics. The union held community events, staged solidarity marches that built on ethnic symbolism, and through selective benefit programs, generated extensive community solidarities. The NFLU and AWOC, by contrast, invested little in preparatory organizing and emphasized collective economic gains. The UFW organizers also used bloc recruitment tactics, holding house meetings and initially concentrating on the more cohesive local workers. They trained indigenous organizers, setting off an expanding wave of grass-roots organizing. The predecessors, the AWOC especially, had mistakenly tried organizing the most transient segment of the workers.

The UFW also mobilized massive external support, securing organizing resources and political support that finally forced the growers to concede. The favorable political environment was decisive, yet it is also true that the UFW pursued this avenue more persistently and skillfully than its predecessors. The key was staging dramatic protest events that captured media attention and created images of grower intransigence and farm worker powerlessness. Chavez went on fasts, led religious pilgrimages, and staged arrests to protest repression. The boycott extended this strategy, spreading the protest campaign to storefronts throughout the country. The union also used these campaigns to mobilize farm workers. Chavez's fasts stirred farm workers and brought in political support. Pilgrimages restored the union's contact with dispersed supporters as well as generating boycott support. The UFW also escalated its tactics, shifting to more militant measures as external support became less problematic and central.

The most dramatic change, however, was in the political environment. The polity is normally restrictive, elites blocking challenges while potential sponsors watch quietly on the sidelines. The NFLU and, to a lesser degree, the AWOC faced major political opposition. The local police and courts harassed organizing campaigns and strikes. Bracero strikebreaking ultimately destroyed both challenges. Federal courts and labor officials halted the NFLU boycott. The UFW, by contrast, received sustained sponsorship and political protection. Student radicals volunteered for the boycotts, civil rights activists provided training in boycott tactics, clerics rallied to the picket lines, unionists contributed strike funds and marched out on sympathy strikes, consumers boycotted grapes and wines, and liberal politicians courted the challenge. Although local political opposition was still intense, state and national elites no longer automatically sided with the growers. This gave the challenge greater organizing space and opportunities to generate external support. After national political alignments became less favorable, the UFW rallied its California allies to secure favorable labor legislation. By the late 1970s, the UFW was organizing effective mass strikes, signalling that its impact would be lasting.

8

The Politics of Turmoil: Political Realignment and the Social Movements of the 1960s

Postwar American suburbs, glorious world! To be Superkids! One's parents remembered the sloughing common order, War & Depression—but Superkids remembered only the emotional surge of the great payoff, when nothing was common any longer—the Life! A glorious place, a glorious age, I tell you!

Tom Wolfe
The Electric Kool-Aid Acid Test (1971)

America's history as a nation has reached its end. The American people will of course survive. But the ties that make them a society will grow more tenuous with each passing year. There will be undercurrents of tension and turmoil, and the only remaining option will be to learn to live with these disorders. For they are not problems that can be solved.

Andrew Hacker
The End of the American Era (1970)

In the two decades between Dwight Eisenhower's reign over a tranquil if not happy populace and Richard Nixon's forced renunciation of his crown, the United States experienced a transformation. The civil rights movement emerged, bringing blacks into the political arena and supporting a broad set of social reforms. A new student Left developed, turning the quiet groves of academe into a battleground as students organized teach-ins and draft resistance campaigns, occupied buildings, and closed down entire campuses. By the late 1960s, the political turmoil had become generalized as new insurgencies arose among women, Native Americans, Chicanos, Puerto Ricans, farm workers, welfare recipients, homosexuals, middle-class consumers, environmentalists, radical ecologists, white ethnics, and even a sprinkling of blue-collar workers. The United Farm Worker challenge emerged during the upswing of this political surge and, as we have seen, effectively harnessed the newly unleashed political energies to its successful bid for power.

What created this broad political explosion? The favorite theories have been analyses of cultural transformation. Charles Reich (1970) provided one of the earliest and most evocative analyses, arguing that the demographic expansion of youth and the arrival of economic affluence had created *The Greening of America* that prefigured a new mode of life and consciousness, which he promptly dubbed "Consciousness III." A more analytic version was offered by Theodore Roszak (1969) who spoke of *The Making of a Counter-Culture* among affluent youth alienated from the narrow materialism and linear rationality of the technocratic society. Those less enamored of the cultural ferment offered less flattering appraisals. Andrew Hacker (1970), looking down from his lofty perch at Cornell, offered a funeral oration, arguing in *The End of the American Era* that affluence, geographic mobility, and the growth of the middle class had created a "nation of 200 million egos" no longer restrained by authority. A more eloquent attack was advanced by Daniel Bell (1976) who argued that consumer capitalism had created a new class which, by assimilating the bohemian culture of the modernist literati, had adopted a destructive quest for self-fulfillment.

These analyses of the links between economic affluence, cultural changes, and the "new politics" had hardly been advanced before a more cynical interpretation was offered emphasizing the concealed economic interests behind the rise of "new class" political activism (Kirkpatrick 1976; Kristol 1978; Bruce-Briggs 1981; Tucker 1982). The seminal statement was, appropriately enough, Daniel Moynihan's (1968) analysis of the origins of the War on Poverty. Pointing to the initiatives of upper-middle class administrators and policy researchers, Moynihan argued that mass-based social movements had been replaced as agencies of social reform by "professional reformers" who, advocating the cause of the poor, pressed for governmental programs that actually advanced their own interests. The problem of poverty was, of course, intractable, but the professional reformers managed to seize an expanding share of the federal budget, while their extravagant promises radicalized the poor by encouraging them to mistakenly believe that their burdens could be lifted. A decade later, Irving Kristol (1978) generalized the argument, asserting that the humanitarian rhetoric of the "new class" reformers in the social service bureaucracies was actually no more than a cover for self-interest, poorly concealing a general class-wide attack on the capitalist institutions that had generated the new affluence.

A more provocative use of the "professionalization of reform" argument was made by John McCarthy and Mayer Zald (1973, 1975, 1977) who refashioned it into a general theory of social movements. Their major departure was to argue that there had not actually been a genuine political upsurge but rather a series of professional social movements launched by a new cadre of political entrepreneurs. The center of their theory was the contrast between "professional" and "classical" social movements. Classical movements were indigenously based, drawing their resources and leadership from aggrieved groups and directly advancing their collective interests. Professional movements, by contrast, had weak or non-existent memberships and were initiated by political entrepreneurs drawn from the outside who, speaking in the name of the excluded, mobilized resources from "conscience constituencies." Structural trends had created a conducive context for these political entrepreneurs. Rising discretionary income created a growing pool of potential contributors. Professional and college students with discretionary time-schedules could serve as "transitory teams" of activists. The mass media could be manipulated to create dramatic images of social injustice that sold the message much like mouthwash and deodorant. The growth of the welfare state and social service sector created new careers in which professional social critics could articulate their views without the inconveniences of actual suffering. Although these new social movements had given off the appearance of genuine turmoil, they were actually Potemkin armies that would soon pass, destroyed by the transiency of media attention and their vulnerability to elite controls.

All three theories receive some support from broad structural trends. The period between the early 1950s and the late 1960s was one of economic prosperity. Per capita income roughly doubled, and real disposable income rose by almost three-fourths, with the highest rates occurring during the early 1960s. Affluence made plausible the psychological underpinnings of the cultural transformation theory, namely that, to use Maslow's (1968) theory of the hierarchy of human needs, Americans were increasingly freed from lower level economic concerns to pursue higher level needs for self-fulfillment. It also meant that there was rising disposable income to invest in social causes, supporting the theory of professional movements. There were also major changes in the economy and the occupational hierarchy. The service sector of the economy boomed, expanding to almost a third of the economy. Professional or "new class" occupations, especially those tied to governmental spending, doubled from around 8 percent to over 16 percent of the work force. The new ranks of affluent professionals presumably adhered to the new culture and had a stake in expanding governmental budgets. They had the discretionary income and time to invest in professional reform efforts. There was also a "baby boom" that created a youth bulge and an academic revolution. Youth grew from around ten percent to almost a quarter of the population, and college enrollments zoomed to over six million or roughly one-third of the prime age population (U.S. *Census*, 1976). Finally, the mass media developed into a pervasive institution, creating a national forum for political debate. Those bent on exposing social injustice and advocating social reforms had a medium for their messages.

Each theory also had special virtues. The cultural transformation theory was borne out by studies of the new youth culture and the new student activists. The creation of a post-adolescent "youth" stage in the life cycle coupled with young people's segregation in high schools and colleges created a new youth culture that prized self-expression and leisure activities. The new generation grew up in the midst of affluence, automatically assuming that the problems of poverty and discrimination were readily solvable (Flacks 1967, 1971; Yankelovich 1971). Yet despite these generational changes, the new student activists largely mirrored their parental political values, differing only in holding these in stronger form. The new rebels came overwhelmingly from upper-middle class families, typically tied to the liberal professions and the governmental social service sector, where the liberal values of self-fulfillment and tolerance for the views of others were prized. The student activists were also concentrated in the social sciences and humanities where disciplinary materials emphasized critical assessments of social problems, and the knowledge base was largely nonapplied and nonvocational (Keniston 1968; Pinckney 1968; Wood 1975; Westby 1976). The theory also received support from studies of western Europe where the same structural trends appeared to give rise to the same "post-materialist" culture and approval of political protest despite divergent national political traditions (Ingelehart 1977). This cultural interpretation also made sense of the high rhetoric and introspective moralism of the new social movements. As Hodgson (1976:367) noted, the new social movements expressed a moral search: "The question was not that with which Lenin had launched his revolution: What is to be done? It was more introspective, less urgent, more of a luxury than that. It was: Is America morally sick?" The cultural theory, however, lacked any specification of the politicization of these new values. Why was it that the new movements suddenly sprang up in the early 1960s when the cultural changes had been taking place over several decades? Even more seriously, why did the turmoil suddenly subside in the mid-1970s while the new culture steadily gained adherents throughout the society (Yankelovich 1979; Veroff, Douvan and Kulka 1981)? The theory also offered little insight into the insurgencies of the excluded. Black sharecroppers and farm workers were inspired by more than visions of cultural revolution.

The neoconservative interpretation of the new movements had the virtue of pointing at the new political coalition between the social service sector of the "new class" and the excluded. Traditionally the upper middle class had been politically conservative, allying with the business community. But increasingly the "new class," especially those in the liberal professions and the social services, moved to the left, supporting liberal Democrats and social reforms (Ladd and Hadley 1978). What was in question, however, was the basis for this move. Although material interests were certainly a constraint, the cultural interpretation made better sense of the activism, especially the more intense forms. Student volunteers who went south to risk their lives in voter registration work, draft resisters who risked imprisonment for their beliefs, and young professionals who shunned lucrative careers as corporate lawyers and managers to serve the poor or the environmental movement could not be interpreted in terms of narrow economic self-interest. The cultural transformation theory was on stronger ground in emphasizing the "public regarding" values that guided much of the "new class" activism. The neoconservative theory also downplayed the indigenous grievances and mobilization among the excluded, acting as if they had simply risen up in response to the call of their more privileged allies when, in fact, the insurgency began first among the excluded.

The theory of professional social movements also offered significant insights, especially into the critical role of sponsors and the rise of a new cohort of political entrepreneurs supported by government and foundation grants and direct mail solicitations (Berry 1977; McFarland 1976; Sabato 1980). Student radicals, church leaders, and trade unionists played a critical support role in farm worker insurgency as well as the civil rights and women's movements (Pinckney 1968; Freeman 1975). Likewise, movement entrepreneurs helped launch several poor people's movements as well as an array of public interest lobbies and law firms (Kotz and Kotz 1977; Jackson and Johnson 1974; Helfgot 1981; Jenkins 1986). Yet the theory seriously overstated the significance of the professional movements. The major social movements of the 1960s were indigenous, mass-based insurgencies. The cultural transformation and "new class" theories were on stronger ground on this point. As we will see, the political turmoil was rooted in a genuine "participation revolution" (Bell 1973) that cannot be explained away simply in terms of political entrepreneurs and their professional movements. In fact, the professional movements were more a product than a producer of this general wave of insurgency. Many of the entrepreneurs were trained by earlier insurgencies and then set out to launch new causes. Others played on elite fears about generalized disorders to secure their grants. Finally, as McAdam (1982) has shown for black insurgency, elite support was generally a response rather than a cause of insurgency and operated as a social control, channelling dissidence into acceptable channels rather than simply facilitating its further development.

The major limit of all these theories, however, is their failure to account for the generalized nature of the turmoil. Why was there a simultaneous rise of multiple social movements advancing the interests of a wide array of excluded and previously unorganized groups? Although the structural trends affected groups throughout the society, it seems doubtful that the supporters of all these challenges were affected simultaneously. All three theories were also economic theories at their root and neglected the political processes involved in the rise and decline of social movements. In particular, they failed to explore the interaction between routine political changes and insurgency. Finally, the theories provided no insight into the sudden contraction of turmoil in the mid-1970s, a major problem since the structural trends persisted or even deepened through the late 1970s.

The "Participation Revolution"

Was there actually a broad upsurge in political participation, especially in nonroutine forms of political action? A key point in McCarthy and Zald's (1973) analysis was that political participation rates remained unchanged from the quiescent 1950s through the tumultuous 1960s. Their evidence, however, was extremely weak, coming from studies of voting turnout. Voting is the most institutionalized form of political participation and certainly cannot be taken as a general indicator of political participation. In fact, recent studies have demonstrated that there was a general surge in political participation. The excluded and the upper-middle class were the major carriers of this explosion. Most important of all, this "participation revolution" overspilled conventional political channels into an escalating wave of unruly protests, riots, and demonstrations that demanded "an enlarged scope of individual participation in the setting of societal goals and practices" (Ladd and Hadley 1978:206).

The participation explosion is evident from concurrent changes in public opinion and political action. Beginning in the early 1960s, Americans became increasingly concerned about domestic social problems—chiefly race, poverty and the environment—and less confident of the ability of political officials to solve these problems (Cantril and Hoopes 1971:29–73; Lipset and Schneider 1983). There was also heightened interest in political issues. As Nie, Verba, and Petrocik (1980:283) described it, politics during the 1950s was "low-keyed, party ties firm, citizens satisfied or relatively so. Politics are, comparatively speaking, dull. The main issues are nondivisive ones—foreign threats." The Kennedy-Nixon context generated heightened interest, and the Johnson-Goldwater campaigns "crystallized the issue positions of that more interested citizenry." Political ideologues who viewed politics in terms of issues rather than personalities increased steadily from 1 percent in the early 1950s to 19 percent by the early 1970s (Nie, Verba, and Petrocik 1980:367). There was also a general liberalization trend, especially in support for civil liberties and social equality (Smith 1981). Significantly, the major supporters of these liberal views were, in addition to excluded groups, upper-middle class professionals involved in the social services who became a major factor in the Democratic party (Ladd and Hadley 1978:357–359). In general, the "dependent" voter who was unresponsive, unknowing, nonrational, and apathetic (Larzarsfeld et al. 1948) gave way to the "responsive" voter who was knowledgeable, rational, ideological, generally reformist, and issue-oriented (Pomper 1975).

These changes were connected to a general increase in political participation. Despite a steady decline in electoral turnout, membership in civic associations and political clubs rose from 2.8 percent in 1956 to 4.4 percent in 1974 (Davis et al. 1981). Those politically active outside of elections increased from the 5–12 percent range in the 1950s (Campbell, Converse, Miller, and Stokes 1960:51–52; Milbrath 1965) to the 15–20 percent range in the late 1960s and early 1970s (Converse 1972:332–336; Rosenau 1974:44–86; Milbrath and Goel 1977:18–19; Ladd and Hadley 1978:363). Similarly, the intensity of political participation rose as these activists, especially the young and well-educated, committed greater resources to electoral campaigns (Beck and Jennings 1979). Most significant of all, the participation revolution overflowed the bounds of routine political processes, creating an explosive wave of protests, demonstrations, and riots that grew steadily throughout the decade and subsided only in the early 1970s. In short, between 1969 and 1975 the United States experienced a period of political turmoil based on a genuine political upsurge. Although the upsurge may not have included all groups, it was significantly general to shake a political system accustomed to relatively low levels of political participation. Significantly, this upsurge peaked precisely at the point that the United Farm Workers was scoring its first victories and, as we will see, it critically shaped the political environment that made for the union's success.

Political Realignment, the New Regime, and Growing Turmoil

Changes in mass politics always develop in interaction with shifts among elites. This broad political upsurge pushed forward a political realignment which led to the rise of a new center-left governing coalition. This new regime, in turn, promoted further increases in participation and, most significantly, the rise of new insurgencies. Although the realignment did not eventually produce the kind of durable electoral changes that the "system of 1896" and the New Deal realignments had created (Burnham 1970), it did generate new political coalitions at both mass and elite levels and, at least for a short time, opportunities for new social movements.

The first signs were electoral shifts by groups already inside the polity yet marginal to prevailing party coalitions who would later become the core supporters of concerted challenges. Beginning in the mid-1950s, two critical groups—the white Protestant upper-middle class and urban blacks—became swing voters whose loyalties became increasingly pivotal to national elections. The upper middle class, which had traditionally been solidly Republican, became increasingly Democratic, and supportive of ideological politics. Although this "new class" gradually became ideologically split between those tied to the welfare state who supported the "new left" and those in the large corporations who supported the "new right," both segments became increasingly disgruntled with the traditional patronage-cum-personality politics of the major parties (Ladd and Hadley 1978:357–359). This made them unpredictable voters and fickle albeit critical contributors to electoral campaigns. At the same time, urban blacks who had been loyal Republicans became restive, supporting liberal Democrats who promised civil rights reforms (Lomax 1962:228–230; Brink and Harris 1963). Meanwhile, the traditional constituencies for the New Deal coalition—blue collar workers, white ethnics, Jews, and southerners—drifted slowly towards the center. These shifts produced a new ideological spectrum of mass allegiances: a right populated by "new class" ideologues, business conservatives, and upper-class southerners; a center occupied by blue collar workers, white ethnics, and working class southerners; and a left filled with "new class" ideologues, women and minorities. In the context of a series of closely contested national elections in which the margin of victory was often less than one percent, the two swing voting blocs became increasingly decisive in the electoral calculations of political elites.

The impact of these trends on governing coalitions depended on the rate at which particular changes were occurring. The polar moves to the left and the right were occurring more rapidly than the move to the center. The Democratic party seized the opportunity to assemble a center-left electoral coalition by courting these restive voters, gradually strengthening their standing in Congressional and Presidential contests.

In 1954 the Democrats narrowly regained control over Congress and, despite losing the Presidency by a larger margin, steadily gained Congressional seats through the mid-1960s. In 1960 Kennedy narrowly won the Presidency, giving the Democrats nominal control of the White House and the Congress. The decisive break, however, came in 1964. The ideological right seized control of the Republican party and mounted an extravagant ideological campaign, giving the Democrats the opportunity to forge a broad center-left coalition. The Democratic landslide produced the largest margin of presidential victory to date (22.7 percent), a Congressional margin that resembled the Republican hegemony

Table 8.1

Governmental Coalitions in the United States (1948–1980)

| | Presidential Control | | Congressional Control | |
| | | % Margin | House Plurality | Senate Plurality |
Year	President	Popular Vote	(No. seats)	(No. seats)
1948	Truman	Democrat, 4.5	Democrat, 92	Democrat, 2
1952	Eisenhower	Republican, 10.7	Evenly Divided	Republican, 1
1956	Eisenhower	Republican, 15.4	Democrat, 33	Democrat, 2
1960	Kennedy	Democrat, 0.2	Democrat, 90	Democrat, 30
1964	Johnson	Democrat, 22.7	Democrat, 77	Democrat, 34
1968	Nixon	Republican, 0.7	Democrat, 51	Democrat, 14
1972	Nixon	Republican, 23.2	Democrat, 47	Democrat, 14
1976	Carter	Democrat, 0.9	Democrat, 149	Democrat, 11
1980	Reagan	Republican, 9.8	Democrat, 50	Republican, 7

of the 1920s, and, for the first time since the early 1940s, a single party with unified control of both the White House and both Houses of Congress (table 8.1).

All three elements of this new regime—the margin of victory, the unity of the regime, as well as its center-left composition—were critical. As Janowitz (1978:92–96) has noted, postwar American politics has been marked by divided and weak governments. At least one chamber of Congress has been held by the opposition party, or the margin of governmental control has been too weak to provide a coherent program. The 1964 election was unique in bringing a new regime to power with sufficient margin to pursue a consistent political program. Because of its ties to minorities and the "new class" liberals, the new regime advanced a series of social reforms—the Civil Rights Acts of 1964 and 1965, the War on Poverty legislation, fiscal and monetary policies to promote full employment, a Model Cities program to rebuild the cities, and the beginnings of environmental and consumer reforms. The reform stance was also strengthened by Congressional reapportionment which, following the 1960 census returns revealing the shift from rural areas to large cities, weakened the coalition of conservative rural Democrats and Republicans whose seniority and control over key committees had given them Congressional power.

The Democrats immediately became the champion of the excluded, pressing for reforms that would incorporate new groups while strengthening their electoral base. Several of these measures inevitable weakened the traditional controls of entrenched antagonists. The excluded had greater opportunities to mobilize, and insurgents secured their more moderate demands. The civil rights movement provided the model experience. Under intense pressure from the White House, Congress passed the Civil Rights Acts of 1964 and 1965, fulfilling the demands articulated in the March on Washington in 1963. By the late 1960s, the federal protections insured a growing and solidly Democratic black vote which, in turn, gave rise to a dramatic increase in black elected officials and an end to race-baiting campaigns and Jim Crow practices (Lawson 1976).

Similarly, the Democrats launched a concerted attack on the bracero program, helping to initiate the UFW challenge by removing a major obstacle to farm worker strikes (Hawley 1966). At the peak of the grape boycott, the Democrats held Congressional hearings on farm worker powerlessness and unsuccessfully supported national labor legislation, and Presidential contenders courted Chavez's campaign endorsement. In the early 1970s, the UFW proved its ability to weather political attacks, and the Democrats again supported reforms, although limited to the demonstrable base of support in California. In each case the basic bargain was incorporative reforms that protected rights to organize in exchange for electoral loyalty. Democratic leaders supported the boycotts and the Agricultural Labor Relations Act in return for a growing Mexican-American vote in Democratic columns.

The insurgent successes of the early 1960s unleashed a broad wave of new social movements by providing models of effective action, identifying new resources and giving proof of the new opportunities. As Freeman (1979) has argued, social movement successes tend to stimulate new challenges by training the cadre and furnishing the strategic models for new challenges. The UFW built off the cadre and strategies of the civil rights movement, much in the same way that the women's movement drew on the student movement (Evans 1979). The earlier challenges also opened up sources of institutional support and political alliances. Church leaders and foundation executives, once involved in the civil rights successes, found it logical to move on to farm worker organizing, worker-controlled coops, and homosexual rights. Finally, the successes provided incontrovertible evidence that social change was now possible. Previously quiescent groups came to perceive their own conditions as unjust and susceptible to change. Dual consciousness dissolved in favor of insurgent consciousness. The less easily mobilized migrant workers rose up following the successful grape boycotts much in the same way that Native Americans, Puerto Ricans, homosexuals, and other excluded groups mounted challenges in the late 1960s and early 1970s.

The generalized turmoil had paradoxical consequences. On the one hand, it maximized the pressure on elites to make concessions, especially for the moderate challengers, and thereby accelerated the success rate. On the other hand, it threatened more powerful actors, set off a wave of counter-movements, and weakened the center-left political coalition, eventually bringing a more restrictive polity. In a sense, the Nixon administration was correct. The dynamic of expanding turmoil was self-perpetuating if left unchecked. The insurgent successes stimulated new challengers, creating an expanding wave of turmoil that might eventually restructure the entire polity.

The Nixon advisers were also right about the possibilities of halting this dynamic by strengthening controls and appeals to polity members newly threatened by the new movements. The insurgents stepped up their demands, challenging more entrenched traditions and alienating former allies. Black leaders such as Martin Luther King became advocates of a general poor people's movement, the new class war that would convert the civil rights struggle into a bid for general economic redistribution. The target was no longer southern conservatives but the national corporate elite, the middle classes, perhaps even blue collar workers. The radical wing of the women's movement advocated comprehensive changes in sex roles. Powerful corporations, deep-seated traditions as well as conservative women were now the target. Radical demands not only provoked more concerted social control efforts but also alienated former

221

allies. Moderate church leaders were more skeptical about redistributionist demands, and liberal foundations channeled their support towards less controversial reforms like protecting the environment and consumer rights. Counter-movements emerged, borrowing many of their tactics from the new movements and attempting to mobilize those threatened by the new demands. The center-left electoral coalition began to dissolve. In 1968 blue collar voters joined southern reactionaries to support George Wallace's third party bid. Insurgency continued to escalate, however, through the 1972 election. The "new politics" coalition seized the Democratic party, restructured its rules to insure the access of the new groups, but faced with the mass defection of the centrist blue collar workers, white ethnics, and southerners, went down to a devastating defeat. The election marked the beginning of the end of a political period. New challenges ceased to proliferate, and those already in motion like the UFW's and the environmentalists' found it necessary to locate a more limited terrain to consolidate their victories. A period of turmoil had come to a close, leaving behind a rich legacy of social change, not the least of which was the unionization of California farm workers.

9

The Politics of Insurgency

The generalized political turmoil of the 1960s grew out of long-term structural trends and political realignments. The transformation of southern agriculture created a massive black migration to the cities. Excluded from mainstream institutions yet freed from the powerful controls of the plantation owners, the black middle class in these urban ghettoes created a new array of churches, student associations, social clubs, and NAACP chapters. By the late 1950s, this new organizational base provided the context for organizing a sustained challenge against the Jim Crow system. About the same time, a new progressivism emerged among the new middle class created by the expansion of the welfare state and the service economy. Professionally committed to developing solutions to social problems, this economically secure yet marginal segment of the middle class became the general advocate for a wide variety of social reforms advanced in the name of the general public and the excluded.

Both insurgencies were facilitated by the political opportunities created by shifting political alignments. The collapse of McCarthyism led to a leftward shift in electoral alignments and elite coalitions. In a series of closely divided elections, political elites found themselves competing for two new sets of restive voters: the newly urbanized blacks who were no longer wedded to the party of their grandfathers or their plantation masters, and the new middle class that was increasingly non-partisan and interested in ideological visions. By the early 1960s, the Democratic party had emerged as the victor, forging a loose coalition between these new contenders and the New Deal coalition. Democratic victories created new opportunities for insurgency, and after the 1964 electoral sweep, the Democrats were in a position to institutionalize a series of social re-

223

forms. Inspired by the civil rights and student successes, a new wave of insurgencies emerged among groups that had previously been unorganized and excluded from routine decision making.

The United Farm Worker challenge was one of the more successful of this new wave of insurgencies. Drawing off the resources and strategic models created by the civil rights and student movements, the UFW organized a mass base of farm worker support and a series of broadly supported boycotts and political campaigns that eventually transformed rural California and gave farm workers a permanent voice in major decisions affecting their lives. The new political alignments weakened their grower antagonists and created opportunities for mobilizing external support on an unprecedented scale.

Does the UFW experience provide a model for insurgency among powerless, excluded groups? The UFW confronted obstacles similar to those of other insurgencies among the powerless. The growers were politically entrenched, having built their empire out of organization and political access. Farm worker movements had been routinely destroyed by political repression. The structure of the labor market also weakened the mobilization base for such challenges. Although conditions did improve slightly in the period before the UFW challenge, the farm workers were still structurally powerless. The key factor leading to a sustained challenge that eventually succeeded was the new political alignments that tempered political repression, removed the bracero strikebreaking force, and made it possible to mobilize broad external support. The UFW leadership was also prepared to seize these opportunities, adopting a dual strategy of simultaneously organizing farm workers as well as gaining external support.

A critical element of this dual strategy was an extremely effective organizing approach. A key problem in organizing powerless groups is their lack of solidarity and indigenous leaders. By building a permanent membership association led by professional organizers, the UFW created a sustained basis for organizing efforts. These organizing campaigns were also effectively designed. By emphasizing collective incentives and using bloc recruitment tactics that built on existing solidarities and trained indigenous organizers, the organizers generated a solid base of farm worker support. Although this support was not initially sufficient for effective strikes, it did sustain the challenge against the Teamster attack and pressure the growers to accept unionization. The UFW also tried to adhere

224

to a pyramiding strategy, investing in preparatory efforts and gradually escalating actions in line with capacities. Under the protections of the Agricultural Labor Relations Act, this mobilization strategy eventually paid off in a series of highly effective strikes in the late 1970s.

This experience runs at odds with Piven and Cloward's (1977) assessment of poor people's insurgencies. They advocate a "cadre organization" that shuns a permanent membership and concentrates exclusively on mobilizing mass defiance. In their view, powerless groups cannot be organized into permanent membership associations. At best, membership organizing diverts energies from mass defiance and, at worst, creates organizational brakes on disruptions. The central problem with this interpretation is that membership associations and mass defiance are not exclusive options. Piven and Cloward are correct that the powerless are an unpromising base for organizing permanent membership associations. In addition to being excluded, they are deprived, disorganized, and often sufficiently marginal that their defiance creates only small institutional disruptions. By this measure, farm workers are an advantaged segment of the American underclass. At least they enjoy a better strategic position than welfare recipients and the unemployed. But, as the UFW demonstrated, the powerless can be organized into permanent associations that provide the basis for mass defiance. The organizing may require infusions of external support, especially salaries for professional organizers and technical assistance such as legal and tactical advice. It may also be the case that the more marginal segments of the powerless lack sufficient leverage to extract significant gains. Sporadic insurgency nurtured by transitory cadres may be all that welfare recipients can mount. But at least for those with a strategic position, a permanent association affords greater promise of a sustained challenge and long-term gains. Piven and Cloward may also be correct that insurgent leaders can blunt insurgency and divert dissidence, but these are strategic choices, not organizational imperatives. Insurgent leaders are sufficiently independent that their strategic decisions can push a challenge towards or away from institutional disruptions. In general, poor people's movements should be able to borrow from the United Farm Worker organizing model.

The UFW also built off the other half of the dual strategy by mobilizing widespread external support. Polity members provided organizing resources, political protection, and external leverage. This support overrode many of the traditional obstacles to organizing farm workers, especially lack of organizing resources and problems in sustaining strikes. Yet, as the experience of most insurgencies testifies, the polity is normally closed. Antagonists use their political access to block challenges, and even polity members without a direct stake generally oppose the entry of new groups because this raises the spectre of a restructuring of polity rules. External support, especially of a sustained character, is rare. The state is an inherently conservative institution. The problem then is how this bias of the state becomes neutralized, polity members rallying to the support of insurgency.

I have argued that the central dynamic is the development of internal political realignments that make the support of new challengers advantageous to polity members. As Tilly (1978:213–214) has argued, a closely divided polity in which rival governing coalitions battle for control increases the likelihood of such member-challenger coalitions. In liberal democratic regimes, elite realignments are mediated by the currents of electoral politics. Parties court enfranchised voting blocs, attempting to forge broad coalitions on the basis of diverse appeals. Changes or instability in the partisan orientation of these voting blocs, especially those that promise the margin of victory, focus elite attentions on the interests of these swing groups. If electoral contests are close, the advantages of bringing new groups into the polity may more than offset the risks of restructuring the polity. Of course, the excluded group has to constitute a significant potential voting bloc, and the insurgents have to advance demands that are compatible with the interests of other coalition partners. The ascendance of center-left governing coalition also strengthens sponsors, reducing the costs of support and increasing their ability to carry through significant reforms.

These realignments and accompanying reforms may also set off a general wave of insurgencies that creates generalized political turmoil and broader opportunities. Successful challenges excite potential insurgents, provide new models of action, and dislodge resources for groups that had previously been quiescent. Sponsors perceive further gains from supporting new challengers. Entrenched antagonists lose their footing. As the political pulse rate heightens, electoral alignments become less stable. Under pressure from proliferating insurgencies, political elites may grant concessionary reforms and fashion incorporative devices to bring the more moderate insurgents into centers of power. Groups with less mobilization potential rise up, pressing their own special cause. Although most of these demands will not be met, if only because the proliferation of insurgency also generates backlash effects, the spread of generalized turmoil will increase the short-term opportunities for the more powerful challenges. As these groups scramble aboard, securing a modicum of their demands, new challengers rise up that make even more radical bids. Previous bystanders feel threatened and sponsors withdraw support, bringing the period of turmoil and reform to a close.

This analysis of the politics of insurgency runs at odds with conventional theories of political power. The core issue is the role of the liberal democratic state. Pluralists have erroneously assumed that the liberal democratic state is, to use Gamson's (1975) term, structurally "permeable." Normally the state is a central agency in the battle against insurgency. Polity members use their access to block challenges, and the excluded are kept out because their interests clash with those on the inside. Yet during exceptional periods of realignment and turmoil, polity members may develop a stake in supporting the entry of new groups. The liberal democratic state temporarily lives up to E. E. Schattschneider's (1960) vision of it as an "alternative power system" in which the force of organized numbers outweighs institutionalized structures of power. The decentralized structure of the American state also provides an advantage. Scrappy challengers have the opportunity to play on regional divisions, concentrating their efforts in particular locales and using external allies to support their demands. In unitary states, different levels of political authority tend to automatically reinforce one another, but in decentralized federal structures, national levels can be at odds with and neutralize or even counteract local authorities. The UFW played on this cleavage quite effectively, mobilizing national elites against local power structures and then later developing strong political ties in California to consolidate gains.

By the same token, elite and Marxist theories of the state have erroneously assumed that the liberal democratic state is an impregnable fortress that consistently supports the prevailing powers. If reforms occur, they have to be preemptive ones that coopt insurgent leaders while denying genuine benefits to the excluded. This picture, however, is almost as much of a caricature as the pluralist myth of permeability. The polity is normally closed, but political realignments and close divisions can create short-term incentives for polity members to sponsor challenges. The liberal democratic state tempers the bias of the state by creating an electoral arena through which the force of organized numbers can have a decisive say. Although such periods of opportunity are exceptional and insurgents have to delicately balance their demands and unruliness to keep from upsetting such coalitions, these member-challenger coalitions can neutralize the state and generate sufficient leverage to force significant concessions. The liberal democratic state has sufficient potential autonomy from existing structures of social power that it can, at least temporarily, serve as a facilitative agency for the institutionalization of genuine social reforms. The translation of this potentiality into actuality depends, of course, on realignments and the spread of generalized turmoil.

This interpretation also casts light on the relative importance of political opportunities and strategies in bringing about successes and the processes leading to political crisis periods (Goldstone 1980; Gamson 1980). Political opportunities have to exist for insurgencies to become sustained and eventually succeed. By the same token, not all challengers during a period of increasing opportunity will succeed. The UFW was accompanied by a broad wave of poor people's movements, the majority of which failed. Weak organizing strategies, radical demands, and premature militancy destroyed fragile political coalitions and induced repression. Opportunities without effective strategies are like thoroughbred horses with inexperienced jockeys. Their potentials will be unmatched by successes at the finish line. The processes creating these opportunities are based in political turmoil and the development of political crisis. If my analysis of the crisis of the 1960s is a reliable guide, however, those emphasizing profound societal dislocations such as major economic depressions and war losses have overstated their case (cf. Piven and Cloward 1977; Goldstone 1980). Although structural dislocations may give rise to crisis periods, this is mediated by the impact of these dislocations on political alignments. The key is a series of political realignments that give rise to generalized turmoil.

What then is the prospect for further insurgencies that advance the interests of the powerless and excluded? The social movements of the 1960s left behind a rich legacy of social reforms and new organizational bases for mounting challenges. There is no lack of significant grievances around which new challenges could be organized. The major factor is the lack of significant political opportunities. The dominance of center-right governments since the mid 1970s has raised the costs of insurgency and discouraged sponsorship. The continued decomposition of political parties and their electoral supports, especially for the Democratic party, have further eroded the chief mechanism through which political re-alignments have traditionally been structured. By these calculations, the prospects for another period of political turmoil appear dim. Yet the UFW experience does offer a promising model for mobilizing the powerless. If new realignments should again create opportunities for challenges, the UFW experience provides a fertile set of lessons for successful insurgency.

Notes

Agenda and Objectives

1. Insurgencies, then, are "power-oriented" social movements, in Turner and Killian's (1972) terms, pursuing changes in the structure of economic and political power. Gamson's (1975) conception of "challenging groups" is similar in that the constituency is initially unorganized and attacks an outside antagonist. The difference is that insurgencies are centered in groups excluded from the political system. For a similar conceptualization, see Tilly (1978, 1979) and McAdam (1982).

2. "Protest action" has here the technical sense of dramatic actions used to galvanize external or third-party support (Lipsky 1968, 1971; Garrow 1978).

3. In constructing this classical model I have synthesized the arguments of many analysts and inevitably ignored significant differences among them. In several cases, these propositions have been "domain assumptions" (Gouldner 1970) that guide but remain implicit throughout the analysis. The collective behavior tradition represents the most complex and eclectic case, having long been divided between the functionalists (Smelser 1963) and the interactionist traditions (Lang and Lang 1961; Turner and Killian 1957, 1972). For a similar treatment of the classical tradition, see McAdam (1982:5–19).

4. The seminal statements of the resource mobilization perspective can be found in Oberschall (1973), McCarthy and Zald (1973, 1977), Tilly (1975, 1978), Gamson (1968, 1975), Useem (1975), and Schwartz (1976). For recent reviews, see Perrow (1979), McAdam (1982), and Jenkins (1981, 1983b), and for the critics' side, Zurcher and Snow (1982), Turner (1982), and Gusfield (1982).

5. The "rationality" theorem means simply that movement actions are instrumentally oriented towards controlling the social environment. As Schwartz (1976:150–155) has argued, insurgents are often misinformed about the structure of their social environment but, in the course of insurgency, draw on their experiences to develop a more accurate picture of their problems and possible solutions. Since emotive and value-laden elements are always interwoven with material interests, the question of rationality is one of orientation, not the particular interests at stake.

1. Theories of Insurgency

1. As Traugott (1978) has argued, a key problem with the classical theories has been their attempt to analyze the entire range of social movements, covering cultural and per-

sonal change movements as well as attempts to change institutional structures. The focus here will be limited to social movements that attempt to alter "elements of social structure and/or the reward distribution of society" (McCarthy and Zald 1977:1218), in particular the exclusion of groups from centers of social power.

2. The critical literature has grown enormously in the past decade, virtually defying comprehensive summary. The main critical points have been that basic concepts such as "structural strain" (Smelser 1963) have been so broad as to be vacuous (Currie and Skolnick 1970; Marx and Wood 1975:376); the measurement of key concepts such as "relative deprivation" has been ad hoc (Portes 1971; J. Wilson 1973:55–90); and key propositions such as the hypothesis of social isolation/anomie (W. Allen 1976; Pinard 1971; Oberschall 1973:104–113; Tilly, Tilly, and Tilly 1975) and relative deprivation or status inconsistency (Tilly and Snyder 1972; Orum 1972) have empirically failed to explain social movement participation. For general summaries of this literature, see Oberschall (1973), J. Wilson (1973), Useem (1975), Marx and Wood (1975:375–383), Schwartz (1976), Wilson and Orum (1976), McAdam (1982:11–35), and Jenkins (1981, 1983b).

3. Olson offers two other irrelevant solutions to the free-rider problem: small-N groups in which individuals receive more from the collective good than it costs; and "privileged groups" in which costs to affluent parties are sufficiently marginal to offset individual benefits. Significant insurgencies, however, require the mobilization of large groups, and affluent parties are rare among disorganized excluded groups.

4. See Piven and Cloward's (1977) discussion of "permanent membership organizations" as opposed to "cadre organizations" and the criticisms of Starr (1978), Hobsbawm (1978), Kesselman (1979), Jenkins (1979), Roach and Roach (1980), and Gamson and Schmeiler (1984).

5. The following criteria subsume those advanced by other analysts. Turner and Killian (1972:256–257), for example, distinguish member benefits and power changes from the realization of a "program for the reform of society." Similarly, Gamson (1975:28–37) distinguishes tangible gains from acceptance by antagonists, while Piven and Cloward (1977) restrict their analysis to short-term tangible gains. Handler (1978:34–41) simply distinguishes short-term tangible gains from symbolic ones. The first category—benefits and short-term tangible gains—constitute policy changes in my scheme. Symbolic gains are merely a different "coin" of receipt. Gamson's "acceptance" measures are forms of regime change, and Turner and Killian's "realization of a reform program" approximates my distributional changes. All, of course, are fundamentally changes in social power.

2. California Agriculture and Grower Power

1. This policy of "overhiring" of labor was first analyzed by Fisher (1951) and, despite contrary arguments by Sosnick (1978:359–361), has only recently been restricted by union hiring halls.

2. The census data reflect physically separated farms and not their actual ownership or fiscal operations. Given the importance of leasing, geographically dispersed farms under single ownership, and dummy ownership, the actual amount of centralization is certainly greater than these figures indicate.

3. California Agriculture and Farm Worker Powerlessness

1. For contemporary evidence of the "ideal" character of immigrant labor, see the data compiled by Sosnick (1978:236–241) with regard to hours and working conditions pre-

ferred by braceros and domestic workers. Bonachich's (1972, 1976) analysis of "split" labor markets captures the general context.

2. For a more detailed analysis of bracero dependency, see Galarza (1964:94, 96–97) and Salandini (1969).

3. Figures arc derived from U.S. Dept. of Agriculture and U.S. Dept. of Labor wage surveys. Corroborating evidence is too plentiful to list. For highlights see: President's Commissions on Migratory Labor (1951, 1960); U.S. Department of Labor (1958:188–190); Galaraza (1964); Salandini (1969:esp. 211); Glass (1966:63); Wolf (1964:184, 289–296); Schmidt (1964); and Fineberg (1971:25). In 1957 corruption in the Placement Service became the target of political attack, giving rise to a revealing investigation of cronyism and grower favoritism under then Governor Earl Warren (see especially *Los Angeles Times*, March 3, 1957). Chavez's early experiences in farm labor organizing centered on abuses in the Placement Office in the Oxnard area (Levy 1975: chs. 6–8).

4. Estimates are derived from California Department of Employment (1949–1970). Measuring the composition of the labor force is, to say the least, hazardous. For a critical review of the labor reporting systems, see Salandini (1969).

5. Unfortunately the surveys conducted by William Metzger underestimated the number of statewide Mexican workers because they centered on the San Joaquin Valley and excluded the bracero and probably illegal workers. They are, however, sufficiently indicative to allow broad comparisons.

4. The Agony of the NFLU (1946–1952)

1. For Mitchell's and Hasiwar's biographies, see Mitchell (1980: esp. 247–249). The STFU's experiences during the 1930s are also recounted in Kester (1936), Jamieson (1945), and Grubbs (1971).

2. See the *Plan of Organization, Southern Tenant Farmer Union Papers* (hereafter *STFU Papers*), December 28, 1947.

3. Untitled and undated newspaper clippings, *STFU Scrapbook of Newspaper Clippings* (hereafter *STFU in the News*), Film 647 (1934–1949), Tamiment Library, New York; Mitchell and Hasiwar (1974:1, 23).

4. Untitled newspaper clipping, *STFU in the News*, July 11, 1947.

5. Mitchell and Hasiwar (1974:1, 25, 31); U.S. House of Representatives (1951b:577).

6. U.S. House of Representatives (1950:577); Kern County Sheriff Lousalot confirmed union estimates of support at the strike meeting, U.S. House of Representatives (1950:617–618); see also Galarza (1977:103) and the conflicting testimony of H. L. Mitchell in U.S. House of Representatives (1949:1003); Robert Schmeiser, President of the Associated Farmers, U.S. House of Representatives (1950:1445–1450); and DiGiorgio foreman Mr. Webdell, U.S. House of Representatives (1950:548).

7. See the *San Francisco Chronicle*, October 7, 1947; *Bakersfield California*, October 9, 1947; both in *STFU in the News*, Tamiment Library, New York.

8. *San Francisco Chronicle*, October 24, 1947; Mitchell and Hasiwar (1975:1, 32); *Commonweal*, November 1947, 117; the Mexican government earlier made use of the threat to cancel the program, apparently in an effort to secure better wages and treatment for its citizens.

9. *San Francisco Chronicle*, October 29, 1947; letter of Jim Wrightson to H. L. Mitchell, November 13, 1947, *STFU Papers*.

10. U.S. House of Representatives (1950:578); *Christian Science Monitor*, December 26, 1947; Strike Bulletin #5, November 28, 1947, *STFU Papers*.

4. THE AGONY OF THE NFLU

11. U.S. House of Representatives (1950:578) the ordinance had been passed on March 3, shortly after Hasiwar's arrival to initiate the organizing drive discussed in *Central Valley Labor*, November 8, 1947 (*STFU in the News*, Tamiment Library, New York).

12. *San Francisco Chronicle*, October 24, 1947; U.S. House of Representatives (1950:579).

13. List of Donors, November 7, 1947, *STFU Papers*; List of Donors, December 15, 1947, *STFU Papers*; Galarza (1974:107).

14. U.S. House of Representatives (1950:578); *Labor*, November 8, 1947; undated articles (probably December 1947), *STFU in the News*.

15. Letter of H. L. Mitchell to Hank Hasiwar, October 1, 1948, *STFU Papers*.

16. Strike Bulletin #9, December 28, 1947, *STFU Papers*; *Fresno Bee*, March 25, 1948; Galarza (1974:107).

17. Letter of Jim Wrightson to H. L. Mitchell, January 12, 1948, *STFU Papers*; Galarza (1977:110).

18. See copy, December 1947, *STFU Papers*.

19. Strike Bulletin #14, *STFU Papers*, February 6, 1948; U.S. House of Representatives (1950:579): Mitchell (1980:255–256).

20. *Bakersfield Californian*, February 10, 1948 (in the hearing and testimony the incident is apparently dated incorrectly as February 22, 1948); *Los Angeles Examiner*, February 10, 1948.

21. "Organizational Report" by Ernesto Galarza, April 1, 1948, *STFU Papers*; Strike Bulletin #17, February 29, 1948, *STFU Papers*; see also testimony of Ernesto Galarza, U.S. House of Representatives (1950:615); U.S. House of Representatives (1950:579); "Organizational Report" by E. Galarza, May 1, 1948, *STFU Papers*.

22. The practice of calling in the Immigration Service was related to the author in a personal interview with Henry Hasiwar, Yonkers, New York, January 27, 1975.

23. Letter of E. Galarza to H. L. Mitchell, May 1, 1948, *STFU Papers*.

24. *Los Angeles Examiner*, May 14, 1948, *STFU in the News*.

25. Untitled article, May 18, 1948, *STFU in the News*.

26. Author's interview with Henry Hasiwar, January 27, 1975.

27. Untitled article, March 21, 1948; untitled article, March 25, 1948, *STFU in the News*; Mitchell (1980:257).

28. Telegram, H. Hasiwar to H. L. Mitchell, June 17, 1948.

29. U.S. House of Representatives (1950:579); the major events of the NLRA case are summarized in the hearings of the U.S. House of Representatives (1949:580); especially see the legal testimony of Alexander Schullman (U.S. House of Representatives 1951b:710–713); also, *New York Times*, April 30, 1948; Galarza (1968, 1977).

30. Letter of H. L. Mitchell to Hank Hasiwar, November 26, 1948, *STFU Papers*; Galarza (1968:28).

31. Galarza (1968: chapters 2 and 3); letter of H. L. Mitchell to Hank Hasiwar, May 8, 1950, *STFU Papers*.

32. Cited Meister and Loftis (1977:78). In Taft's (1968:209) words, labor support for the NFLU was "token."

33. Letters of Ernesto Galarza to H. L. Mitchell, December 1, 1948 and October 20, 1949, *STFU Papers*.

34. Letter of Ernesto Galarza to H. L. Mitchell, December 27, 1948, *STFU Papers*; Galarza (1977:122).

35. Letters of H. Hasiwar to Governor Earl Warren, September 7, 1949; Ernesto Galarza to H. L. Mitchell, September 22, 1949; NFLU News Release, September 24, 1949; E. Galarza to H. L. Mitchell, October 3, 1949; Bertha Rankin to H. L. Mitchell, September 25, 1949; *STFU Papers*; Galarza (1977:126).

5. FLAWED STRATEGY: AWOC

36. Letter of E. Galarza to H. L. Mitchell, September 7, 1950; Press Release, October 30, 1950, *STFU Papers*.

37. Letter of Ernesto Galarza to H. L. Mitchell, April 7, 1950, *STFU Papers*; Galarza (1968:76).

38. Galarza (1977:127). For the troubles with union locals that disappeared like sand castles before the tide, see the letter of Ernesto Galarza to H. L. Mitchell, April 7, 1950, *STFU Papers*.

39. Letter of E. Galarza to H. L. Mitchell, November 31, 1950, *STFU Papers*; Galarza (1977:148–152).

40. H. L. Mitchell and H. Hasiwar, (1974:111, 27); leter of H. Hasiwar to H. L. Mitchell, June 2, 1951, *STFU Papers*; Galarza (1977:160); "The Wetback Strike", page 7, *STFU Papers*.

41. Letter of Ernesto Galarza to H. L. Mitchell, December 31, 1950, *STFU Papers*.

42. See NFLU report, inappropriately titled "The Wetback Strike," June 13, 1951, *STFU Papers*. "The Bracero Strike" would have been more apt.

43. Letter of H. Hasiwar to H. L. Mitchell, April 30, 1951, *STFU Papers*.

44. Letter of H. Hasiwar to H. L. Mitchell, June 21, 1951, *STFU Papers*.

45. *Fresno Citizen*, June 8, 1951, *STFU in the News;* letter of L. Lave to H. L. Mitchell, June 19, 1951, *STFU Papers;* Galarza (1977:163).

46. Letters of E. Galarza to H. L. Mitchell, January 30, 1951 and April 4, 1951, and of H. Hasiwar to H. L. Mitchell, June 2, 1951; also "The Wetback Strike," June 1951, page 3, *STFU Papers*.

47. "The Wetback Strike," pages 3, 22; NFLU Press Release, May 28, 1951, *STFU Papers;* Galarza (1977:168).

48. Letter of H. Hasiwar to H. L. Mitchell, May 31, 1951; also numerous telegrams to Mitchell throughout June 1951, *STFU Papers*.

49. "The Wetback Strike", June 1951, *STFU Papers;* author's interview with H. Hasiwar, January 19, 1975.

50. "The Wetback Strike," page 20, *STFU Papers*.

51. Letter of L. Lave to H. L. Mitchell, June 19, 1951, *STFU Papers*.

52. Letter of Acting Secretary of Labor Galvin to H. L. Mitchell, June 21, 1951, *STFU Papers*.

53. "The Wetback Strike," June 1951, page 19, *STFU Papers;* Galarza (1977:169–170); Mitchell (1980:269); H. L. Mitchell and H. Hasiwar (1974:III, 12–13).

54. See Galarza (1977:171–186) and the letters of Bill Becker to H. L. Mitchell, April 7, 1951, and to California Central Labor Council, June 5, 1951; Ernesto Galarza to H. L. Mitchell, October 25, 1951, April 24 and 26, 1952; and the minutes of the NFLU National Board Meeting, October 24–25, 1952, *STFU Papers*.

5. The Flawed Strategy: The AWOC (1959–1965)

1. Author's interview, H. L. Mitchell.

2. Author's interview with Father Thomas McCullough, former head of Spanish Mission Band and organizer of the Agricultural Workers Association, Berkeley, Calif., April 17, 1975.

3. Author's interview, H. L. Mitchell.

4. Author's interviews with Father Thomas McCullough, April 17 and 29, 1975, Berkeley, Calif.; McNamara (1968, 1970); London and Anderson (1970:79–90).

6. La Causa Ascendant: Building the United Farm Workers Challenge (1962–1970)

1. For an introduction to the Alinsky approach, see Alinsky (1947, 1971), Bailey (1974), Ecklein and Laufer (1972), Hagstrom (1965), Prager and Specht (1969), Fish (1975), and Boyte (1980). Ross' early efforts are recounted in Levy (1975:95–105).

2. R. Taylor (1975: ch. 5), and Levy (1975:55–61); for Chavez's own version, see Chavez (1966).

3. Levy (1975:111). As Chavez once noted: "The most important thing about signing up a member was that you made a friend. You visited a place, and they would later write to you. Then we would write back to them. If I would be in the neighborhood, I would try to stop in to visit" (Chavez 1969:6).

4. A full listing of the NFWA benefits is provided in the application for OEO funding ("The People," located in California Migrant Ministry Collection, Archives for Labor History and Urban Affairs, Wayne State University, Detroit, Michigan [hereafter CMM Collection], Box 13, Folder 10) of group insurance, social case work, credit union, newspaper, citizenship education, money management education, and an auto repair cooperative.

5. Chris Hartmire, *Director's Report: California Migrant Ministry,* September 15–16, 1965 (CMM Collection, Box 2, Folder 4); Hartmire (1967:12).

6. Author's interview with Chris Hartmire and James Drake, May 2–5, 1975, Los Angeles, Calif.

7. Shotwell (1960); National Migrant Ministry (1961).

8. Author's interview with John Regier, Syracuse, New York, April 14–15, 1975. The early definitions of "community development" advanced by Douglas Still dealt only with educational programs, e.g., literacy, English language, health care, etc. ("CMM Goals," December 8, 1960, in CMM Collection, Box 1, Folder 3. By the time Chris Hartmire assumed the directorship of the CMM in 1961, community development was primarily a question of politics, especially voting rights.

9. For evidence on upper-class Protestant conservatism, see Hamilton (1973) and Quinley (1974).

10. Hartmire (1967:12); Chris Hartmire, *Report to the Rosenburg Foundation,* November 12, 1965, p. 6; CMM Collection, Box 26, Folder 10; "CMM Executive Board Minutes," August 1965; CMM Collection, Box 1, Folder 4.

11. Author's interview with Chris Hartmire, Executive Director of the National Farm Worker Ministry, May 2, 1975, Los Angeles, Calif. "Goals: Some More Thoughts on Where the CMM is Going," April 15, 1965 (CMM Collection, Box 2, Folder 13); and Hartmire (1967:11).

12. Author's interviews with UFW Staff, Delano and LaPaz, California, April 25–30, 1975.

13. Author's interview with Bill Kircher, former Director of Organization, AFL–CIO, Cincinnati, Ohio, August 25, 1975, and Paul Schrade, former west coast director, UAW, Los Angeles, Calif., May 4, 1975.

14. Author's interview with Jack Conway, formerly director of Center for Community Change, Washington, D.C., July 12, 1979.

15. Author's interview with Dolores Huerta, UFW Boycott house, New York, April 12, 1975.

16. Author's interviews with Mark Day, Los Angeles, California, May 3, 1975, and Victor Salandini, San Diego, California, May 5, 1975; McNamara (1968:449-485).

17. Author's interview, Philip Vera Cruz, UFW Vice President, Delano, Calif., April 26, 1975.

18. Dunne (1971:75–76); letter of James Drake to Chris Hartmire and Walter Press, May 6, 1975 (CMM Collection, Box 13, Folder 11); R. Taylor (1975:119–120).

19. Author's interview with Jim Drake, Los Angeles, California, May 5, 1975; *Valley Labor Citizen*, June 16, 1965.

20. Author's interview, Eddie Cuellar, Visalia, Calif., April 23, 1975, and Bard Mc-Allister, Visalia, Calif., April 23, 1975; Chavez's decision to avoid a strike is recounted in Levy (1975:154).

21. *Valley Labor Citizen*, June 4, 1965; the AWOC agreement also marked a new departure: "For the first time a grower met in formal talks with union leaders, and agreed to pay what the union was asking, although the union failed to get formal recognition as a bargaining agent" (*Los Angeles Times*, May 13, 1965); R. Taylor (1975:124-125).

22. *El Malcriado*, billed by NFWA as "the Voice of the Farm Worker," in its usual way inflated the number of Filipino strikers to 5,562 (*El Malcriado*, number 24, p. 14); there were probably no more than 5,000 grape workers in the area (*Valley Labor Citizen*, September 17, 1965).

23. R. Taylor (1975:128); author's interview with Bill Kircher, former Director of Organizations for the AFL–CIO, Cincinnati, Ohio, August 23, 1975.

24. For accounts of picketing, see Nelson (1966:24–28); *People's World*, October 2, 1965; R. Taylor (1975:130–136); *San Francisco Chronicle*, December 30, 1964.

25. Estimates vary wildly. Nelson in a clear overstatement claims that ninety percent of the workers walked out (1966:60), while Healy, a right-wing Catholic priest, claims that only ten percent ever walked out (1966:17). Martin Zaninovich, a grower, likewise claimed that only 500 workers struck (testimony, *Senate Subcommittee on Migratory Labor* 1966:592). Kopkind's estimate that 50 percent walked out is probably right (1967:13–14).

26. *Valley Labor Citizen*, October 1, 1965; Draper Papers, Stanford University, Stanford, Calif.; *Valley Labor Citizen*, October 8, 1965; *People's World*, October 9, 1965.

27. Author's interview, Chris Hartmire, Los Angeles, Calif.

28. *The California Farmer*, September 17, 1966; *Valley Labor Citizen*, November 5, 1965; author's interview with Bard McAllister, AFSC.

29. For accounts of the recruitment of strikebreakers, see *Valley Labor Citizen*, October 8, 1965; Brown (1972); testimony of Cesar Chavez, *Senate Subcommittee on Migratory Labor* (1966:379–380); *People's World*, October 23, 1965.

30. United Farm Workers, "A Summary of Events in the Grape Strike" (mimeo); United Farm Workers, "A History of the Delano Grape Strike and the DiGiorgio 'Elections,'" p. 2, CMM Collection, Box 4, Folder 4.

31. *Valley Labor Citizen*, September 24, 1965; *People's World*, November 3, 1965; *San Francisco Chronicle*, November 18, 1965; *People's World*, November 27, 1965; *Valley Labor Citizen*, December 3, 1965.

32. In 1965 only 6 percent of DiGiorgio Corporation revenues came from agricultural sales ("Report to Shareholders of DiGiorgio, Inc.," year ending December 12, 1965); as for Schenley, it is rumored that the vineyards were actually purchased for the purpose of a tax write-off (author's interview with David Selvin, editor of *San Francisco Labor*, Berkeley, Calif., April 27, 1975).

33. SDS *Regional Newsletter* March 8, 1966 vol. 1 (no. 8); SNCC's *The Movement* October 1965 vol. 1 (no. 10); the original boycott mailing list consisted entirely of SDS, CORE, and SNCC contacts (CMM Collection, Box 13, Folder 12).

34. Kushner (1974:153); author's interview with Paul Schrade, former UAW Regional

Director of the UAW, Los Angeles, Calif., May 4, 1975; *People's World*, November 20, 1965.

35. R. Taylor (1975:167–180); author's interview with Sam Kushner, former reporter for the *People's World*, Los Angeles, Calif., May 4, 1975.

36. Author's interview, William Kircher, Cleveland, Ohio, August 25, 1975.

37. R. Taylor (1975:168–169); author's interview, William Kircher, Cleveland, Ohio, August 25, 1975.

38. Author's interview with Jim Drake, head of the Los Angeles boycott, May 3, 1975; according to Drake, at that point the boycott was taken within the NFWA as something of a joke.

39. R. Taylor (1975:175–177); Dunne (1971:135–137). Paul Schrade brought to my attention the role played by the liquor industry's norms on publicity.

40. *Newsweek*, April 18, 1966, p. 42–43; R. Taylor (1975:829); Levy (1975:206–218).

41. Author's interview, Ben Gines, former AWOC and Teamster organizer, Delano, Calif., April 25, 1975; R. Taylor (1975:145, 170–173); Dunne (1971:155).

42. "History of the Grape Strike," Ronald Haughton Collection, Box 5, Folder 18, housed in Archives for Labor History and Urban Affairs, Wayne State University, Detroit, Mich.

43. The role of marketing practices in the boycott was first pointed out by Ron Haughton, author's interview, Detroit, Mich., April 1, 1975.

44. Author's interview, Bill Kircher, Cleveland, Ohio, August 25, 1975.

45. Author's interviews with UFW cadre, Delano and LaPaz, California, April 25–30, 1975, and with Bill Kircher, Cleveland, Ohio, August 25, 1975.

46. See, for example, Progressive Labor's (SDS) "Unionization of the Unorganized: Delano Grape Strike" *Progressive Labor* November 1967 6(2):42–49.

47. Author's interview, Ronald Haughton, Detroit, Mich., April 1, 1975.

48. Letter of Chris Hartmire to the "Action List," February 20, 1967, CMM Collection; *San Francisco Examiner*, February 15, 1967; undated letter of Leroy Chatfield to Bishop Donohoe and Brother West (FSC), Leroy Chatfield Collection, Archives of Labor History and Urban Affairs, Wayne State University, Detroit, Mich.

49. Nicolas Mills, "Workers on the Farms" *New Republic*, 117, September 23, 1967.

50. Various letters of Irwin DeShetler, Part I, Folder 87, Irwin DeShetler Collection, Archives of Labor History and Urban Affairs, Wayne State University, Detroit, Mich.

51. Author's interview with Chris Hartmire, Los Angeles.

52. Kircher estimated that half the wine growers had been signed but later discovered that it was around twenty percent. Author's interview, William Kircher, Cincinnati, Ohio, August 25, 1975; Levy (1975:263–268); author's interviews with James Drake, Los Angeles, California, May 5, 1975.

53. UFWOC, "Information Sheet: Grape Boycott"; R. Taylor (1975:217–218).

54. Author's interview with Terry Rosenberg, one of the Boston boycott team, Stony Brook, New York, February, 1975, and Fred Ross, Jr., head of the San Francisco area boycott, San Francisco, Calif., April 28, 1975.

55. Brown (1972); Dunne (1971:ch. 15); author's interview with Bill Kircher, Cincinnati, Ohio, August 23, 1975.

56. See, for example, *New York Times*, February 29, 1968.

57. R. Taylor (1968); the AFL–CIO never completely recovered from the announcement, partly because they also feared that the demand for labor legislation might reopen the possibility of even more restrictive labor legislation as well as create interunion rivalry (author's interview with Bill Kircher, Cincinnati, Ohio, August 23, 1975).

58. Brown (1972:165–170); quote from margin notes of Victor Salandini, from a meeting

with Cesar Chavez, dated October 18, 1969, Victor Salandini Collection, Archives of Labor History and Urban Affairs, Wayne State University, Detroit, Mich., Box B, Folder 1.

59. Drawn from the author's own boycott experience on Long Island, during the lettuce boycott of the summer of 1973.

60. Amalgamated Food Employees, Local 590, v. Logan Valley Plaza, Inc., 391 U.S. 308; Brown (1972:165–175).

61. U.S. Senate (1969); *New York Times*, February 21, 1969; R. Taylor (1975:236–237); Meister and Loftis (1977:155–156); "Boycott Effect Report," September 18, 1968, De-Shetler Collection, Box 8, Folder 14; *Los Angeles Times*, June 14, 1969.

62. *Los Angeles Times*, August 5, 1969; *Bakersfield Californian*, August 24, 1969; *Stockton Record*, November 5, 1969; *The Packer*, January 31, 1970; *Fresno Bee*, February 1, 1970; Meister and Loftis (1977:162).

63. For an analysis of the favorable political environment of the late 1960s, see Jenkins and Perrow (1977).

7. La Causa on Trial: Counterattack and Renewal (1970-1980)

1. *Salinas Californian*, August 6 and 8, 1970; Levy (1975:335–339).

2. *Salinas Californian*, August 21, 1970; Meister and Loftis (1977:169).

3. *Modesto Bee*, November 18, December 16 and 31, 1970; *San Jose Mercury*, September 25, 1974; Levy (1975:406–407, 434–435).

4. *Salinas Californian*, November 26, 1971; *New York Times*, July 13, 1973; Meister and Loftis (1977:170).

5. Author's personal interview, Cincinnati, Ohio, August 25, 1975; Levy (1975:406–407).

6. *Salinas Californian*, August 25, 1970; Levy (1975:382–384).

7. *Salinas Californian*, August 26, 1970; Meister and Loftis (1977:168).

8 Author's interview with Fred Ross, Jr., head of San Francisco boycott, April 20, 1975; Friedland and Thomas (1974); Meister and Loftis (1977:172).

9. *Los Angeles Times*, May 3, 1972; R. Taylor (1975:262–264); Meister and Loftis (1977:178–179).

10. *Los Angeles Times*, October 6, 1972; R. Taylor (1975:281–284); Meister and Loftis 1977:181–182).

11. Author's personal interview with Dolores Huerta, UFW Vice-President, New York, N.Y., November 29, 1974.

12. *New York Times*, July 20, 1973; *New York Times*, April 18, 1973; Levy (1975:472–474); Meister and Loftis (1977:184–185).

13. R. Taylor (1975:271); *Los Angeles Times*, June 7, 1973; *New York Times*, April 30, 1974.

14. *New York Times Magazine*, September 15, 1974; *New York Times*, June 26, 1973.

15. *New York Times*, April 19, 1973; R. Taylor (1975:297); Levy (1975:478).

16. Cited in R. Taylor (1975:300); *Los Angeles Times*, June 12, 1973.

17. *New York Times*, March 24, 1974; *Los Angeles Times*, March 22, 1974.

18. Cesar Chavez, cited in Levy (1975:496).

19. *New York Times*, July 19 and 31, 1973; *Los Angeles Times*, July 20, 26, and 31, 1973; *San Francisco Chronicle*, July 23 and 31, 1973.

20. *Los Angeles Times*, August 2, 1973; R. Taylor (1975:308).

21. Author's interviews, Phillip Vera Cruz, Delano, Calif., April 15, 1975, and Dolores Huerta, New York, N.Y., April 20, 1974.

22. *Los Angeles Times*, June 17, 1973; *New York Times*, June 27, 1973; Meister and Loftis (1977:192).

23. *San Francisco Chronicle*, November 17, 1973; *Los Angeles Times*, November 22, 1973; *New York Times*, November 23, 1973; Meister and Loftis (1977:196–197).

24. *San Francisco Chronicle*, November 17, 1973; *Los Angeles Times*, March 29, 1974; Meister and Loftis (1977:199).

25. *San Francisco Chronicle*, March 27, 1974; *Los Angeles Times*, April 9, 1974.

26. *Sacramento Bee*, May 6, 1975; Meister and Loftis (1977:216); *Los Angeles Times*, May 29, 1975; Sosnick (1978:378–379).

27. *Los Angeles Times*, August 17, 1975; Meister and Loftis (1977:219–220).

28. *New York Times*, September 14, 1975; Meister and Loftis (1977:222).

29. *New York Times Magazine*, September 15, 1974:18.

30. *New Republic*, December 7, 1974:13.

31 *Los Angeles Times*, October 28, 1977; May 9 and August 17, 1978; March 10, 1977.

32. *Los Angeles Times*, January 1 and March 10, 1977; Sosnick (1978:383).

33. *Los Angeles Times*, July 6, 1976; Meister and Loftis (1977:227).

34. R. Taylor, 1975:321–322; *Los Angeles Times*, March 29 and June 6, 1979; *New York Times*, November 20, 1983.

35. Derived from USDA *Farm Income Situation* (1966–80) and USDL *Labor Statistics* (1966–80).

Bibliography

Adams, James L. 1970. *The Growing Church Lobby In Washington*. Grand Rapids, Mich.: William B. Eerdmans.

Aiken, Michael et al. 1968. *Economic Failure, Alienation, and Extremism*. Ann Arbor: University of Michigan Press.

Alinsky, Saul. 1947. *Rules for Radicals*. New York: Random House.

—— 1971. *Reveille for Radicals*. New York: Random House.

Allen, R. H. 1935. "The Spanish Land Grant System as an Influence in the Agricultural Development of California." *Agricultural History* 9:127–142.

Allen, William S. 1965. *The Nazi Seizure of Power*. Chicago: Quadrangle.

Andersen, Kristi. 1979. *The Creation of a Democratic Majority, 1928–1936*. Chicago: University of Chicago Press.

Aronowitz, Stanley. 1973. *False Promises*. New York: McGraw-Hill.

Ash-Garner, Roberta. 1977. *Social Movements in America*. Chicago: Markham.

Auerbach, Jerome. 1966. *Labor and Liberty*. Indianapolis, Ind.: Bobbs-Merrill.

Averitt, Robert, 1968. *The Dual Economy*. New York: Norton.

Bailey, Robert. 1974. *Radicals in Urban Politics*. Chicago: University of Chicago Press.

Bailis, Lawrence N. 1974. *Bread or Justice*. Lexington, Mass.: Lexington Books.

Bain, Joe S., Richard E. Caves, and Julius Margolis. 1966. *Northern California's Water Industry*. Baltimore, Md.: Johns Hopkins University Press.

Baker, George and Ronald Taylor. 1972. "The Corporate Green Giant." *The Nation*, March 13.

Ball, Gordon A. and Earl O. Heady. 1972. *Size, Structure and Future of Farms*. Ames: Iowa State University Press.

Ballis, George. 1960. *The California Water Plan: An Evaluation*. Washington, D.C.: Public Affairs Press.

—— 1966. *Basta! The Tale of Our Struggle*. Delano, Calif.: Farm Worker Press.

—— 1972. "Profile of the Power Structure in the San Joaquin Valley." In U.S. Senate Subcommittee on Migratory Labor, *Farm Workers in Rural America*, 3-A:694–724.

Barnes, Peter. 1971. "Land Reform: The Great American Land Grab." *New Republic*, June 5.

Beck, Paul A. and M. Kent Jennings. 1979. "Political Periods and Political Participation." *American Political Science Review* 73:737–750.

Bell, Daniel. 1961. *The End of Ideology*. New York: Free Press.

—— 1973. *The Coming of the Post-Industrial Society*. New York: Basic Books.

BIBLIOGRAPHY

—— 1976. *The Cultural Contradictions of Capitalism.* New York: Basic Books.

Benedict, M. R. 1946. "The Economic and Social Structure of California Agriculture." In Claude B. Hutchinson, ed., *California Agriculture*, pp. 395–435. Berkeley: University of California Press.

—— 1953. *Farm Policies of the United States, 1790–1950.* New York: Twentieth Century Fund.

Berger, Samuel R. 1971. *Dollar Harvest: The Story of the Farm Bureau.* Lexington, Mass.: D.C. Heath.

Berk, Richard. 1974. "A Gaming Approach to Crowd Behavior." *American Sociological Review* 39:355–373.

Berkman, Richard and Kip Viscusi. 1971. *Damning the West: Nader Task Force on the Bureau of Reclamation.* Washington, D.C.: Center for Responsive Law.

Berry, Jeffrey M. 1977. *Lobbying for the People.* Princeton, N.J.: Princeton University Press.

Blackford, Mansel G. 1977. *The Politics of Business in California, 1890–1920.* Columbus: Ohio State University Press.

Block, Fred. 1977. "The Ruling Class Do Not Rule." *Socialist Revolution*, 33:6–38.

Bonachich, Edna. 1972. "A Theory of Ethnic Antagonism: The Split Labor Market." *American Sociological Review* 37:547–559.

—— 1976. "Advanced Capitalism and Black-White relations in the U.S.: A Split Labor Market Interpretation." *American Sociological Review* 41:34–51.

Bonnen, James T. 1968. "Distribution of Benefits from Selected Farm Programs." In U.S. President's National Advisory Commission on Rural Poverty, *Rural Poverty in the U.S.* Washington, D.C.: GPO.

Boyte, Harry. 1980. *The Backyard Revolution.* Philadelphia: Temple University Press.

Brill, Harry. 1971. *Why Organizers Fail.* Berkeley: University of California Press.

Brink, William and Louis Harris. 1963. *The Negro Revolution in America.* New York: Simon & Schuster.

Brody, David. 1960. *Steelworkers in America.* New York: Harper & Row.

—— 1980. *Workers in Industrial America.* New York: Oxford University Press.

Brown, Jerald. 1972. *The United Farm Worker Grape Strike and Boycott, 1965–1970: An Evaluation of the Culture of Poverty Theory.* Ph.D. dissertation, Department of Anthropology, Cornell University, Ithaca, N.Y.

Bruce-Briggs, ed. 1981. *The New Class?* New Brunswick, N.J.: Transaction Books.

Burnham, Walter Dean. 1970. *Critical Elections and the Mainsprings of American Politics.* New York: Norton.

Burowoy, Michael. 1979. *Manufacturing Consent.* Chicago: University of Chicago Press.

Burstein, Paul. 1979. "Public Opinion, Demonstrations and the Passage of Antidiscrimination Legislation." *Public Opinion Quarterly* 43:157–172

—— 1981. "Social Protest, Public Opinion and Public Policy." Paper presented at annual meeting of the American Sociological Association.

Burstein, Paul and William Breudenburg. 1978. "Changing Public Policy: The Impact of Public Opinion, Antiwar Demonstrations and War Costs on Senate Voting on Vietnam War Motions." *American Journal of Sociology* 84:99–122.

Button, J. W. 1978. *Black Violence.* Princeton, N.J.: Princeton University Press.

Campbell, Angus, Philip Converse, Warren Miller, and Donald E. Stokes. 1960. *The American Voter.* New York: John Wiley.

Cantril, Hadley and S. N. Hoopes. 1971. *The Hopes and Fears of Americans.* Washington, D.C.: Potomac Books.

Caute, David. 1977. *The Great Fear.* New York: Simon & Schuster.

BIBLIOGRAPHY

Chambers, Clarke. 1952. *California Farm Organizations*. Berkeley: University of California Press.

Chavez, Cesar. 1966. "The Organizer's Tale." In Staughton Lynd, ed., *American Labor Radicalism*, pp. 138–147. New York: John Wiley.

Chester, Lewis, et al. 1969. *American Melodrama*. New York: Viking Press.

Chiu, Ping. 1967. *Chinese Labor in California*. Madison: State Historical Society of Wisconsin.

Cleland, Robert Glass. 1944. *From Wilderness to Empire: A History of California, 1542–1900*. New York: Knopf.

—— 1947. *California In Our Time*. New York: Knopf.

—— 1951. *The Cattle on a Thousand Hills*. San Marino, Calif.: The Huntington Library.

—— 1963. *This Reckless Breed of Men*. New York: Knopf.

Coffman, George W. 1971. *Corporations with Farming Operations*. USDA-ERS Report #209. Washington, D.C.: GPO.

Cohn, Norman. 1961. *Pursuit of the Millenium*. New York: Harper & Row.

Coleman, James. 1969. *Resources for Social Change*. New York: John Wiley.

Converse, Philip. 1972. "Change in the American Electorate." In A. Campbell and P. Converse, eds., *The Human Meaning of Social Change*, pp. 263–338. New York: Russell Sage.

Corwin, Arthur F., ed. 1978. *Immigrants—and Immigrants: Perspectives on Mexican Labor Migration to the United States*. Westport, Conn.: Greenwood Press.

Craig, Richard C. 1971. *The Bracero Program*. Austin: University of Texas Press.

Cumberland, William. 1917. *Cooperative Marketing*. Princeton, N.J.: Princeton University Press.

Currie, Elliott and Jerome Skolnick. 1970. "A Critical Note on Conceptions of Collective Behavior." *Annals of the American Academy of Political and Social Science* 391:34–45.

Dahl, Robert. 1967. *Pluralist Democracy in the United States*. Chicago: Rand McNally.

Dahrendorf, Ralf. 1959. *Class and Class Conflict in Industrial Society*. Palo Alto: Stanford University Press.

Daniels, Cletus E. 1981. *Bitter Harvest*. Ithaca, N.Y.: Cornell University Press.

Davies, James C. 1969. "The J-Curve of Rising and Declining Satisfactions as a Cause of Some Great Revolutions and a Contained Rebellion." In Hugh Davis Graham and Ted Robert Gurr, eds., *Violence in America*, pp. 671–709. New York: Bantam Books.

—— 1971. *Why Men Revolt?* New York: Free Press.

Davis, James A., T. W. Smith, and C. B. Stephenson. 1981. *General Social Survey*. Ann Arbor: Inter-University Consortium on Political and Social Research.

Davis, Mike. 1980. "The Barren Marriage of Labor and the Democratic Party." *New Left Review* 123:3–44.

Day, Mark. 1971. *Forty Acres: Cesar Chavez and the Farm Workers*. New York: Praeger Publishers.

Dean, Gerald W. and Harold Carter. 1960. *Cost-Size Relationships for Cash Crop Farms in Yolo County, California*. Giannini Foundation. Report #238. Davis, Calif.: University of California.

Delmatier, Royce, Clarence McIntosh, and Earl G. Waters. 1970. *The Rumble of California Politics, 1848–1970*. New York: John Wiley.

Derber, Milton and Edwin Young. 1957. *Labor and the New Deal*. Madison: University of Wisconsin Press.

Dereshinsky, Ralph M. 1972. *The NLRB and Secondary Boycotts*. Philadelphia: University of Pennsylvania Press.

Devine, Donald J. 1970. *The Attentive Public*. Chicago: Rand McNally.

BIBLIOGRAPHY

Doeringer, Peter B. and Michael Piore. 1971. *Internal Labor Markets and Manpower Analysis*. Lexington, Mass.: D. C. Heath.

Domhoff, G. William. 1978. *The Powers That Be*. New York: Vintage.

—— 1979. *Who Really Rules*. Santa Monica, Calif.: Goodyear.

Dumke, Glenn S. 1944. *The Boom of the Eighties in Southern California*. San Marino, Calif.: The Huntington Library.

Dunbar, Tony and Linda Kravitz. 1976. *Hard Traveling*. Cambridge, Mass.: Ballinger.

Dunne, John Gregory. 1967. *Delano*. New York: Farrar, Straus & Giroux.

—— 1971. *Delano: Revised and Updated*. New York: Farrar, Straus & Giroux.

Ecklein, Joan and Armand Laufer. 1972. *Community Organizers and Social Planners*. New York: John Wiley.

Engle, Senator Claire. 1955. "Testimony." In *Hearings before the House Subcommittee on Irrigation and Reclamation of the Committee on Interior and Insular Affairs*. 84th Congress.

Erdman, H. E. 1958. "The development and significance of California cooperatives, 1900–1915." *Agricultural History* 32:179–184.

Etzioni, Amitai. 1961. *Comparative Organizations*. New York: Free Press.

Evans, Sarah. 1979. *Personal Politics*. New York: Vintage Books.

Fainstein, Norman and Susan Fainstein. 1974. *Urban Political Movements: The Search for Power by Minority Groups in American Cities*. Englewood Cliffs, N.J.: Prentice-Hall.

Fairs, J. E. and D. L. Armstrong. 1963. *Economies Associated with Farm Size, Kern County Cash Crop Farms*. Giannini Foundation Report #269. Berkeley, Calif.: Giannini Foundation.

Feavis, Donald F. 1971. *The California Farm Worker 1930–1942*. Ph.D. dissertation. Davis, Calif.: University of California.

Feierabend, I. K., R. L. Feierabend, and B. A. Nesvold. 1969. "Social Change and Political Violence." In H. D. Graham and T. R. Gurr, eds., *The History of Violence in America*, pp. 632–689. New York: Praeger.

Fellmeth, Robert C. 1973. *The Politics of Land*. New York: Grossman.

Fineberg, Richard A. 1971. *Green Card Workers in Farm Labor Disputes*. Ph.D. dissertation. Claremont, Calif.: Claremont Graduate School and University Center.

Fireman, Bruce and William A. Gamson. 1979. "Utilitarian Logic in the Resource Mobilization Perspective." In Mayer Zald and John McCarthy, eds., *The Dynamics of Social Movements*, pp. 8–44. Cambridge, Mass.: Winthrop.

Fish, F. H. 1975. *Black Power/White Control*. Princeton, N.J.: Princeton University Press.

Fisher, Lloyd. 1953. *Harvest Labor Market in California*. Cambridge, Mass.: Harvard University Press.

Flacks, Richard. 1967. "The Liberated Generation: Exploration of the Roots of Student Protest." *Journal of Social Issues* 23:53–75.

—— 1971. *Youth and Social Change*. Chicago: Markham.

Foster, James C. 1975. *The Union Politic: The CIO Political Action Committee*. Columbia: University of Missouri Press.

Freeman, Jo. 1973. "The Origins of the Women's Liberation Movement." *American Journal of Sociology* (January) 78:792–811.

—— 1975. *The Politics of Women's Liberation*. New York: David McKay.

—— 1979. "Resource Mobilization and Strategy: A Model of Analyzing Social Movement Organization Actions." In J. McCarthy and M. Zald, eds., *The Dynamics of Social Movements*, pp. 167–189. Cambridge, Mass.: Winthrop.

—— 1983. "On the Origins of Social Movements." In *The Social Movements of the Sixties and Seventies*, pp. 8–32. New York: Longman.

244

BIBLIOGRAPHY

Friedland, William. 1981. "Seasonal Farm Labor and Worker Consciousness." *Research in the Sociology of Work* I:351–380.

Friedland, William H., Amy E. Barton, and Robert J. Thomas. 1981. *Manufacturing Green Gold*. New York: Cambridge University Press.

Friedland, William and Dorothy Nelkin. 1971. *Migrant: Agricultural Workers in America's Northeast*. New York: Holt, Rinehart & Winston.

Friedland, William and Robert J. Thomas. 1974. "Paradoxes of Agricultural Unionism." *Society* 10:54–62.

Friedrich, Carl. 1937. *Constitutional Government and Politics*. New York: Harper & Row.

Fry, John. 1964. *The Church and Community Organization*. New York: National Council of Churches.

Fujimoto, Isao. 1968. *Is This The Dream?* Unpublished manuscript, Department of Applied Behavioral Science. Davis: University of California.

—— 1978. "The Communities of the San Joaquin Valley." In U.S. Senate, *Priorities in Agricultural Research of the U.S. Department of Agriculture*, pp. 1374–1396. Washington, D.C.: GPO.

Fuller, Varden. 1940. *The Supply of Agricultural Labor as a Factor in the Evolution of Farm Organization in California*. Ph.D. dissertation, Department of Economics, University of California, Berkeley.

—— 1969. "Political Pressures and Income Distribution in Agiculture." In Ruttan et. al. *Agricultural Policy in an Affluent Society*, pp. 255–263. New York: Norton.

Fuller, Varden and John Mamer. 1978. "Constraints on California Farm Worker Organization." *Industrial Relations*, 17:143–155.

Fuller, Varden and William van Vuuren. 1972. "Farm Labor and Labor Markets." In A. Gordon Ball and Earl O. Heady, eds., *Size, Structure and Future of Farms*, pp. 38–174. Ames: Iowa State University Press.

Gaffney, Mason. 1969. "Economic Aspects of Water Resource Policy." *American Journal of Economics and Sociology* 28:131–144.

Galarza, Ernesto. 1964. *Merchants of Labor: The Mexican Bracero Story*. San Jose, Calif.: Rosicrucian Press.

—— 1970. *Spiders in the House and Workers in the Field*. Notre Dame: University of Notre Dame Press.

—— 1977. *Farm Workers and Agri-business in California, 1947–77*. Notre Dame: University of Notre Dame Press.

Galenson, Walter. 1960. *The C.I.O. Challenge to the A.F.L.* Cambridge, Mass.: Harvard University Press.

Gamson, William. 1968. "Stable Unrepresentation in American Society." *American Behavioral Scientist* (November/December) 12:15–21.

—— 1968. *Power and Discontent*. Homewood, Ill.: Dorsey Press.

—— 1975. *The Strategy of Protest*. Homewood, Ill.: Dorsey Press.

—— 1980. "Understanding the Careers of Challenging Groups." *American Journal of Sociology* 85:1043–1601.

Gamson, William and Emilie Schmeiler. 1984. "Organizing the poor." *Theory and Society*. Forthcoming.

Garner, Roberta and Mayer Zald. 1983. "Social Movements and Systemic Constraints." CRSO Working Paper #238. Center for Research on Social Organization, University of Michigan, Ann Arbor.

Garrow, David. 1978. *Protest at Selma*. New Haven: Yale University Press.

Gates, Paul W. 1959. "Adjudication on Spanish-Mexican Land Claims in California." *Huntington Library Quarterly*, no. 3.

245

BIBLIOGRAPHY

—— 1960. *The Farmer's Age*. New York: Holt, Rinehart & Winston.

—— 1962. "California's Embattled Settlers." *California Historical Society Quarterly* 41:33–68.

—— 1967a. "Pre-Henry George Land Warfare in California." *California Historical Society Quarterly* 46:22–38.

—— 1967b. *California Ranchos and Farms, 1846–1862*. Madison, Wisc.: State Historical Society of Wisconsin.

—— 1968. *The History of Public Land Law Development*. Washington, D.C.: GPO.

—— 1975. "Public Land Disposal in California." *Agricultural History* 49:158–178.

Gaventa, John. 1980. *Power and Powerlessness*. Urbana: University of Illinois Press.

Gelb, Joyce and Marian Palley. 1982. *Women and Public Policy*. Princeton, N.J.: Princeton University Press.

Georgi, Peter Hugh. 1969. *The Delano Grape Strike and Boycott*. B.A. honors thesis, Department of Economics, Massachusetts Institute of Technology, Boston, Mass.

Genovese, Eugene. 1973. *Roll Jordan Roll!* New York: Random House.

Gerlach, Luther P. and Viriginia Hine. 1970. *People, Power, Change: Movements of Social Transformation*. Indianapolis, Ind.: Bobbs-Merrill.

Geschwender, James. 1971. *The Black Revolt*. Englewood Cliffs, N.J.: Prentice-Hall.

—— 1983. "The social context of strategic success." In Jo Freeman, ed., *The Social Movements of the Sixties and Seventies*, pp. 235–251. New York: Longman.

Gitlin, Todd. 1980. *The Whole World Is Watching: The Media in the Making and Unmaking of the New Left*. Berkeley: University of California Press.

Glass, Judith Chanin. 1966. *Conditions Which Facilitate Unionization of Agricultural Workers: A Case Study of the Salinas Valley Lettuce Industry*. Ph.D. Dissertation, Department of Economics, University of California, Los Angeles.

Gohman, Ervin. 1961. *Asylums*. Garden City, N.Y.: Doubleday.

Goldberg, Ray A. 1972. "Profitable Partnerships: Industry and Farmer Coops." *Harvard Business Review* (March–April):108–121).

Goldenberg, Edie. 1975. *Making the Papers*. Lexington, Mass.: Lexington Books.

Goldfarb, Ronald. 1981. *A Caste of Despair*. Ames: Iowa State University Press.

Goldschmidt, Walter. 1978. *As You Sow*. 2d edition. New York: Alanheld-Osmun.

Goldstein, Robert. 1978. *Political Repression in Modern America*. Cambridge, Mass.: Schenkman.

Goldstone, Jack A. 1980. "The Weakness of Organizations: A New Look at Gamson's *The Strategy of Social Protest*." *American Journal of Sociology* 85:1017–1042.

Goodall, Merrill R., John D. Sullivan, and Timothy De Young. 1978. *California Water: A New Political Economy*. New York: Allanheld-Osmun.

Gouldner, Alvin. 1970. *The Coming Crisis of Western Sociology*. New York: Basic Books.

Gramsci, Antonio. 1957. *The Modern Prince and Other Writings*. New York: International Publishers.

Granovetter, Mark. 1978. "Threshold Models of Collective Action." *American Journal of Sociology* 83:1420–1443.

Grebler, Leo, Joan W. Moore, and Ralph Guzman. 1970. *The Mexican-American People*. New York: Free Press.

Greene, Sheldon. 1969. "Immigration Law and Rural Poverty-Like Problem of the Illegal Entrant." *Duke Law Journal* 3:479.

Greenstone, J. David. 1969. *Labor in American Politics*. New York: Vintage Books.

Gregor, Howard F. 1951. "A Sample Study of the California Ranch." *Annals of the Association of American Geographers* 41:285–306.

BIBLIOGRAPHY

——— 1962. "The Plantation in California." *Professional Geographer* 14:1–4.

——— 1969. "Farm Structure in Regional Comparison: California and New Jersey Vegetable Farms." *Economic Georgraphy* 45:208–225.

——— 1970a. "The Large Industrialized American Crop Farm." *Geographical Review* 60:152–175.

——— 1970b. "The Industrial Farm as a Western Institution." *Journal of the West* 9:78–92.

Grubbs, Donald. 1971. *Cry From the Cotton: The Southern Tenant Farmers Union and the New Deal*. Chapel Hill: University of North Carolina Press.

Gurr, Ted Robert. 1970. *Why Men Rebel*. Princeton, N.J.: Princeton University Press.

Gusfield, Joseph R. 1968. "The Study of Social Movements." In D. L. Sills, ed., *Encyclopedia of the Social Sciences* 14:445–452. New York: MacMillan & Free Press.

——— 1970. *Protest, Reform, and Revolt*. New York: John Wiley.

——— 1982. "Social Movements and Social Change." *Research on Social Movements, Conflicts and Change* 4:283–316.

Hacker, Andrew. 1970. *The End of the American Era*. New York: Atheneum.

Hadden, Jeffrey. 1969. *The Gathering Storm in the Churches*. Garden City, N.Y.: Doubleday & Co.

Hadley, Eleanor M. 1956. "A Critical Analysis of the Wetback Problem." *Law and Contemporary Problems* 21:334.

Hamilton, Richard. 1972. *Class and Politics in the U.S.* New York: John Wiley.

Handler, Joel F. 1978. *Social Movements and the Legal System*. New York: Academic.. Press.

Hardin, Charles. 1948. "Reflections on Agricultural Policy Formation in the U.S." *American Political Science Review* 42:881–905.

——— 1952. *The Politics of Agriculture*. Glencoe, Ill.: Free Press.

Hathaway, Dale E. 1963. *Government and Agriculture*. New York: Macmillan.

——— 1969. "The Implications of Changing Political Power on Agriculture." In V. Ruttan, Waldo and Houck, eds., *Agricultural Policy in an Affluent Society*, pp. 63–68. New York: W. W. Norton.

Hawley, Ellis. 1966. "The Politics of the Mexican Labor Issue 1950–1965." *Agricultural History* (July) 40(3):157–176.

Heirich, Max. 1972. *The Spiral of Conflict*. New York: Columbia University Press.

Helfgot, Joseph. 1981. *Professional Reforming*. Lexington, Mass.: Lexington Books.

Hibbs, Douglas. 1973. *Mass Political Violence*. New York: John Wiley.

Higbee, Edward. 1963. *Farms and Farmers in an Urban Age*. New York: Twentieth Century Fund.

Hightower, James. 1973. *Hard Tomatoes, Hard Times*. New York: Quadrangle.

——— 1975. *Eat Your Heart Out: Food Profiteering in America*. New York: Quadrangle.

Hill, Richard B. 1972. *California Farm Labor Contractors*. Ph.D. dissertation, University of Missouri, Columbia.

Hilton, Bruce. 1969. *The Delta Migrant Ministry*. New York: Macmillan.

Hobsbawn, F. J. 1959. *Primitive Rebels*. New York: Schocken Books.

——— 1978. "Should the Poor Organize?" *New York Review of Books* 14:558–570.

Hodgson, Godfrey. 1976. *America in Our Time*. Garden City, N.Y.: Doubleday.

Hoffmann, Abraham. 1974. *Unwanted Mexicans*. Tuscon, Ariz.: University of Arizona Press.

Hopper, Rex. 1950. "The Revolutionary Process." *Social Forces* 28:270–279.

Howe, Charles and K. W. Easter. 1971. *Interbasin Transfers of Water*. Baltimore, Md.: Johns Hopkins University Press.

Hudley, Norris. 1975. *Water and the West*. Berkeley: University of California Press.

BIBLIOGRAPHY

Hutchinson, Cecil A. 1969. *Frontier Settlement in Mexican California.* New Haven, Conn.: Yale University Press.

Hutchinson, W. H. 1965. *Oil, Land and Politics: The California Career of Thomas Robert Baird.* Norman: University of Oklahoma Press.

Hyman, Herbert H. and Charles R. Wright. 1971. "Trends in Voluntary Association Memberships of American Adults." *American Sociological Review* 36:191–206.

Inglehart, Ronald. 1977. *The Silent Revolution.* Princeton, N.J.: Princeton University Press.

Issac, Larry and William Kelly. 1981. "Racial Insurgency, the State and Welfare Expansion." *American Journal of Sociology* 86:1348–1386.

Iwata, Masakazu. 1962. "The Japanese Immigrants in California Agriculture." *Agricultural History* 36:25–37.

Jackson, Larry R. and William R. Johnson. 1974. *Protest by the Poor.* Lexington, Mass.: Lexington Books.

Jackson, Maurice, E. Petersen, J. Hull, S. Monsen, and P. Richmond. 1960. "The Failure of an Incipient Social Movement." *Pacific Sociological Review* 3:35–40.

Jamieson, Stuart. 1945. *Labor Unionism in American Agriculture.* USDL Bulletin #836. Washington, D.C.: GPO.

Janowitz, Morris. 1979. *The Last Half Century.* Chicago: University of Chicago Press.

Jenkins, J. Craig. 1977. "Radical Transformation of Organizational Goals." *Administrative Science Quarterly* 22:568–585.

—— 1979. "What Is To Be Done: Movement or Organization?" *Contemporary Sociology* 8:222–228.

—— 1981. "Sociopolitical Movements." *Handbook of Political Behavior* 4:81–154.

—— 1983a. "The Transformation of a Constituency into a Movement". In J. Freeman, ed, *The Social Movements of the Sixties and Seventies.* pp. 512–570. New York: Longman.

—— 1983b. "Resource Mobilization Theory and the Study of Social Movements." *Annual Review of Scoiology* 9:527–553.

—— 1986. "Nonprofit organizations and policy advocacy." *Handbook of Nonprofit Organizations.* New Haven: Yale University Press.

Jenkins, J. Craig and Charles Perrow. 1977. "Insurgency of the Powerless: Farm Worker Movements in the U.S." *American Sociological Review* 42:429–468.

Jennings, Edward T. 1979. "Urban Riots and Welfare Policy Change." In H. Ingram and D. Mann, eds. *Why Policies Succeed or Fail.* Beverly Hills, Calif.: Sage.

Johnson, Chalmbers. 1966. *Revolutionary Change.* Boston: Little, Brown.

Jones, Lamar B. and James W. Christian. 1965. "Some Observations on the Agricultural Labor Market." *Industrial and Labor Relations Review* (July) 18:527–529.

Katznelson, Ira. 1973. *Black Men/White Cities.* Chicago: University of Chicago Press.

——1981. *City Trenches.* New York: Pantheon.

Kelley, Dean. 1957. *The Churches View Their Mission in Christian Life and Mission.* New York: National Council of Churches. Mimeo.

Keniston, Kenneth. 1968. *The Young Radicals.* New York: Harcout Brace Jovanovich.

Kester, Howard. 1936. *Revolt Among the Sharecroppers.* Covici-Friede.

Kirkpatrick, Jeanne. 1976. *The New Presidential Elite.* New York: Russell Sage Foundation and Twentieth Century Fund.

Knoke, David. 1976. *Change and Continuity in American Politics.* Baltimore, Md.: Johns Hopkins University Press.

Knott. 1956. "Fruits and Vegetables." In Gifford M. Ziever, ed., *California and the Southwest.* New York: John Wiley.

BIBLIOGRAPHY

Kolko, Gabriel. 1963. *The Triumph of Conservatism*. New York: Free Press.

Kopkind, Andrew. 1967. "Poverty Politics in California." *New Republic* (February) 156:19–20.

—— 1970. "What To Do Till the Movement Arrives." *Working Papers for A New Society* 4:43–49.

Korpi, Walter. 1978. *The Working Class in Welfare Capitalism*. London: Routledge and Kegan Paul.

Kornhauser, William. 1959. *The Politics of Mass Society*. New York: Free Press.

Kotz, Nick. 1971a "Farm to Market Control: "Conglomerates Reshape Food Supply." *Washington Post* (Oct. 3).

—— 1971b "Agribusiness Threatens Family Farm." *Washington Post* (Oct. 4).

Kotz, Nick and Mary Kotz. 1977. *A Passion for Equality*. New York: W. W. Norton.

Koziara, Karen S. 1968. "Collective Bargaining on the Farm." *Monthly Labor Review* 91:3–9.

Krebs, A. V. 1972. *A Profile of California Agribusiness*. Washington, D.C.: Agribusiness Accountability Project.

—— 1973a *The BankAmerica Corporation*. Washington, D.C.: Agribusiness Accountability Project. Mimeo.

—— 1973b. *Summary Report on Major U.S. Corporations Involved in Agribusiness*. Washington, D.C.: Agribusiness Accountability Project. Mimeo.

Kriesberg, Louis. 1973. *The Sociology of Social Conflicts*. Englewood Cliffs, N.J.: Prentice-Hall.

Kristol, Irving. 1978. *Two Cheers for Capitalism*. New York: Basic Books.

Kushner, Sam. 1975. *Long Road to Delano*. New York: International Publishers.

Kyle, Leonard R., W. B. Sundquist, and Harold A. Guither. 1972. *Who Will Control U.S. Agriculture?* Special Publication #27. Extension Service, College of Agriculture, University of Illinois.

Ladd, Everett C. 1978. *Transformations of the American Party System: Political Coalitions from the New Deal to the 1970s*. New York: W. W. Norton.

Lane, Robert. 1965. "The Politics of Consensus in an Age of Affluence." *American Political Science Review* 59:874–895.

Lang, Kurt and Gladys Engel Lang. 1961. *Collective Dynamics*. New York: Thomas Y. Crowell.

Lawson, Ronald. 1983. "The Decentralized but Moving Pyramid." In J. Freeman, ed., *The Social Movements of the Sixties and Seventies*, pp. 119–132. New York: Longman.

Lawson, Steven. 1976. *Black Ballots*. New York: Columbia University Press.

Lazarsfeld, Paul. 1956. *Personal Influence*. New York: Free Press.

Lazarsfield, Paul, Bernard Berelson, and Helen Gaudet. 1948. *The People's Choice*. New York: Columbia University Press.

Lee, Robert and Russell Galloway. 1969. *The Schizophrenic Church: Conflict Over Community Organization*. Philadelphia, Penn.: Westminster.

Levy, Jacques. 1975. *Cesar Chavez: An Autobiography of La Causa*. New York: W. W. Norton.

Lincoln, James. 1978. "Community Structure and Industrial Conflict." *American Sociological Review* 13:199–200.

Lindblom, Charles. 1977. *Politics and Markets*. New York: Basic Books.

Lipset, Seymour Martin. 1950. *Agrarian Socialism*. New York: Free Press.

—— 1960. *Political Man*. Garden City, N.Y.: Doubleday.

Lipset, S. M. and William Schneider. 1983. *The Confidence Gap*. New York: Free Press.

Lipsky, Michael. 1968. "Protest as a Political Resource." *American Political Science Review* 62:1144–1158.

—— 1971. *Protest in City Politics: Rent Strikes, Housing and the Power of the Poor*. Chicago: Rand McNally.

Lockwood, David. 1956. *The Blackcoated Worker*. Cambridge: Cambridge University Press.

London, Joan and Henry Anderson. 1970. *So Shall Ye Reap*. New York: Thomas Y. Crowell.

Lowi, Theodore. 1977. *The Politics of Disorder*. New York: Basic Books.

—— 1979. *The End of Liberalism*. 2nd edition. New York: W. W. Norton.

Lukes, Steven. 1974. *Power*. New York: Macmillan.

Lyman, Stanford. 1974. *Chinese Americans*. New York: Random House.

Maass, Arthur. 1951. *Muddy Waters*. Cambridge: Harvard University Press.

Maass, Arthur M. and Raymond Anderson. 1978. *. . . and the Desert Shall Rejoice: Conflict, Growth and Justice in Arid Environments*. Cambridge, Mass.: MIT Press.

MacCannell, Dean. 1980. *Report on Current Social Conditions in the Communities in and Near the Westlands Water District*. Report of California Macrosocial Accounting Project. Davis, Calif.: University of California Experimental Station.

Madden, J. Patrick. 1967. *Economics of Size in Farming*. USDA-ERS Report #107, Washington, D.C.: GPO.

Madden, J. Patrick and Earl J. Partenheimer. 1972. "Evidence of Economies and Diseconomies of Farm Size." Pp. 91–107 In G. A. Ball and E. O. Heady, ed., *Size and Structure of Farms*. Ames: Iowa State University Press.

Majka, Theo. 1978. "Regulating Farmworkers." *Contemporary Crises* 2:141–155.

Mann, S. A. and J. M. Dickinson. 1978. "Obstacles to the Development of a Capitalist Agriculture." *Journal of Peasant Studies* 4:13–36.

—— 1980. "State and Agriculture in Two Eras of American Capitalism." In Federick Buttel and Howard Newby, eds., *The Rural Sociology of Advanced Societies*, pp. 73–95. Montclair, N.J.: Allanheld Osmun.

Martin, Roscoe. 1957. *Grass Rotts Administration*. Birmingham, Ala.: University of Alabama Press.

Marx, Gary T. and James L. Wood. 1975. "Strands of Theory and Research in Collective Behavior." *Annual Review of Sociology* I:363–428.

Marx, Karl. 1979. *The Letters of Karl Marx*. Ed. Saul Padover. Englewood Cliffs, N.J.: Prentice-Hall.

Maslow, Abraham. 1968. *Towards a Psychology of Being*. Boston: Van Nostrand.

Matthiewsen, Peter. 1969. *Sal Si Puedes: Cesar Chavez and the New American Revolution*. New York: Random House.

Matusow, Allen J. 1967. *Farm Policies and Politics in the Truman Years*. Cambridge, Mass.: Harvard University Press.

McAdam, Doug. 1982. *Political Process and the Development of Black Insurgency*. Chicago: University of Chicago Press.

McCarthy, John and Mayer Zald. 1973. *The Trend of Social Movements in American*. Morristown, N.J.: General Learning Corporation.

—— 1977. "Resource Mobilization and Social Movements." *American Journal of Sociology* 82:1212–1241.

McClure, Arthur F. 1969. *The Truman Administration and the Problems of Postwar Labor. 1945–1948*. Cranbury, N.J.: Associated University Presses.

McConnell, Grant. 1953. *The Decline of Agrarian Democracy*. New York: Atheneum.

BIBLIOGRAPHY

McCune, Wesley. 1943. *The Farm Bloc*. Garden City, N.J.: Doubleday, Doran & Co.

—— 1956. *Who's Behind Our Farm Policy?* New York: Praeger.

McFarland, Andrew. 1976. *Public Interest Lobbies*. Washington, D.C.: American Enterprise Institute.

McWilliams, Carey. 1939. *Factories in the Fields*. Boston, Mass.: Little, Brown.

—— 1942. *Ill Fares the Land*. Boston, Mass.: Little, Brown.

—— 1949. *California: The Great Exception*. New York: Current Books.

Meister, Dick and Anne Loftis. 1977. *A Long Time Coming*. New York: Macmillan.

Metzler, William. 1965. *Farm Mechanization and Labor Stabilization*. Giannini Foundation. Berkeley: University of California Press.

—— 1966. *Farm Workers in a Specialized Seasonal Crop Area*. Giannini Foundation Report #289. Berkeley, Calif.: Giannini Foundation.

Metzler, William and Afife Sayin. 1948. *The Agricultural Labor Force in the San Joaquin Valley. California: 1948*. Washington, D.C.: GPO.

Migdal, Joel. 1974. *Peasants, Politics and Revolution*. Princeton, N.J.: Princeton University Press.

Milbrath, Lester. 1965. *Political Participation*. Chicago: Rand McNally.

Milbrath, Lester and M. L. Goel. 1977. *Political Participation*. Chicago: Rand McNally.

Miller, A. H., L. H. Bolce, and M. Halligan. 1977. "The J-Curve Theory and the Black Urban Riots." *American Political Science Review* 71:964–82.

Mills, C. Wright. 1947. *The New Men of Power*. New York: Harcourt Brace Jovanovich.

Mitchell, Ronald L. and William S. Hoofnagle. 1972. *Contract Production and Vertical Integration in Farming: 1960 and 1970*. USDA-ERS Report #479, Washington, D.C.: GPO.

Mitchell, H. L. 1980. *Mean Things Happening in This Land*. New York: Allanheld Osmun.

Mitchell, H. L. and Henry Hasivar. 1974. *The NFLU*. Oral interview in STFU Papers.

Moe, Terry. 1980. *The Organization of Interests*. Chicago: University of Chicago Press.

Montgomery, David. 1980. *Worker's Control in America*. New York: Cambridge University Press.

Moore, Barrington. 1978. *Injustice*. White Plains, N.Y.: Sharpe.

Morre, C. V. and J. Snyder. 1970. "Corporate Farming in California." *California Agriculture* (March).

Morin, Alexander. 1952. *The Organizability of Farm Labor in the U.S*. Cambridge, Mass.: Harvard University Press.

Moynihan, Daniel Patrick. 1965. "The Professionalization of Reform." *The Public Interest* I:6–20.

—— 1968. *Maximum Feasible Misunderstanding*. New York: Free Press.

Mueller, Willard. 1969. "Public Poligy Towards Mergers in Food Retailing." In Ruttan et. al., *Agricultural Policy in an Affluent Society*, pp. 186–191. New York: W. W. Norton.

Nash, Gerald N. 1959. "Henry George Reexamined: William Campman's View on Land Speculation in Nineteenth-Century California." *Agricultural History* 33:135–187.

—— 1964. "The California State Land Office, 1858–1898." *Huntington Library Quarterly* 27:347–356.

National Migrant Ministry. 1961. *National Goals for the Fifth Decade*. New York: National Migrant Ministry.

Navasky, Victor. 1975. *Kennedy Justice*. New York: Atheneum.

Nelson, Eugene. 1966. *Huelga!* Delano, Calif.: Farm Worker Press.

Newby, Howard. 1975. *The Deferential Worker*. New York: Cambridge University Press.

Nie, Norman H., Sidney Verba, and John R. Petrocik. 1980. *The Changing American Voter* 2nd edition. Cambridge, Mass.: Harvard University Press.

North, David S. 1970. *The Border Crossers*. Washington D.C.: Trans-Century Corporation.

North, David and Marion Houstoun. 1976. *The Characteristics and Role of Illegal Aliens in the U.S. Labor Market*. Washington, D.C.: Linton & Co.

Oberschall, Anthony. 1973. *Social Conflicts and Social Movements*. Englewood Cliffs, N.J.: Prentice-Hall.

—— 1978a. "The Decline of the 1960's Social Movements." *Research in Social Movements, Conflicts and Change* 1:257–289.

—— 1978b. "Theories of social conflict." *Annual Review of Sociology* 4:291–315.

O'Brien, J. David. 1975. *Neighborhood Organization and Interest Groups Processes*. Princeton: Princeton University Press.

Oliver, Pamela. 1982. "The Mobilization of Paid and Volunteer Activists in the Neighborhood Movement." Paper presented at annual meeting of the American Sociological Association, Toronto, Canada.

Olson, Mancur. 1965. *The Logic of Collective Action*. Cambridge, Mass.: Harvard University Press.

Orum, Anthony. 1972. *Black Students in Protest*. Washington, D.C.: American Sociological Association.

Padfield, Harland and Wiliam Martin. 1965. *Farmers, Workers and Machines*. Tucson, Ariz.: University of Arizona Press.

Paige, Chris. 1968. "Farm Worker Organizing and the AWOC." Unpublished paper, Department of History, University of California, Berkeley.

Paige, Jeffrey. 1975. *Agrarian Revolution*. New York: Free Press.

Perelman, Michael. 1978. *Farming for Profit in a Hungry World*. Montclair, N.J.: Allanheld Osmun.

Perelman, Michael and Kevin P. Shea. 1972. "The Big Farm." *Environment* (Dec.) 14:10–15.

Perrow, Charles. 1979. "The Sixties Observed." In Mayer Zald and John McCarthy, eds., *The Dynamics of Social Movements*, pp. 192–211. Cambridge, Mass.: Winthrop.

Petersen, Paul and J. David Greenstone. 1977. "Racial Change and Citizen Participation." In R.H. Haveman, ed., *A Decade of Federal Antipoverty Programs*, pp. 241-278. New York: Academic.

Pinard, Maurice. 1971. *The Rise of a Third Party: A Study in Crisis Politics*. Englewood Cliffs, N.J.: Prentice-Hall.

Pinckney, Alfonso. 1968. *The Committed*. New Haven, Conn.: College & University Press.

Pitt, Leonard. 1966. *The Decline of the Californios*. Berkeley: University of California Press.

Piven, Francis and Richard Cloward. 1977. *Poor People's Movement*. New York: Pantheon.

Pomper, Gerald. 1975. *Voter's Choice: Varieties of American Electoral Behavior*. New York: Dodd, Mead.

Portes, Alexandro. 1971. "On the Logic of Post Factum Explanation." *Social Forces*, 50: 26–44.

—— 1974. "Return of the Wetback." *Society* (March–April) 11, (3):40–49.

—— 1977. "Labor Functions of Illegal Aliens." *Society*, 15:31-37.

Portes, Alejandro and John Walton. 1981. *Labor, Class and the International System*. New York: Academic Press.

Poulantzas, Nicos. 1973. *Political Power and Social Classes*. London: New Left Books.

Prager, Robert and Harry Specht. 1969. "Assessing Theoretical Models of Community Organization Practice: Alinsky as a Case in Point." *Social Service Review* (June) 43:123–135.

Pratt, Henry J. 1972. *The Liberalization of American Protestantism*. Detroit, Mich.: Wayne State University Press.

Preis, Art. 1964. *Labor's Giant Step: Twenty Years of the CIO*. New York: Pioneer Publishers.

Quinley, Richard. 1974. *Prophetic Clergy*. New York: John Wiley.

Raper, Howard. 1969. *The Tragedy of Lynching*. New York: Arno.

Rasmussen, Wayne D. (ed.) 1975. *Agriculture in the United States: A Documentary History*. New York: Random House.

Reed, H. 1956. "Irrigation and Agricultural Development." In Clifford M. Zievev, ed., *California and the Southwest*. New York: John Wiley.

Reich, Charles. 1970. *The Greening of America*. New York: Random House.

Reisler, Mark. 1976. *By the Sweat of Their Brow: Mexican Immigrant Labor in the United States, 1900–1940*. Westport, Conn.: Greenwood Press.

Ripley, Randall and S. Franklin. 1978. *Congress, the Bureaucracy and Public Policy*. New York: W.W. Norton.

Rodman, Walter. 1975. "California Agriculture." In W. D. Rasmussen ed., *Agriculture in the United States*. New York: Random House.

Romer, Sam. 1962. *The International Brotherhood of Teamsters*. New York: John Wiley.

Roos, Robert de. 1948. *The Thirsty Land: The Story of the Central Valley Project*. Palo Alto, Calif. Stanford University Press.

Rose, Arnold. 1967. *The Power Structure*. New York: Oxford University Press.

Rosenau, James. 1974. *Citizenship Between Elections*. New York: Free Press.

Roszak, Theodore. 1969. *The Making of the Counter-Culture*. Garden City, N.Y.: Doubleday.

Rule, James and Charles Tilly. 1975. "Political Process in Revolutionary France: 1830–1832." In J. Merriman, ed., *1830 in France*, pp. 41–85. New York: New Viewpoints.

Rushing, William. 1972. *Class, Culture and Alienation*. Lexington, Mass.: Lexington Books.

Sabato, Andrew. 1980. *The Rise of the Political Consultants*. New York: Basic Books.

Salandini, Victor. 1969. *The Short-Run Socio-Economic Effects of the Termination of Public Law 78 on the California Farm Labor Market for 1965–1967*. Ph.D. dissertation, Catholic University, Washington, D.C.

Samora, Julian. 1971. *Los Mojados: The Wetback Story*. Notre Dame, Ind.: University of Notre Dame Press.

Schattschneider, E. E. 1960. *The Semi-Sovereign People*. New York: Holt, Rinehart & Winston.

Schlesinger, Arthur Jr. 1965. *A Thousand Days*. New York: Houghton Mifflin Co.

Schmidt, Fred H. 1964. *After the Bracero*. Institute of Industrial Relations. Los Angeles: University of California.

Schumaker, Paul D. 1978. "The Scope of Political Conflict and the Effectiveness of Constraints in Contemporary Urban Protest." *Sociological Quarterly* 19:168–184.

Schwartz, Michael. 1976. *Radical Protest and Social Structure*. New York: Academic Press.

Scofield, Williams. 1969. "Corporations in Farming." In *Corporation Farming: What are the Issues?* North Central Workshop. Department of Agricultural Economics, Report #53. Lincoln, Nebr.: University of Nebraska.

Selznick, Phillip 1949. *TVA and the Grass Roots*. Berkeley: University of California Press.

—— 1970. "Institutional Vulnerability to Mass Society." In J. R. Gusfield, ed., *Protest Reform and Revolt*, pp. 258–274. New York: John Wiley.

Shanon, Fred A. 1968. *The Farmer's Last Frontier: Agriculture, 1860–1897*. New York: Harper & Row.

Shear, S. K. 1956. "Fruit and Nut Industry." In Clifford M. Zievev, ed., *California and the Southwest*, pp. 146–159. New York: John Wiley.

Shils, Edward. 1955. "The End of Ideology?" *Encounter* 5:52–62.

Shorter, Ed and Charles Tilly. 1974. *Strikes in France, 1830–1968*. New York: Cambridge University Press.

Shotwell, Louisa R. 1960. *Four Decades of the Migrant Ministry: 1920–1960*. National Migrant Ministry. Mimeo.

Shrode, Ida May. 1956. "Early Settlement of California and the Southwest. In Clifford M. Zievev, ed., *California and the Southwest*, pp. 110–121. New York: John Wiley.

Skocpol, Theda. 1979. *States and Social Revolution*. New York: Cambridge University Press.

—— 1980. "Political Response to Capitalist Crisis." *Politics and Society* 10:155–187.

Smelser, Neil. 1963. *The Theory of Collective Behavior*. New York: Free Press.

Smith, Tom W. 1981. "General Liberalism and Social Change in Post-World War II America." *Social Indicators Research* 10:1–28.

Show, David. Louis Zurcher, and Sheldon Eckland-Olson. 1980. "Social Networks and Social Movements." *American Sociological Review* 45:787–801.

Snyder, David. 1975. "Institutional Setting and Industrial Conflict." *American Sociological Review* 40:259–278.

Snyder, David and Charles Tilly. 1972. "Hardship and Collective Violence in France. 1830 to 1960." *American Sociological Review* 37:520–532.

Sosnick, Stephen. 1978. *Hired Hands*. Santa Barbara, Calif.: McNally and Loftin.

Steedly, Homer R. and John W. Foley. 1979. "The Success of Protest Groups: Multivariate Analyses." *Social Science Research* 8:1–15.

Stein, Walter J. 1973. *California and the Dust Bowl Migration*. Westport, Conn.: Greenwood Press.

Steinbeck, John. 1939. *The Grapes of Wrath*. New York: Viking Press.

Stephenson, W. A. 1937. "Appropriation of Water in Arid Regions." *Southwestern Social Science Quarterly* 18:215–226.

Stinchcombe, Arthur. 1961. "Agricultural Enterprise and Rural Class Relations." *American Journal of Sociology* 4:168–187.

Taft, Phillip. 1967. *The Labor Movement in California*. Berkeley: University of California Press.

Talbot, Ross B. and Don F. Hadwiger. 1968. *The Policy Process in American Agriculture*. San Francisco, Calif.: Chandler.

Tangri, Beverly. 1967. *Federal Legislation as an Extension of US Public Policy Towards Agricultural Labor: 1914–54*. Ph.D. dissertation, Department of Economics, University of California, Berkeley.

Taylor, Paul. 1949. "Central Valley Project: Water and Land." *Western Political Quarterly* 2:228–253.

—— 1958. "The Excess Land Law: Legislative Erosion of Public Policy." *Rocky Mountain Law Review* 30:30–45.

—— 1971. "The 160-Acre Limitation." In David Seckler, ed., *California Water*, pp. 251–262. Berkeley: University of California Press.

—— 1975. "The Battle for Acreage Limitation." Pp. 113–117 In Peter Barnes, ed., *Land for the People*, pp. 113–117. Emmaeus, Penn.: Rodale Press.

Taylor, Ronald. 1975. *Chavez and the Farm Workers*. Boston, Mass.: Beacon Press.

BIBLIOGRAPHY

Thompson, Mark. 1963. *The Agricultural Workers Organizing Committee, 1959–1962.* Masters thesis, Dept. of Economics, Cornell University, Ithaca, N.Y.

Thomas, Robert J. 1981a. "Citizenship, Gender and Work Organization." *American Journal of Sociology* 85:1185–1200.

—— 1981b. "Undocumented Workers in Industrial Agriculture." Unpublished paper.

Tilly, Charles. 1975. "Revolutions and collective violence." In Fred I. Greenstein and Nelson W. Polsby, eds., *The Handbook of Political Science.* Reading, Mass.: Addison-Wesley.

—— 1978. *From Mobilization to Revolution.* Reading, Mass.: Addison-Wesley.

—— 1979. "Social Movements and National Politics." CRSO Working Paper #197. Center for Research on Social Organization. University of Michigan, Ann Arbor.

Tilly, Charles, Louise Tilly, and Richard Tilly. 1975. *The Rebellious Century.* Cambridge, Mass.: Harvard University Press.

Traugott, Mark. 1978. "Reconceiving Social Movements." *Social Problems* 26:38–49.

Truman, David. 1951. *The Governmental Process.* New York: Knopf.

Tucker, William. 1982. *Progress and Privilege.* New York: Norton.

Turner, Ralph. 1964. "Collective Behavior and Conflict: New Theoretical Frameworks." In B. McLaughlin, ed., *Studies in Social Movements,* pp. 63–72. New York: Free Press.

—— 1970. "Determinants of Social Movement Strategies." In Tomotsu Shibutani, ed., *Human Nature and Collective Behavior,* pp. 145–164. Engelwood Cliffs, N.J.: Prentice-Hall.

—— 1982. "Collective Behavior and Resource Mobilization as Approaches to Social Movements." *Research on Social Movements, Conflicts and Change* 4:1–24.

Turner, Ralph and Lewis Killian. 1957. *Collective Behavior.* 1st edition. Englewood Cliffs, N.J.: Prentice-Hall.

—— 1972. *Collective Behavior.* 2nd edition. Englewood Cliffs, N.J.: Prentice-Hall.

Useem, Michael. 1975. *Protest Movements in America.* Indianapolis, Ind.: Bobbs-Merrill.

Veblen, Thornstein. 1917. *The Theory of the Business Enterprise.* New York: Viking Press.

Verba, Sidney and Norman H. Nie. 1972. *Participation in America.* New York: Harper & Row.

—— 1975. "Political Participation." In Fred I. Greenstein and Nelson Polsby, eds., *Handbook of Political Science.* Vol. 4. Reading, Mass.: Addison-Wesley.

Verhoff, Joseph, Elizabeth Douvan and Richard Kulka. 1981. *The Inner American.* New York: Basic Books.

Vogeler, Ingolf. 1981. *The Myth of the Family Farm.* Bolder, Colo.: Westview.

Von Eschen, Donald, Jerome Kirk, and Maurice Pinard. 1971. "The Organizational Substructure of Disorderly Politics." *Social Forces* (June) 49:529–544.

Waskow, Arthur. 1967. *From Race Riot to Sit-In.* Garden City, N.Y.: Doubleday.

Watson, Don. 1977. *Rise and Decline of Fruit Tramp Unionism in the Western Lettuce Industry.* Unpublished manuscript. San Francisco, Calif.

West, Guilda. 1981. *The National Welfare Rights Movement.* New York: Praeger.

Westby, David. 1976. *The Clouded Vision: The Student Movement in the United States in the 1960s.* Lewisburg, Penn.: Bucknell University Press.

Wik, Reynold M. 1975. "Some Interpretations of the Mechanization of Agriculture in the Far West." *Agricultural History* 49:73–83.

Wilcox, Walter, Willard Cochrane, and Robert W. Herdt. 1973. *Economics of American Agriculture.* Englewood Cliffs, N.J.: Prentice-Hall.

Wilson, James Q. 1961. "The Strategy of Protest: Problems of Negro Civic Action." *Journal of Conflict Resolution* 3:291–303.

BIBLIOGRAPHY

—— 1973. *Political Organizations.* New York: Basic Books.

Wilson, John. 1973. *An Introduction to Social Movements.* New York: Basic Books.

Wilson, Kenneth and Anthony Orum. 1976. "Mobilizing People for Collective Political Action." *Journal of Political and Military Sociology* 4:187–202.

Wilson, William J. 1973. *Power, Racism and Privilege.* New York: Free Press.

Wolfe, Alan. 1977. *The Limits of Legitimacy.* New York: Free Press.

Wolf, Eric. 1969. *The Peasant Wars of the Twentieth Century.* New York: Harper & Row.

Wolf, Jerome. 1964. *Imperial Valley as an Index of Agricultural Labor Relations in California.* Unpublished Ph.D. Dissertation. Los Angeles: University of California Press.

Wood, James L. 1975. *The Sources of the American Student Movement.* Lexington, Mass.: D. C. Heath.

Wrong, Dennis. 1980. *Power.* New York: Harper & Row.

Yankelovich, Daniel. 1979. *New Rules.* New York: Random House.

Yankelovich, Daniel and Ruth Clark. 1971. *The New Morality.* New York: McGraw-Hill.

Yinger, Winthrop B. 1970. *History of UFWOC: A Chronology.* California Migrant Ministry.

Zald, Mayer and John McCarthy. 1975. "Organizational Intellectuals and the Criticism of Society." *Social Service Review* 49:344–362.

Zurcher, Louis and David Snow. 1981. "Collective Behavior: Social Movements." In M. Rosenberg and R. Turner, eds., *Social Psychology,* pp. 447–482. New York: Basic Books.

Government Documents

Bureau of the Census. 1976. *Historical Statistics on the U.S.* Washington, D.C.: GPO.

California Legislature. Assembly. Committee on Agriculture. 1969. *The California Farm Labor Force: A Profile.* Sacramento,: State of California.

—— 1970. *The Low Income Worker in the California Farm Labor Force.* Supplement. Sacramento: State of California.

California Legislature. Senate. Fact-Finding Committee on Labor and Welfare.

—— 1961. *California's Farm Labor Problems.* Parts 1 and 2. Sacramento: State of California.

California Legislature. Senate. Fact-Finding Committee on Un-American Activities.

—— 1967. *Fourteenth Report.* Sacramento: State of California.

U.S. Department of Labor. 1976. *Labor Statistics.* Washington, D.C.: GPO.

U.S. Congress. House. Special Subcommittee of Committee on Education and Labor, 80th Congress. 1949. *Hearings: National Labor Relations Act of 1949 (HR 2032).* Washington, D.C.

U.S. Congress. House. Special Subcommittee of Committee on Education and Labor, 81st Congress. 1950. *Hearings (HR 75).* Washington, D.C.

U.S. Congress. Senate. Agriculture Committee. 1963. *Hearings on Extension of the Mexican Farm Labor Program.* 88th Congress, 2nd Session.

U.S. Congress. Senate. Committee on Small Business. 1968. *Corporation Farming.* 90th Congress, 2nd Session. Washington, D.C.: GPO.

—— 1973. *The Role of The Giant Corporation.* 92nd Congress, 1st and 2nd Sessions. Washington, D.C.: GPO.

U.S. Congress. Senate. Subcommittee on Migratory Labor. 1968. *Migratory Farm Labor Problems in the U.S.* 90th Congress, 2nd Session. Report 1006. Washington, D.C.

—— 1969. *Migrant and Seasonal Farmworker Powerlessness.* 16 volumes. Washington, D.C.: GPO.

BIBLIOGRAPHY

—— 1971–72. *Farmworkers in Rural America.* Volumes 1–5. Washington, D.C.: GPO.

U.S. Department of Agriculture 1976. *State Farm Income Statistics (Supplement to #557).* Washington, D.C.: GPO.

U.S. Department of Agriculture. Consumer and Marketing Service. Fruit and Vegetable Divisions. Market News Branch. 1966–70. *Fresh Fruit and Vegetable Unloads in Eastern, Southern, Midwestern and Western Cities by Commodities, States and Months.* Washington, D.C.: GPO (Annual Report).

—— 1966–70. *Daily Grape Report.* Fresno, CA.: U.S. Department of Agriculture (Daily Report).

U.S.D.A.-Economic Research Service (ERS). 1946–80a. *The Farm Income Situation.* ERS Report #230. Washington, D.C. (issued quarterly).

—— 1946–80b. *Farm Costs and Returns.* ERS Report #233. Washington, D.C.

—— 1946–80. *Farm Labor.* Washington, D.C.

—— 1969a. *Corporations Having Agricultural Operations.* ERS Report #156. Washington, D.C.: GPO.

—— 1969b. *Corporations Having Agricultural Operations.* ERS Report #209. Washington, D.C.: GPO.

—— 1970. *Domestic Migratory Farm Workers: Personal and Economic Characteristics.* Agricultural Economic Report #121. Washington, D.C.: GPO.

—— 1970. *Our 31,000 Largest Farms.* ERS Report #175. Washington, D.C.: GPO.

—— 1971. *New Moves in the Marketing Game.* Washington, D.C.: GPO.

—— 1972. *Market Structure of the Food Industries.* Market Research Report #971. Washington, D.C.: GPO.

U.S. Department of Commerce. 1950–69. *Census of Agriculture. Statistics for the State and Counties: California.* Vol. 1, Part 48. Washington, D.C.: GPO.

Index